In Defense of French Poetry

Thereon the men in the vaudevilles
sang of peace and of empire
Au douce temps de pascor
And Tchang-tsong wrote of music, its principles
Sun-tong made records of rites
And this was written all in red-character,
countersigned by the assembly
sealed with the Imperial Seal
and put in the hall of the forebears
as check on successors.

What thou lovest well remains,
the rest is dross
What thou lov'st well shall not be reft from thee
What thou lov'st well is thy true heritage

. . . .

To have gathered from the air a live tradition
or from a fine old eye the unconquered flame
This is not vanity.
Ezra Pound, *The Cantos*

IN DEFENSE OF FRENCH POETRY

An Essay in Revaluation

William Calin

THE PENNSYLVANIA STATE UNIVERSITY PRESS
UNIVERSITY PARK AND LONDON

Ezra Pound. *The Cantos of Ezra Pound.* Copyright 1940, 1948 by Ezra Pound.
Reprinted by permission of New Directions Publishing Corporation, New York,
and Faber & Faber Ltd., London, England.

Library of Congress Cataloging-in-Publication Data

Calin, William.
In defense of French poetry.

Bibliography: p.
Includes index.
1. French poetry—History and criticism. I. Title.
PQ401.C35 1986   841'.009   85–43560
ISBN 0-271-00437-1

CONTENTS

Acknowledgments   vii

1   The Problem   1
2   The Persona   13
3   The Language   41
4   The Meaning   71
5   The Creed   99
6   The Public   125
7   The History   151

Appendix   179
Notes   191
Index   199

ACKNOWLEDGMENTS

A few pages of this book were published previously. They are taken from longer studies on the medieval courtly lyric in *L'Esprit Créateur,* on Charles d'Orléans in the *Mélanges Alice Planche,* on Ronsard's *hymnes* and on Voltaire in *Degré Second,* and on Boileau and the mock-epic in my *A Muse for Heroes* (University of Toronto Press).

Françoise Calin contributed the critical insights of a modernist and her unerring sense of style and decorum. Having read the manuscript, she made it much better. So also did the referees for Penn State Press, Professor William Kibler, Department of French and Italian, University of Texas, and Professor Gerard J. Brault, Department of French, Penn State University.

Philip Winsor, senior editor, and Cherene Holland, copyeditor, are the perfect embodiments of their respective professional archetypes. It was a joy to work with both.

Steven Rodgers prepared the index.

I thank them all.

1

THE PROBLEM

In France, in intellectual circles today, it is commonplace to bemoan the "crisis of poetry"—a crisis in the reading, writing, publishing, teaching, and understanding what for centuries stood at the pinnacle of the art world but in recent times allegedly has been removed to the periphery, if not eliminated altogether. As to the nature of the crisis, varied opinions have been offered, but that some sort of crisis exists is irrefutable, if only on the pedagogical or practical level. This is obvious to anyone who has taught a course on French verse to undergraduate students in France or abroad, or who has discussed French poetry with generally well-read, cultivated people, whether in France or abroad. I propose that one cause, and symptom, of the crisis lies in the fact that most readers of poetry—educated French people and foreign students—hold an insufficient concept as to the nature of poetry and that, at the same time, they are not well acquainted with the history of French verse. In other words, they do not have the background to conceive poetry synchronically and diachronically, both as theory and as textual practice.

A surprisingly large number of books have been published recently in France, Belgium, and Switzerland dealing with poetry in general and French poetry in particular. Having consulted many of these, I discovered that the vast majority, including student texts, present a system of esthetics obviously of Romantic and/or Symbolist provenance. The widely accepted view, also prevalent in the literary reviews and in the classroom, can be stated roughly in the following terms: Poetry is a brief lyric distinguished by concrete, striking imagery. It expresses the individual voice of its creator, the poet, who reveals the deepest feelings of his soul with sincerity and authenticity and who discovers, then transmits to the reader, secrets of the universe. The distinctive mark of poetry and testimony to its greatness is originality in language and style: in other words, the *écart* (Barthes's term, derived from Valéry) between poetry and literary prose or everyday common speech.

This view envisages the poetic process from various perspectives. The poet himself is seen as a sublime and/or pathetic creator, alone, standing in opposition to society. He is an outsider, alienated, persecuted, misunderstood. This heroic, unique individual lives and then presents to the reader a unique spiritual adventure, his "way of being" in the world, his moment of consciousness, his soul. His is an individual voice. For the Romantics and for quite a few Moderns, the quality of verse depends upon and has to reflect the author's sincerity, authenticity, and originality—originality conceived as a reflection of sincerity and sincerity as a reflection of originality. Hence the call for subjectivity and for what we can designate as the "personal myth."

The poet not only tells of himself. According to the Romantic-Symbolist esthetic, his spiritual adventures grant him the right to create myths, to elaborate a poetic theology based upon atheistic mysticism. He is or becomes a seer (Rimbaud's *voyant*), a prophet, a modern Orpheus, who discovers poetic truth: the sacred, the unknown, the unsayable, superhuman knowledge, divine mysteries. He seizes the ineffable and the transcendent, then reveals them to his readers as a poetic, secular scripture. In Novalis's words, "Der ächte Dichter ist *allwissend*—er ist eine wirckliche Welt im Kleinen."[1]

It also should be underscored that, for the poet to master such transcendence, he has to be born a genius, for poetic creation comes from the soul. In other words, the source of his creativity is inspiration or, for the Symbolists and Surrealists, imagination, which, even when seconded by intellect, education, hard work, and written models, is defined as a gift from the gods, magical, a *tremendum* associated with the unconscious and the world of dreams.

In *Qu'est-ce que la littérature?* Sartre separates poetry from the rest of literature by declaring that its words do not function as intellectual signs, nor are they meant to express ideas or reality as such. Instead, poetic enunciations exist for their own sake, are things, not signs, and poetry can be defined or envisaged as pure language.[2] In this, Sartre propagates a doctrine held by many, including the Abbé Bremond and Roland Barthes, which states that the nature of poetry is to *be* language and that, in the last analysis, it represents only itself.

A comparable doctrine assumes that the norm of speech is prose and that poetry encompasses breaking away from the norm. This implies, however, that poetry cannot be conceived as the embellishment, ornamentation, or rhetorical amplification of literary prose or the everyday spoken idiom. It is of a different essence, just as each poet's style seeks to be different in essence from prose and from the style of his fellow poets. Ideally, each poet invents his own language. Hence the demand for striking imagery and an unexpected vocabulary, so that the poet will create a sense of shock in the reader, an impression of mystery and the unknown. Hence also the poet's dread of language, for should his text fail to become what he wishes it to be, he has no choice but to relapse into silence.

Last of all, from Poe and Baudelaire to the present, we find a continuous historical elaboration of the concept of *poésie pure*, which assumes that the best poetry, the only real poetry, contains uniquely poetic value, thus is exempt from allegedly nonpoetic values such as the emotive, the moral, and the epistemological.[3] Many nondevotees of pure poetry nonetheless agree that the poem is self-reflexive, existing only for itself; that poetry remakes the world; that poetry's chief function is to question its own nature and function; that in a sense poetry creates itself, proclaims its identity, and *is* ontologically prior to its poet; finally, that the poem or poet is God.

Some notion of the attitudes just summarized can be found in the Appendix, which lists the books that fall into this line and offers a number of representative quotations. The idea of poetry they represent can in one sense be categorized as Romantic or Symbolist (or post-Romantic and post-Symbolist). In fact, it is a modern, reductionist, nondifferentiated view that is not at all a fair or accurate reflection of the opinions of any of the great Romantic or Symbolist poets; neither does it offer an adequate account of the views of leading contemporary scholars on those periods. For one thing, it fails to take into account the evolution from Romanticism to Symbolism to Surrealism. Obviously, the esthetics of Lamartine, Hugo, Mallarmé, and Valéry are by no means identical. Whereas self-expression, sincerity, and the outpouring of personal emotion are hallmarks of Romanticism, the text as a perfectly constructed object and the embodiment of an ideal universe of beauty belongs to a later generation. Leconte de Lisle, Mallarmé, and Rimbaud reacted against Romantic subjectivism and sentiment. The early and late Symbolists strove for an antiprosaic, elevated diction. Laforgue, Corbière, Apollinaire, and the Surrealists then undermined conventional poetical rhetoric under the influence of prose. Indeed, there is an inherent contradiction between literature deemed to be subjective and biographically or psychologically authentic, on the one hand, and self-reflexive and devoid of emotive or moral value, on the other. And we find, in the twentieth century, two converging yet distinct currents: poetry as an Orphic quest for the ineffable, and meta-poetry, nonreferential, turning in upon itself. Nonetheless, at the level and in the books to which I refer, the tenets we can call modern are derived from the Romantics and the Symbolists. The filiation is direct, and today the various doctrines have been fused into a general modern synthesis. And it is this synthesis that has formed the taste of the advanced, culture-oriented student, reader, and poet in French-speaking countries today.

Whether or not the synthesis, reductionist and nondifferentiated as it is, in fact accounts for the sort of verse composed since 1800 is of course open to question. Indeed, whether or not the views of the great poet-theorists taken separately account for their own verse is also questionable. There has to be a certain congruence between the artistic production of the last two centuries and the ideas of literature elaborated during the same time span. The Romantic or Symbolist poetics do express, if nothing else, some of the *intentions* of Hugo and Mallarmé, Baudelaire and Valéry, Claudel and Pierre Emmanuel. The number of poets who, since Vigny and Hugo, have proclaimed comparable notions, who have consciously, willfully meditated on their art, proves the point.[4] Yet, although their theories of literature provide insights into the nature, the substance, the essence of modern verse, we cannot rely upon Hugo's or Mallarmé's personal esthetic or public pronouncements to be the last word concerning their art or that of their contemporaries, any more than we do in the case of Ronsard and Boileau. Poetry is not criticism. Poets are not critics. And the modern critic possesses a cumulative knowledge of and insight into the nature of literature that no writer or critic of the past, Ronsard, Boileau, or Mallarmé, can equal.

But what of the past? What about the eight centuries of verse that extend from *La Chanson de Saint-Alexis* to the discovery of Chénier and the publication of Lamartine's *Méditations poétiques*? One thing is certain: Whatever its validity for the modern, the esthetic of sincerity, originality, linguistic creativity, and pure poetry is neither suitable nor justifiable in the case of *chansons de geste, romans courtois,* and the songs of the trouvères, Machaut and Charles d'Orléans, Marot and Ronsard, Sponde, La Ceppède, and d'Aubigné, La Fontaine, Racine, and Boileau. To apply such criteria to the poetry of the past results in a biased reading of the past. By overmodernizing, we look for the criteria where they do not exist—in one or two modern-seeming poets such as Villon and du Bellay. By overemphasizing Villon or du Bellay, we neglect their contemporaries. Finally, we downgrade entire periods—the early

Middle Ages or the eighteenth century—where no Villon or du Bellay can be found.

Significantly, the vast majority of studies on French verse cited in the Appendix solve this problem by ignoring it, that is, by ignoring the past altogether. They claim to treat the French tradition yet take almost all their examples from the period since Lamartine, if not since Baudelaire. A whole series of books will contain an occasional, isolated allusion to the pre-Romantic past, as a rule limited to Villon, Ronsard, possibly Malherbe, and Racine. That is all. And that is the rule.

True, a number of writers do cope with the past, but not with success. The major contemporary poet Alain Bosquet, in his *Verbe et vertige: Situations de la poésie*,[5] an influential, oft-quoted study and anthology, states that verse in the Middle Ages was concerned only with simple narration and that it was excessively transparent, manifesting no sense of the mysteries, of the unknowable and unsayable. After Villon, the tradition extending from Marot to Lamartine is alleged to be still worse. During this period external form is emphasized, and verse reveals qualities of order, harmony, measure, elegance, rhetoric, abstraction, and psychological insight. These traits, deemed to be specially French, exclude true poetry, as does the purportedly subjective and politically oriented voice of the Romantics. In France, according to Bosquet, real poetry begins with Baudelaire and Nerval.

In *Structure du langage poétique*, Jean Cohen proposes a strikingly original contribution to poetic theory in France.[6] Choosing three figures from each of three major periods—Classicism (Corneille, Molière, Racine), Romanticism (Lamartine, Vigny, Hugo), and Symbolism (Verlaine, Rimbaud, Mallarmé)—Cohen compares the measurable, quantitative frequency of certain traits of style and language, such as nonpunctuated metrical pauses, noncategorical rhymes, and impertinent, redundant, and abnormal epithets. In almost all cases he observes an evolution from the seventeenth to the twentieth centuries in the direction of greater and more numerous *écarts* of poetic language from the language of prose. His conclusion: The essence of poetry is to be found in these *écarts*; a true sense of the nature of poetry comes to the foreground only with the Moderns; poetry becomes truly poetic as it evolves historically in time. Cohen has obviously been influenced by Barthes, who, in *Le Degré zéro de la littérature*, contrasts the verse of the classical age (ornamental prose) with modern verse, genuinely poetic in essence, and who states that true *écriture* has existed only since 1850, during the great period of crisis in bourgeois society.[7] Robert Champigny also distinguishes the quality of poetry from that of eloquence or of the theater; he also believes that only today is poetry in the process of reaching maturity.[8]

Such denigration of the tradition of French verse, whether it be implicit and based upon seemingly rigorous analysis as with Cohen, or explicit and largely subjective as in the case of Bosquet, is by no means a recent phenomenon. To cite three examples: Pierre Louÿs wrote: "L'histoire de la poésie française n'a que trois pages: *Création,* par Ronsard; *Destruction,* par Boileau; *Résurrection,* par André Chénier."[9] A no less peremptory judgment comes from A. E. Housman and André Gide in an anecdote Gide recounted in the Preface to his *Anthologie de la poésie française*:

> —Comment expliquez-vous, M. Gide, qu'il n'y ait pas de poésie française?
> Et comme, interloqué, j'hésitais à le comprendre, il précisa:
> —L'Angleterre a sa poésie, l'Allemagne a sa poésie, l'Italie a sa poésie. La France n'a pas de poésie . . .
> Il vit assurément que je doutais si je devais prendre ces derniers mots pour une boutade impertinente, et continua de sorte que je ne pusse croire, de sa part, à de l'ignorance:
> —Oh, je sais bien, vous avez eu Villon, Baudelaire. . .
> J'entrevis aussitôt ce à quoi il tendait, et pour m'en assurer:
> —Vous pourriez ajouter Verlaine, dis-je.
> —Assurément, reprit-il; quelques autres encore; je les connais. Mais, entre Villon et Baudelaire, quelle longue et constante méprise a fait considérer comme poèmes des discours rimés où l'on trouve de l'esprit, de l'éloquence, de la virulence, du pathos, mais jamais de la poésie.[10]

Finally, Rimbaud's famous letter to Paul Demeny ought to be cited:

> Toute poésie antique aboutit à la poésie grecque, Vie harmonieuse.—De la Grèce au mouvement romantique,—moyen âge,—il y a des lettrés, des versificateurs. D'Ennius à Theroldus, de Theroldus à Casimir Delavigne, tout est prose rimée, un jeu, avachissement et gloire d'innombrables générations idiotes: Racine est le pur, le fort, le grand. —On eût soufflé sur ses rimes, brouillé ses hémistiches, que le Divin Sot serait aujourd'hui aussi ignoré que le premier venu auteur d'*Origines*. —Après Racine, le jeu moisit. Il a duré deux mille ans![11]

This prejudice can be accounted for in historical terms. Louÿs, Gide, Housman, and the young Rimbaud—all four to some extent neo-Romantics—hold a Romantic attitude toward French verse: the assumption that France has been traditionally a classical nation and as such imposed its esthetic upon the rest of Europe in the seventeenth and eighteenth centuries; that the essence of poetry is, however, Romantic; therefore, the founding countries of Romanticism, England and Germany, are inherently more poetic than France is or was; and that modern Frenchmen have had to rebel against, indeed to deny, their national tradition and its "déficience même du sentiment lyrique," again to quote Gide, in order to become true poets in the modern sense.

Surely not unrelated to this phenomenon is the relative weight granted to the different periods of French literary history in textbooks and anthologies. Having examined a few major anthologies of verse published since World War II, I compared the numbers of pages allotted to the eight centuries before Chénier and those devoted to the modern period, that is, the last 150 to 180 years. Here are the results:

	Number of pages	
Anthology	1050–1800	1800–19—
Cl. Bonnefoy, *La Poésie française*	214	397
S. Brindeau, *La France en poésie*	47	97
A. G. Canfield and W. F. Patterson, *French Poems*	219	259
J. Chiari, *Harrap Anthology of French Poetry*	224	287
L. Decaunes, *Les Riches Heures de la poésie française*	81	313
A. Gide, *Anthologie de la poésie française*	341	433
R. Lalou, *Les Plus Beaux Poèmes français*	92	172
J. Mambrino, *La Poésie mystique française*	50	241
The Oxford Book of French Verse	266	326
The Penguin Book of French Verse	319	329
Les Plus Belles Pages de la poésie française	275	472
G. Pompidou, *Anthologie de la poésie française*	208	276
P. Seghers, *Le Livre d'or de la poésie française*	150	287
W. J. Smith, *Poems from France*	46	152

A comparable situation exists with regard to anthologies used in the schools. Of course, one eminently legitimate explanation for the predominance of the modern is pedagogical. At any level, in any country, students do not necessarily have sufficient command of the language to master older texts. Initiating them to poetry, teaching them to love poetry, may well require some neglect of the past. Whatever the reason, it is true that the *Littérature et langage* series, conceived after 1968 and designed to renew the teaching of literature, is organized according to theme and genre in place of the chronological evolution. Volume 2, *Le conte, la poésie,* contains seventeen French *textes d'étude* from prior to 1800 and twenty-nine from after that date.[12] To be fair to the innovators, however, their coverage is more representative, more universal, than in the somewhat traditional *L'Art de commenter un poème lyrique* by François Germain.[13] Germain, whose "doctorat d'état" revolutionized Vigny studies in the 1950s and remains perhaps the best volume ever devoted to a French Romantic poet, lists the great French lyricists: Ronsard, Jean-Jacques Rousseau, and seven names that extend from Chateaubriand to Valéry. His anthology includes two poems prior to Chateaubriand, thirteen from Romanticism and since. And in a major German publication, a collection of essays on French verse published in 1970 (*Interpretationen französischer Gedichte,* ed. Kurt Wais), eight articles treat five poets from Villon to Chénier, whereas seventeen articles cover thirteen poets of the nineteenth and twentieth centuries.[14] In a comparable publication from 1975 (*Die französische Lyrik,* ed. Hans Hinterhäuser), of the fifty-nine texts studied, nineteen are before the nineteenth century and forty since that time, thirty-two of these after Baudelaire.[15] In his introduction the editor claims that his choice was determined not by personal taste but by history.

Of course, scholars working within their fields of specialization, for the most part the traditional century periods, are aware of the value of composition in verse. Splendid criticism has been done in all areas, rehabilitating schools of poetry and individual poets. Since the 1950s, students of the Baroque period have made the most striking contribution to a revaluation of the canon, and medievalists have worked with enthusiasm and élan. Figures such as Jean Renart and Thibaut de Champagne, Guillaume de Machaut and Jean Lemaire de Belges, Scève, Sponde, La Ceppède, Théophile de Viau, and Saint-Amant, who used to be considered *minores,* are now slowly but surely receiving the recognition they deserve. The problem is, given the state of literary studies in our universities, whether in France, Germany, or the United States, scholars write for other scholars specializing in the same area. No matter how fine the monograph, how important the discovery or revaluation an individual makes, it most probably will be limited to the purview of his fellow *iémistes.* Conversely, although specialists in various centuries are aware of the latest research in their field, often their knowledge of other periods is based upon *idées reçues* long out of date. It is a sad, undeniable fact that for many professors of French the terms *baroque* or *rococo* remain only words. The seventeenth century is still to be characterized by "Corneille, Racine, Molière" and the eighteenth by "les idées des Philosophes." How many teachers of French, or general readers for that matter, know a French epic other than the

Song of Roland and have any idea of what is contained in the *Romance of the Rose?*[16]

An analogous situation, or at least an analogous overemphasis of the nineteenth century, was prevalent in the English-speaking world up to the 1920s. However, it disappeared under the assault of Modernism (Eliot, Pound, Auden) and the New Critics. These men were concerned with the close reading of texts; they emphasized the inherent, unique, literary quality of literature. They also believed in scrutinizing or re-valuating literary history. Thus Eliot, Leavis, Brooks, and Empson all contributed to the revision of the canon of English verse: to rehabilitating Donne, the Metaphysicals, and to a lesser extent Dryden, Pope, and the Augustans, and to a relative downgrading of Milton and of the nineteenth century. Whether or not one agrees with them is irrelevant. The importance of their contribution was and still is to focus attention on the national tradition and to encourage, indeed to insist upon, a rethinking of that tradition as a living bond between contemporary poets and the masters of the past.

Indeed, in contrast to France, it is literally inconceivable for studies on English verse as a whole to neglect everyone prior to Wordsworth or Browning; for that matter, it is no less inconceivable for studies on Italian and Spanish verse to neglect everyone prior to Leopardi and Manzoni or Bécquer and Rubén Darío. In these three countries Chaucer, Spenser, Milton, and Pope; Dante, Petrarch, Ariosto, and Tasso; Juan Ruiz, Garcilaso, Juan de la Cruz, and Góngora, for the university professor and the practicing poet, in the student texts and artistic reviews, form the heart of the tradition, are an honor to the muses and to the nation.

Unfortunately, the French *nouveaux critiques* have done little to counter the trend. Although their theory of literature and their analy-sis of individual texts follow in the traces of their Anglo-American predecessors, they have tended to limit their purview to the contempo-rary period and a few French classics. They are concerned with a universal grammar of narrative or with the theory of *différance*, not with revising the norms of literary history and revaluating the standard academic canon.

Such is the situation in general. Of course, some structuralists or poststructuralists have chosen to work with poetry and have made valu-able contributions. The most famous attempt is an article co-authored by Jakobson and Lévi-Strauss on Baudelaire's "Les Chats," which launched an ongoing debate on that text and on structuralism.[17] Jakob-son is a world-renowned linguist, the author of a number of studies on poems in several languages. In the same general current we can place

Julia Kristeva, Jean Cohen, and Michael Riffaterre.[18] Collections of new-critical essays on poetry have appeared in recent years. Among the more striking are *Essais de sémiotique poétique,* edited by Greimas; *Sémantique de la poésie,* edited by Todorov; and a *Rhétorique de la poésie,* ascribed to "Le Groupe μ."[19]

In opposition to this current, however, Henri Meschonnic and others have criticized the Jakobson-Cohen assumption that prose represents a linguistic norm, therefore that poetry has to be considered the *écart* from that norm.[20] On this point Greimas joins the revisionists. Meschonnic furthermore castigates the linguistic structuralists and semioticians, including Greimas, for excessive formalism, for their implicit postulate that the kernel of poetry and of poetic analysis lies in stylistics, to the neglect of other critical approaches or aspects of the text. There is certainly some justification to reservations of this kind. For example, the Todorov collection includes contributions on semantics, figures, and rhetoric, but not on poetry itself. Another problem concerns the fact that Jakobson, Greimas, and their followers are indeed structural linguists; their insights are predicated upon precise, rigorous knowledge of and formation in that discipline. Therefore, their analyses have not had the impact they deserve because nonlinguistically trained scholars can scarcely comprehend the line of argument. And, resembling their predecessors in one respect, structuralists concentrate on modern verse almost exclusively. Just as Riffaterre specializes in the stylistic analysis of Victor Hugo and Kristeva is fascinated by Mallarmé, the Greimas group offers semiotic-linguistic studies of Jarry, Bataille, Rimbaud, Michaux, and Mallarmé; they also discuss Apollinaire, Baudelaire, Hugo, Nerval, and Jacques Roubaud.

I do not seek to paint a distorted, unfair, or uncharitable picture of contemporary attitudes toward poetry. I admire Sartre, Barthes, Jakobson, Greimas, Bosquet, and for that matter all who contribute to the defense and illustration of French verse. Polemic is not my aim. Nor am I unaware of the exceptions, men of letters who respect the past and propose something other than post-Romantic notions of poetry: Eluard, who edited the influential *Première Anthologie vivante de la poésie du passé*; Thierry Maulnier, who, in his *Introduction à la poésie française* (1939), ascribes the golden age of French verse to the sixteenth and seventeenth centuries and places Villon, Scève, du Bellay, Ronsard, d'Aubigné, and Racine ahead of Baudelaire and Rimbaud; Roger Caillois, who, in *Les Impostures de la poésie* and *Art poétique,* insists upon clarity, hard work, metrical constraint, and imitation as central to the poetic process; and Francis Ponge, author of *Pour un Malherbe,* apologist for a return to rigor, control, and reason in contemporary writing.[21] This is the heritage of Valéry as well as of Malherbe. Nonetheless, it is a fact that Eluard, Maulnier, Caillois, and Ponge form a tiny minority. As stated earlier, the vast majority of books on French verse, student texts, and reviews uphold an esthetic emphasizing sincerity, originality, lyricism, rebellion, and mystical insight while at the same time ignoring or denigrating most poetry prior to the nineteenth century. That is the position I hope to contest and to correct.

In the course of this book I shall examine questions central to the neo-Romantic and neo-Symbolist esthetic and, for that matter, to any esthetic of poetry. Chapters will discuss the poet's voice and persona, levels of style, genre and the problem of message, poetry as religion and transcendence, the poet and his public. I shall base my enquiry upon evidence provided by the French poets, concentrating upon the early masters, the tradition that extends from the *Song of Roland* to Voltaire and Chénier. It will come as no surprise that my findings shall be in antithesis to those offered by the Romantic and Symbolist schools. The longest, most important section will scrutinize the problem of literary history, seeking to explore the evolution of French verse and calling for a change in the canon. These last chapters will also consider the present state of poetry in France and prospects for the future. Throughout I shall comment on individual texts, consciously limiting myself to the older poetry (pre-1800) because it is less known to the general reader and because it forms the tradition that I seek to explore and to defend.

In my opinion, the standard view, derived from Romanticism and Symbolism, is not absolute but historically determined and limited, and it fails to come to grips with the continuity of French verse. It behooves us to become more aware of a tradition that has played so great a role in French and world culture. Otherwise, a unique segment of our heritage will be lost forever. One of the doctrines of modern criticism states that all writers work within a common literary culture, made up of rules, conventions, registers, genres, modes, styles, archetypes, common themes, and motifs. American New Criticism, the myth-criticism of Frye and his disciples, French structuralism, Franco-American deconstructionism, and German esthetics of reception all emphasize the inherent literariness of literature. In the last analysis, poetry is based on and derived from other poetry; it is an ontological whole in and of itself. Furthermore, poetry reaches out across the ages. The vocation of letters is handed down in the tradition of the "clerks," forming an unbroken historical succession and a professional brotherhood. Eliot and Leavis bequeathed to England a sense of their tradition. France needs to become aware of her own, which she ought to have but, up to now, has largely failed to obtain. I am committed to the elaboration of such a notion of tradition, to Curtius's ideal of cultural continuity as the *exempla maiorum,* a perpetual celebration, preservation, rediscovery, and restoration of our culture.[22] To contribute to the ideal is the purpose of this book.

2

THE PERSONA

Poetry expresses the individual voice of its creator, the poet, who reveals the deepest feelings of his soul with sincerity and authenticity. The poet is seen as a sublime and/or pathetic creator, a heroic, unique individual, and his is an individual voice. The quality of verse depends upon and has to reflect the author's sincerity, authenticity, and originality—originality conceived as a reflection of sincerity and sincerity as a reflection of originality.

This "personal myth" or "biographical fallacy"[1] is not unique to the modern world. Throughout history the public associates poetry with the poet and relates artistic creation to the creator's life and personality. Even in the Middle Ages trouvères proclaimed an esthetic comparable to the Romantics in one respect, however much they differ in others: that good love poetry is sincere; that it proceeds from an outpouring of love in the heart; that ladies ought therefore to recognize true lovers and true poets, distinguishing them from false ones; and that the poet is a lover, and the lover a poet. This is the notion of *convenance,* stating that the form and contents of a courtly song correspond to, derive from, and reflect a comparable state, both inspiration and authentic sentiment, inside the poet.

We also know that the medieval public did project the subject matter of songs onto their authors' lives, that they invented appropriate love stories to explain the love songs these men composed. This accounts for the *Razos* and *Vidas* of the troubadours and, in the thirteenth and fourteenth centuries, for a series of romances or of *dits amoureux* that contain lyrical inserts ascribed by the narrator-implied author to the hero, either to an independent character or to himself in his role as protagonist-lover. These texts can be called poetic pseudobiographies or poetic pseudoautobiographies; in them the lyrics comment on the story, and the story purportedly tells how the lyrics came into being. The allegedly personal experiences recounted in the narrative attest to the authenticity of the lyrics, to the reality behind their composition. They tell us something about the historicity and quality of the songs, just as the songs, as historical evidence, guarantee the historicity and authenticity of the frame-narrative.

However, modern scholarship informs us that the medieval trouvère partakes of shared conventions and works within preexisting registers of expression, based upon stylistic and thematic decorum. He readily sacrifices his personal experience, even his identity, in order to participate in the tradition. The work of art is made up of rhetorical commonplaces, elaborated in an organic relationship with his public, a group of connoisseurs who judge him largely on formal criteria. The truth these songs reveal is uniquely esthetic. And the pseudobiographies and pseudoautobiographies are uniquely works of fiction, fascinating esthetic constructs, intertexts containing interior duplication, but fiction nonetheless. *Le Roman du Castelain de Couci* is a courtly romance, a novel based upon an old folkloric motif, that, to the best of our knowledge, tells us nothing historical about the poet, Gui, Châtelain de Couci. Nor do tales of love authored by Guillaume de Machaut reveal accurate autobiographical information about him.

The same is true when we approach more recent verse. For generations a romantic biography was projected onto Pierre de Ronsard, his life highlighted by a series of passionate love affairs, or at least passionate longings, with and for Cassandre, Marie, Sinope, Genèvre, Astrée, and Hélène, each recipient of the Master's verse purported to be a genuine flesh-and-blood beloved. More recent scholarship has shown that Ronsard probably never was in love with Isabeau de Limeuil, a member of Catherine de' Medici's "flying squadron," Prince Louis de Condé's mistress, or with the prototype for Astrée, Françoise d'Estrées, mistress of the Duke of Anjou, the future Henry III; the "Sonnets sur la mort de Marie" were written for King Henry, mourning the death of another mistress, Marie de Clèves. We have no reason to believe that a Marie Dupin from Bourgueil in Anjou ever existed at all. It is probable that Ronsard, deciding to shift from middle style to low style, from verse based upon Petrarchan convention and abstruse mythology to a pastoral mode with sensual overtones, evoking the body in addition to roses, simply invented a country girl, Marie, to balance off the courtly lady Cassandre. Even when a specific beloved is mentioned, even when we think we have found a woman to whom Ronsard addressed his verse, biographical truth proves to be illusory. There was an Hélène de Surgères; she was the official narratee of the *Sonnets pour Hélène*. Nonetheless, Ronsard wrote about her cruelly to his friend Scévole de Sainte-Marthe; his other friend, the Cardinal du Perron, mocked her to her face. Was Hélène de Surgères ever loved by the poet other than as the object of his next cycle, designated as such by the queen? After all, Petrarch had Laura, Scève had Délie, du Bellay had Olive, Baïf had Francine. The Prince of Poets determined that he would have Cassandre, Marie, Hélène, and many more.

Similarly, in modern times, although Lamartine published a series of love elegies directed to Elvire, several real women inspired his muse: Antoniella, Lena, Julie Charles, for that matter his wife, and quite a few of the poems were of strictly literary origin. Indeed, the author took the trouble to cover his traces, to convince mistress "X" that most or all of the pieces in his collection were composed for her, and that the exceptions concerned only a very old flame ("Y"), now deceased, whereas "Z" had never existed at all. Perhaps the greatest single volume of lyrics in the nineteenth century proves to be *Les Contemplations* (1856), in which Victor Hugo elaborates a structure of unusual power and simplicity, whereby poems of tranquillity and joy (the first three books of *Les Contemplations*: "Autrefois") allegedly precede the death of his daughter Léopoldine in 1843, and poems of suffering (the last three books: "Aujourd'hui") come after that date. Unfortunately, literary space in the book does not correspond to chronological time of composition or of inspiration. In order to create his fiction, Hugo falsifies the dates ascribed to his texts, for indeed one of the painful poems was written prior to 1843 and most of the joyful ones afterward.

A sonnet sequence or a book of elegies is first and foremost literature, a verbal pattern in which private biographical inspiration may indeed play a role, but only one, relatively minor part of the whole. What counts is the dramatic function of the "poet as lover" or "poet as creator" in a literary structure determined by the genre and mode the author chooses to cultivate. Were Ronsard and Lamartine in love with Hélène de Surgères and Julie Charles? Were they in love with an ideal woman, an *Ewig-Weibliche*: Helen of Troy and Elvire? Were they in love with love? Or were they passionately, committedly, in love with literature and desperate to imitate Petrarch? The answer will be, most likely, all four, none of the four, and each of the four in succession, from day to day and week to week, as the poet lives and as he creates.

Even when we can discover a specific, concrete trace of influence between an author's work and events in his personal life (Charles d'Orléans, Villon, and Théophile de Viau in prison; Aragon in adoration before Elsa Triolet), the trace in question most often proves to be trivial and irrelevant to our reading of the work. This is because a poem is never the direct expression of events in an author's life or even of his personality or state of mind vis-à-vis these events. Although a poem can express an archetype, a myth, a mentality, the writer is withdrawn from the mentality he himself has created. In other words, poets write as poets, not as men, consciously or unconsciously erecting a barrier between themselves and their work. Conversely, our experience of the greatness or uniqueness of a work of art does not derive from, nor does it in any way serve as evidence for, the personality or life experience of the artist. The text causes us to recognize, even to share, universal human feelings and experience, not the idiosyncratic reactions of one person. Because an emotion has been felt strongly by a poet does not guarantee that he will communicate it strongly to the reader; on the contrary, a poem expressing strong emotion may have been composed by an emotionless, ultrabookish author. We can no longer accept the Romantic doctrine that poets inherently possess more enthusiasm, sensitivity, and passion than other men. Similarly, nothing prevents us from appreciating verse produced by scoundrels, individuals who may have led despicable lives. A poet has to be defined as a person who makes poems; therefore our domain of study is the poem and the effect it has on readers, not the biography and psychology of its maker.

Perhaps Eliot's greatest contribution to criticism was his recognition of certain truths:

> . . . the more perfect the artist, the more completely separate in him will be the man who suffers and the mind which creates. . . .

> The business of the poet is not to find new emotion, but to use the ordinary ones and, in working them up into poetry, to express feelings which are not in actual emotions at all.

> Poetry is not a turning loose of emotion, but an escape from emotion; it is not the expression of personality, but an escape from personality.[2]

A distinction has to be made between natural discourse and fictive discourse, the latter defined as the representation of natural discourse in a work of art.[3] Imaginative literature—novels, plays, poems—is always and by definition fictive. This is the case whether the author adopts an impersonal, omniscient stance (the implied author-narrator in Chrétien de Troyes or Zola), assumes the personality of a literary character obviously to be distinguished from himself (the Comtesse de

*** in *La Vie de Marianne*; Jacob recounting *Le Paysan parvenu*), or appears as a version of himself, as a character who takes the author's name and at least some of his personal traits (much lyric poetry, Machaut's *dits*, Proust's *roman*).

For at least one generation now critics in the Anglo-American world no longer refer to the "I" of a poem as "Donne," "Pope," and "Shelley," nor do they refer to him as "the poet." The "I" is designated as "the Speaker" or "the Narrator," and we never confuse him with the author, not even with the "implied author." The Speaker is treated as a literary character, who may or may not share traits and experiences with the author, and who represents the author per se no more than Hamlet and Lear represent Shakespeare, or Pyrrhus, Néron, and Phèdre stand for Racine. All poems are said by a Speaker. Indeed, a poem can be defined as verse utterances delivered by a Speaker; the poem is the Speaker speaking. The poem is also the Speaker's vision of the world discovered by the reader, for the Speaker-Narrator does not perorate in the void; he performs for a Narratee and/or an implied reader-audience. Furthermore, the Speaker can be reliable or unreliable. He can speak with something approaching the implied author's authority and seek to mold the beliefs and norms of the implied reader, be a dramatized, active participant, a reliable commentator, with whom we sympathize because the poem is filtered uniquely through his consciousness, because he has full control of the inside vision, and his is the central intelligence, most likely the only voice we hear. Or, on the contrary, the author may create a situation in which distance intervenes, in which the implied reader withdraws from the Speaker and judges him in turn. These are some of the options open to the writer, the voices he adopts, the masks he wears; hence we are correct to say that they serve as his personae.

Now for some examples. The dominant trait in early medieval letters was that of a poetic or universal "I", an Everyman representative of mankind. As a reliable Narrator with a valid claim to authenticity, he would generally be objective, unobtrusive, and unself-conscious. However, each of the truly great troubadours chose to play a role, to adopt a persona that distinguished him and his work within the tradition: Thus we can account for Bernart de Ventadorn, the humble, timid wooer; Jaufre Rudel, the lover from afar; Arnaut Daniel, the "lunatic"; and Peire Vidal, the boaster. In the late Middle Ages a new persona, the naïve, blundering comic hero, developed into a convention, largely because of Guillaume de Machaut, though it existed already in Jean de Meun. The Machaut-Narrator can serve as a witness, as nonhero or nonlover to provide comic relief, or act as a foil to the aristocratic, amorous protagonist. However, in *Le Jugement dou Roy de Behaingne, Le Jugement dou Roy de Navarre,* and *La Fonteinne amoureuse,* the "I" is not only the center of consciousness but also the single focus for the plot. What he says is to be given credence; he participates actively in the tale as hero. Indeed, since the mode of the *dit amoureux* is highly dramatic—the Narrator shows rather than tells, his technique is scenic rather than panoramic—Machaut succeeds in creating the illusion of objectivity. On the other hand, for this reason, focalization remains external to the Narrator's deepest feelings. We recognize him to be obtuse and naïve, not aware of comic overtones in his story. Even though he may identify with the Narrator, Machaut erects a barrier between himself and his all-too-human literary creation. He is more sophisticated than his Narrator, and his attitude toward the events recounted in his tales may be quite different.

Machaut the author appears inside and outside the plot: as a literary character, participant or witness, actively engaged in events; as the same character, telling the story of these events later; and as himself, the implied author, pulling the strings. From this situation emerges distance and control, given that the unself-conscious, unobtrusive Narrator is separated from the only too self-conscious, obtrusive hero-witness and from the author hiding behind the scenes. Machaut the author provides both support and correction, sympathy for and criticism of, the Narrator as hero.

François Villon is often credited with being the first "personal poet" and, as *le bon folastre,* a rebel against society and public morals, a precursor of the Romantics, Rimbaud, and Genet. However, the genre Villon chose to adopt—the mock-testament—and the satirical mode he chose to write it in determine in large measure the themes and style of his work. Just as Machaut sought to appear as a naïve, blundering nonlover witness-poet and Charles d'Orléans adopted the stance of an aging, indifferent prince, given to *nonchaloir,* so Villon incarnates intermittently the roles of repentant sinner, disconsolate lover, loyal friend, scourge of vice, gay trickster, and shameless lecher. He cultivates both the elegiac and ironic modes, both poetry and counterpoetry. Furthermore, narrative voice and point of view vary according to the demands of the text. For example, the "Ballade pour Robert d'Estouteville" and the "Ballade pour prier Nostre Dame," bequeathed to the provost of Paris and the author's mother, respectively, are written from their point of view and in their voice. The latter text especially is a masterpiece of dramatic displacement. Villon succeeds in entering into the consciousness of an ignorant woman of the people, filtering ideas, imagery, even speech through her imagination. The Speaker's naïve Christian belief, her commitment to faith over good works, her obsessive restatement of the Credo (it is all she has!), her confession of illiteracy, her evoking the simplest, most conventional, most popular religious motifs (harps and lutes in heaven, boiling pitch in hell; the legends of Theophilus and Mary the Egyptian), the assimilation of herself as woman to the Virgin Mary (she speaks as a mother to the Mother of God) and to a repentant Saint Mary the Egyptian—all this is appropriate to the mentality of Villon's mother as a persona in the text and should be read as a fictional or semifictional projection of her, but of course it tells us nothing about the beliefs, religious and otherwise, of the poet or his real, historical mother.

Even when Villon speaks in his own voice, the context of the poem determines its style and register. The dramatized, obtrusive mock-poet is at times brought close to the reader; he demonstrates qualities of sincerity, honesty, pathos, and sympathetic wit. The reader, sharing his ethical norms, can even identify with him. Thus the speaker appears as a reliable narrator; we can take him seriously and believe what he says. The *Lais* begins and ends with personal reminiscence: In the cold of winter, the dead season, we see Villon the poor scholar shivering in his room. He is assimilated to the wolf, outcast and enemy of society, who has to feed on the wind. He falls asleep alone. The fire is extinguished and his flickering candle has blown out. The room is so cold that his ink has frozen. Poetry, consciousness, and the flame of life cannot abide winter, a season which, because of Christmas, should remind us of eternal life but which instead brings famine, cold, and ultimately death for wolves and the impoverished poet.

However, we do not know under what conditions Villon composed the *Lais*. That particular Christmas he may have been burglarizing the Collège de Navarre! Furthermore, unless we accept for all verse the principles of inspiration endemic to Romanticism, it must be assumed that the historical Villon did not literally compose a series of perfect *huitains* in the cold of a winter evening, doze off, and then conclude his legacy with other perfectly constructed *huitains* written without a candle to see by and in frozen ink. Villon the poet has elaborated some traditional exordium and conclusion topics in a highly original way by recounting an incident in the life of Villon the narrator that may well not have had the slightest historical foundation.

A still more striking example is the "Ballade de la Grosse Margot," in which the Narrator-Speaker, choosing to bequeath a poem to a low-class prostitute, lowers the style and contents to her level, rendering them commensurate to her point of view, adopting the role of her lover and procurer. This is of course a literary tour de force that tells us nothing about Villon the author's experiences or lack thereof among the fleshpots of Paris. To what extent the poet shares the Narrator's normative judgments either when he wrote this *ballade* or when he elaborated the *Testament* in its ultimate form, to what extent the incident described in the *ballade* is nonfictional and whether or not Margot existed historically, remain open to conjecture. The Narrator, as Margot's procurer, is playing a role, different from but not necessarily more reliable than that of the chaste, anguished lover perishing from his lady's glancing eyes.

Du Bellay's *Regrets* is in no sense an autobiography, any more than is Villon's *Testament*. The author chooses to write satire, and for that reason adopts a persona, assuming a self-conscious Horatian voice that employs the appropriate Horatian register. The Speaker appears to denigrate himself but in fact is only renouncing the sublime and middle styles, characterized by *gravitas* and *delectatio,* in which Ronsard excels. As a satirist and as a practitioner of *genus tenue,* he has to persuade the implied reader, to manipulate him, to impose his own values and norms. An important arm in the persuasion is the illusion of sincerity, established through a conversational tone, the evocation of concrete external reality, and the forthright statement of *saeva indignatio,* of an allegedly passionate response from himself to that reality. Du Bellay is also one of the first practitioners of the "esthetics of negligence" motif, whereby a Speaker-implied author admits to being inferior to court poets in technique, in mastery of composition, and in stylistic elegance.[4] He does so, however, not out of true humility or need for some sort of personal confession. In fact, this topic asserts a claim to excellence on the part of the negligent poet. I am an aristocrat, he says, not a mere pedant of the court; I embody *fortitudo* as well as *sapientia*; I am a man of the world, and I know whereof I speak; if I disregard the rules, my verse is all the better because of the qualities of authenticity and true nobility I bring to it. This is of course as much a matter of style, of rhetoric, of *captatio benevolentiae,* as any claim to formal perfection. And (in this he will be followed by Baudelaire and Mallarmé) at the very moment du Bellay admits sterility, incapacity to write in Ronsard's manner, he does so in perfectly composed sonnets that give the lie to his own pose and are proof of his supreme creative capacities and attainments.

Almost a century later, in the High Baroque period, we find an exciting lyric and epic poet, Antoine Gérard de Saint-Amant, who, like du Bellay, has been taken too readily at his own word. Despite scholarly findings to the contrary, Saint-Amant still has a reputation of ignorance and debauchery, of having written in the fumes of wine, of performing splendidly in the descriptive, bacchic, or grotesque genres but being incapable of high seriousness. This is because he specialized, so to speak, in the bacchic and grotesque, because he wrote encomia on wine, cider, and cheese and introduced into France the Burlesque. I submit that *le goinfre, le bon gros,* is a persona, a literary convention that the young provincial from Rouen assumed for a specifically literary purpose when speaking of food and drink; he then adopted other personae, other conventions, in order to write about nature, love, God, and war. He did so in order to demonstrate his originality, to proclaim himself resolutely a *modernus* and, practicing the esthetics of negligence, be recognized as an *honnête homme* free from pedantry with a right to frequent the most aristocratic circles in Europe. We know that, in contrast to the *bon gros* singing away in cabarets, Saint-Amant had one of the finest, most vigorous minds of his generation, that he was well-read in Latin, Italian, and Spanish, that he "rewrote" Ovid, Ronsard, and Marino, capturing them intertextually and giving them his stamp. Conscious of his art, with a high opinion of it, Saint-Amant read the theoreticians and justified his own practice at length. This poet of reason knew the rules, especially when he chose to break them, and his achievement, whether in high, middle, or low style, manifests awareness of esthetic decorum and of the hierarchy of literary kinds.

Boileau adopts a stance similar to du Bellay's: *l'ami du vrai,* an honest man, clumsy but fearless, a poet unfit for the sublime but driven to tell the truth to a corrupt world, endowed by the gods with a gift for satire. He is a *vir bonus, ingénu,* and hero all at the same time. Yet this upright, honest friend of truth adores literary parody and pastiche; the free spirit who lashes out at flatterers and sycophants himself indulges in the most flagrant adulation of Louis XIV ("*grand Roy*") and even of Guillaume de Lamoignon. In *Le Lutrin* his persona, the implied author, claims he is not capable of ending the poem properly and that to describe the feats of his hero (Lamoignon) is beyond his powers. Literally speechless, he urges the hero to conclude the story himself:

> Parle donc: c'est à Toy d'éclaircir ces merveilles. . . .
>   Aussi-bien, quelque ardeur qui m'inspire,
> Quand je songe au Heros qui me reste à décrire,
> Qu'il faut parler de Toy, mon Esprit éperdu
> Demeure sans parole, interdit, confondu.[5]

This self-deprecation serves to undermine a traditional motif: the author of epic, the Ronsardian *vates.* An example of Curtius's *Unsagbarkeit* (inexpressibility),[6] it also is a means for winning the reader's sympathy,

again according to the principles of *captatio benevolentiae*. Boileau intervenes obtrusively not out of real humility but in order to serve as a
mediator between his hero and the public, to establish his authority,
and to mold the implied reader's norms and beliefs. He is the charming, ironic, self-conscious master behind the scenes, who keeps us in-
formed and connives with us against his own characters. The satirist
must hold the reader's attention, win his sympathy, and disarm potential criticism. His persona is unusually ambivalent and self-conscious. It
is also as conventional, as artificial, as much of a topos as any other
persona. This being the case takes nothing away from its effectiveness.
Generations of readers have accepted Boileau's pseudoautobiographical declarations, his confessions, even his decision to renounce satire
(while remaining a satirist). Indeed, the public's acceptance of Boileau's
stance represents a tribute to his skill as an artist, to his capacity to
assume the mask and to make it live, move, and breathe.

The Regent of Parnassus's great inheritor in this line is François-Marie Arouet, in my opinion one of France's last great classical
poets. In a text such as *Le Mondain* Voltaire expresses new, dangerous
ideas: that civilization, art, and luxury are good; that they exist in a
modern world, a society of consumption, which is good; and that the
various social and economic forces that contribute to this state of
affairs—hard work, planetary exploration, and the business ethos—
are also good.[7] Therefore, the present is deemed superior to the past,
progress is found to be an observable fact, worthy of praise, and
ideologies exalting the past and denigrating the present (traditional
Christianity, the courtly pastoral myth) are considered both false and
dangerous. This is where the Voltairean Speaker, the Man of the
World, stands, but not necessarily Voltaire himself or his implied
reader. Much of the charm in *Le Mondain* is derived from its light
touch, from the fact that the author has assumed an authorial stance
and voice, a persona that resembles his own but which we ought not
to identify with totally. The Narrator speaks with authority; his ideas
are the only ones we hear in the course of the poem; and the ideological vision is refracted uniquely through his prism, in his consciousness. His is not necessarily a reliable voice, nor does he have absolute
power over the implied reader, his narratee. By grossly overstating
exaggerated moral claims ("Ce temps profane est tout fait pour mes
moeurs. / J'aime le luxe, et même la mollesse. . ."), by appealing to a
dubious consensus ("Tout honnête homme a de tels sentiments"), and
by raising his cook to the level of a classical demigod ("Qu'un cuisinier
est un mortel divin!"), Voltaire undermines his own privileged voice.

He creates distance, and the reader comes to question the Man of the World's ideas just as the Man of the World questioned those found in the Bible and in Fénelon's *Télémaque*.

From Voltaire's death to the decline of Romanticism (and for the general reader up to today), it has become fashionable to assume that the Speaker in a poem is more sincere, more authentic, if his speech is simple instead of ornate, emotional instead of rational, and spontaneous instead of premeditated. Since Baudelaire, it has become fashionable to assume that the Speaker is sincere and authentic if he confesses he is prurient, shameful, even diabolical, as opposed to claiming to be virtuous or at least calling for virtue. However, Gide, Breton, Aragon, and Eluard maintain the old tradition in one sense: They all insist upon a bond of identification between the man and the artist, between the writer and what he writes, for they believe the inner and outer man coincide; and they proclaim that the best poem is in fact the "most virtuous," in that it reveals truth and will convince the reader to live that truth in his life. The result, however, is neither greater truth and virtue nor, since Baudelaire and Lautréamont, greater vice—simply a new set of personae, a new version of the myth of the artist, a new variation on old themes of rhetoric.

In the Western (and French) tradition for the most part, an author assumes a persona not because of some striking, unusual experience in his life or because of private moods and states of mind, but simply because a persona is called for by the genre or mode in which he chooses to write and the public he chooses to address. The Speaker adapts to his public, for his goal is to manipulate the implied reader, working within the latter's mental and moral framework. Since, in general, form determines subject matter, not the other way around, we can interpret a work of art correctly only by relating it to the genre category in which it belongs, the mode, register, or style that gave it birth and against which it has to be measured. Furthermore, shifts in style and mode over the ages are caused not by brusque mutations, by the conscious, willful revolution of genius, but by the natural evolution of genres and genre expectations in both author and public, determined by the esthetics of reception, and contributed to, of course, by men of genius.

It is true that some modern poets practice one genre and develop one style, cultivating a limited number of themes and motifs. Even in the present, however, this kind of author is not unique; in the centuries prior to Baudelaire he is a *rara avis* indeed. The traditional approach required that a writer adopt many genres, modes, and personae over a lifetime, indeed that he assume more than one persona at the same time. The example of Ronsard is striking in this respect. From 1550 to 1560, his most fruitful decade, the Prince of Poets composed Pindaric odes, Horatian odes, love sonnets in the grand Petrarchan style (six-teenth-century *fin' amor*), love sonnets in a more humble register, erotic poems in the lowest style, eclogues, epitaphs, epithalamia, other "public genres," elegies, and *hymnes*. In the very same year (1553) he published *Livret de folastries* and a new edition of *Les Amours* and *Le Cinquiesme livre des Odes*. In 1555 appeared *Les Meslanges,* a new edition of *Les Quatre premiers livres des Odes, Continuation des Amours,* and *Les Hymnes* (1555). The following year (1556) saw *Nouvelle Continuation des Amours* and *Le Second livre des Hymnes.* And later in his career he continued to practice the old genres and to develop new ones, the most important being satirico-religious *discours* and his epic *La Franciade.* According to stance and voice, Ronsard was a noble lover, a sensuous lover, a lover of food and wine, a sublime thinker, a priest of Apollo (the *poeta vates*), and the scourge of Huguenots, more or less concurrently, based upon the needs of genre, style, and decorum, not his private passions.

Saint-Amant, poet of the High Baroque, proved to be, if anything, more varied than Ronsard in his poetic output and the personae he adopted to create it. Thus the author of *Moyse sauvé,* the major epic of the century (a new kind of epic, the *idyle heroïque*), composed in the course of his lifetime mythological poems (brief epics in the style of Marino), poems on nature, meditative poems, erotic poems high and low, the famous *bon gros* texts devoted to food and drink, burlesque poems, caprices (poems of the fantastic), familiar epistles in the Hora-tian style, and religious texts. As in the case of Ronsard, the various modes, stances, and voices recur throughout his career, juxtaposed or even superimposed.

A final example of the protean writer, perhaps the most striking of all, is Jean de La Fontaine, known to the general reader in France uniquely for his fables, which in fact comprise only one-fifth of the total opus. La Fontaine gave birth to fables, lascivious tales (*contes*) in the Ariosto-Boccaccio manner, five long poems, comedies, a ballet, op-era libretti, *chansons, ballades,* sonnets, epigrams, epistles, satires, odes, madrigals, idylls, and descriptions. In 1665 he published a volume of tales and translated verses cited in Saint Augustine's *De civitate Dei*; in 1671, more tales, more fables, and an edition entitled *Recueil de poësies chrestiennes et diverses*; in 1673 and 1674 *Poëme de la Captivité de saint Malc* and still more tales. It is wrong on our part to neglect the *contes* or the religious verse or both in favor of the fables, whether for literary or moral reasons, thus to presume the religious texts are trivial or inau-

thentic, for that matter to claim that the Boccaccio-style tales are also
trivial or inauthentic. La Fontaine is the great master of the fable in
French literature. He is also the great master of the *conte,* and his
Captivité de saint Malc is a masterpiece in its own right, as is his brief
mythological epic *Adonis.* Nothing prevents him from being creative, in
Saint Malc and in bawdy stories, in the fables and in *Adonis.* Nothing
prevents Saint-Amant from being as creative in *Moyse sauvé, l'Arion,* and
La Plainte de Lyrian et de Sylvie as in "Le Melon," "Le Cantal," and "Le
Mauvais Logement."

In contrast to the modern esthetic of shock or originality, the traditional French poet assumed an esthetic of recognition, aiming at clarity,
continuity, and a sense of community. For the Pléiade and their successors, up to and including Chénier, the key to writing is "invention," one
of the five categories of rhetoric, a poetic process that involved finding
appropriate material, then copying or rearranging it. This is the esthetic of the *topos,* or commonplace, known in advance to author and
reader alike, based upon a shared literary culture. Poems refer to other
poems or to universal archetypes, not to "real life," the poet's or anyone else's. And the history of poetry is a history of conventions and
archetypes, not of poets.

Roger Caillois's aphorism is appropriate in this context: "Malraux dit
quelque part qu'on ne devient pas peintre en regardant la nature, mais
en regardant les tableaux des autres peintres. De même, c'est en lisant
les vers des autres poètes qu'on devient poète."[8] All poets build on the
foundation left by their predecessors, imitating, improving, perfecting,
distorting, and repudiating. Great poets proceed by working within the
tradition. Even when they rebel, they do so from within, by revising the
tradition and misinterpreting it, by what Harold Bloom calls creative
misreading. By twisting and distorting such artistic forms the creator
arrives at new forms, which will become the tradition for his successors.
Thus all poetry is based upon the principle of intertextuality. All great
texts are intertexts, containing and reacting upon pre-texts of an earlier age.

As a matter of course the Renaissance masters took inspiration from
ancient Rome and from modern Italy. They not only welcomed a classical esthetic, adhering to classical norms and imitating the classical triad
of styles, but they incorporated into their own work allusions to and
textual borrowings from the Ancients. Du Bellay or Ronsard seeks
cultural overtones, a sort of allusiveness, and quotes passages, from the
Bible, Virgil, Ovid, Horace, Petrarch, Ariosto, and Bembo. Then later
poets—d'Aubigné, for example, or Saint-Amant—incorporate pre-
textual material from the Bible, Virgil, Ovid, and Petrarch, and from

du Bellay, Ronsard, and du Bartas. The intertextual pattern works as well with native as with foreign *auctores*.

That this is true for the Renaissance has long been a cliché in scholarly circles. However, the same intertextual pattern and concern for tradition dominated the Middle Ages, a period that school histories sometimes present as fresh, primitive and artless vis-à-vis the modern. Chrétien de Troyes, Guillaume de Lorris, or Jean de Meun proceeds no differently than Ronsard—by reading, translating, glossing, and assimilating Virgil, Ovid, Horace, Boethius, and the troubadours. Later masters, say Guillaume de Machaut or Froissart, then assimilate the Roman classics plus the *Romance of the Rose,* now considered, like the classics, a work of authority composed by *auctoritates,* enjoying as much prestige in the thirteenth and fourteenth centuries as Petrarch or Ronsard was to enjoy in the sixteenth.

Indeed, the Middle Ages has never been surpassed in its reverence for the written word, the book. In this age of grammar and rhetoric, when the great civic ideal was a *translatio imperii et studii* from Greece and Rome to France, the book itself became a symbol for history, nature, the world, and, above all, the Word of God: *In principio erat verbum.* . . . The universe itself was conceived as a book written by God, testifying to him and praising his glory. Old authors therefore were endowed with quasi-supernatural powers, were revered with quasi-supernatural awe. The classics provided French romancers with stories, with themes and motifs, with techniques of description and rhetorical amplification, with a sense of the unicity of poetic style. Indeed, much of medieval vernacular literature was composed in order to provide a viable culture for the *illiterati* and *idiotae,* those people of varied social estate who did not read Latin but wished to learn and to know.

As an example of the poetry of convention, I should like to examine first some love songs (*grands chants courtois*) by two of the greatest early trouvères, Gace Brulé and Gui, Châtelain de Couci. Both texts date from the end of the twelfth century.

> Li consirrers de mon païs
> Si longuement me trait a mort,
> Qu'en estranges terres languis,
> Las, sanz deduit et sanz confort,
> Et si dout mout mes anemis
> Qui de moi mesdient a tort,
> Maiz tant sent mon cuer vrai et fort
> Que, se Dieu plaist, ne m'en iert pis.

Ma douce dame, ne creez
Touz ceus qui de moi mesdiront.
Quant vous veoir ne me poez
De vos biauz iex qui soupris m'ont,
De vostre franc cuer me veez.
Maiz ne sai s'il vous en semont,
Quar tant ne dout rienz en cest mont
Con ce que vous ne m'oublïez.

Par cuer legier de feme avient
Que li amant doutent souvent,
Maiz ma loiautez me soustient,
Donc fusse je mors autrement!
Et sachiez de fine Amour vient
Qu'il se doutent si durement,
Quar nus n'aime seürement,
Et false est amours qui ne crient.

Mes cuers m'a guari et destruit,
Maiz de ce va bien qu'a li pens,
Et ce que je perdre la quit
Me fait doubler mes pensemens.
Ensi me vient soulaz et fuit,
Et nonpourquant, selonc mon sens,
Penser a ma dame touz tens
Tieg je, ce sachïez, a deduit.

Chançon, a ma dame t'envoi
Ançoiz que nus en ait chanté,
Et si li dites de par moi,
Guardez que ne li soit celé:
"Se trecherie n'a en foi
Et trahison en loiauté,
Donc avrai bien ce qu'avoir doi,
Quar de loial cuer ai amé."[9]
. . . .

La douce voiz du louseignol sauvage
Qu'oi nuit et jour cointoier et tentir
M'adoucist si le cuer et rassouage
Qu'or ai talent que chant pour esbaudir;
Bien doi chanter puis qu'il vient a plaisir
Cele qui j'ai fait de cuer lige homage;
Si doi avoir grant joie en mon corage,
S'ele me veut a son oez retenir.

Onques vers li n'eu faus cuer ne volage,
Si m'en devroit pour tant mieuz avenir,
Ainz l'aim et serf et aour par usage,
Maiz ne li os mon pensé descouvrir,
Quar sa biautez me fait tant esbahir
Que je ne sai devant li nul language;
Nis regarder n'os son simple visage,
Tant en redout mes ieuz a departir.

Tant ai en li ferm assis mon corage
Qu'ailleurs ne pens, et Diex m'en lait joïr!
C'onques Tristanz, qui but le beverage,
Pluz loiaument n'ama sanz repentir;
Quar g'i met tout, cuer et cors et desir,
Force et pooir, ne sai se faiz folage;
Encor me dout qu'en trestout mon eage
Ne puisse assez li et s'amour servir.

Je ne di pas que je face folage,
Nis se pour li me devoie morir,
Qu'el mont ne truis tant bele ne si sage,
Ne nule rienz n'est tant a mon desir;
Mout aim mes ieuz qui me firent choisir;
Lors que la vi, li laissai en hostage
Mon cuer, qui puiz i a fait lonc estage,
Ne ja nul jour ne l'en quier departir.

Chançon, va t'en pour faire mon message
La u je n'os trestourner ne guenchir,
Quar tant redout la fole gent ombrage
Qui devinent, ainz qu'il puist avenir,
Les bienz d'Amours (Diex les puis maleïr!)
A maint amant ont fait ire et damage;
Maiz j'ai de ce mout cruel avantage
Qu'il les m'estuet seur mon pois obeïr.[10]

Both songs present (or, rather, share) a common worldview, a common poetic universe. In both, the Lover-Speaker sings to or about the Lady. He is the *sujet*; she is the *objet*; the chief *opposants* are *losengiers*: talebearers, slanderers, sowers of discord, who will harm the Lover in his Lady's eyes or harm them both in the eyes of her husband. The other major "character" or "function" is the song itself, which, according to the fiction of the poem, will be an *adjuvant,* will serve as a go-between, a message-messenger, from the Lover to the Lady, will play a role in the story recounted by itself. Thus within the fiction of the text we find elaborated an explicit structure of communication, which reveals a Narrator or Singer-Lover, a persona of the implied author, speaking to his Narratee or Narratees, the Lady, Amor, God, his patron or patroness, other singers, or his song. It also reveals an implied audience, the world of the court: anonymous courtiers, lovers, and poets who admire the Lady as the Singer does and therefore sympathize with him. The Singer's objective, among others, is to convince this implied audience, as well as the Lady, of his courtliness, indeed to win their approbation (*captatio benevolentiae*) rather than to seduce her. They serve as a mirror to reflect his aspirations and the courtly world-within-the-poem he wishes to create. This is a public act, elaborated for an elite audience, those happy few whose sensitivity, taste, and breeding make them worthy of appreciating the art object, a community in which the trouvère himself finds a proper, respected place.

The *grand chant courtois* is almost exclusively a *requête d'amour*. In it the Speaker, in love with a Lady, begs her to grant him her favors, to reserve affection for him, or perhaps simply not to forget him. He loves her. She does not yet return his love; she may not even be aware of his existence. What she thinks, if anything, remains unknown to us, for she does not speak. The unique focus of experience and erotic consciousness, the unique poetic, lyrical voice comes from the male lover, not the female beloved. In this preintercourse stage of the relationship, the Speaker is torn by desire; he is fascinated, dazzled, ravished by the Lady's beauty; he suffers from lovesickness, weeps, endures melancholia, and, as a melancholic man (lover and poet), teeters on the brink of madness. The trouvère song emphasizes longing, not contentment, separation, not togetherness, silence, not community.

At the heart of the courtly love situation we find the obstacle, whatever keeps the lovers apart: separation in space, her superior social status, her husband, talebearers, and slanderers. It is because of the obstacle that good or true love (*fin' amor*) burns ever bright, that it endures and proves to be of worth. The Lady, of course, is superior to her suitor, in social class and in virtue; hence a pattern of motifs containing military-feudal and religious overtones. She is the master; he is her vassal. She has conquered him; he or his heart lies languishing in her prison or as hostage. He owes or desires to owe her feudal service. He also adores her as one ought to adore Christ or the Virgin Mary, and the terms that express his longing (love, adoration, worship, passion) are borrowed from the religious lexicon and thus bear Christian connotations. Because the Speaker's passion is deemed to be good, because as the singing voice he is capable of experiencing and expressing it, we assume that he becomes a better person, ennobled by *fin' amor*. Because of *fin' amor*, he manifests the ecstasy of youth (*joven*), that commitment and forgetfulness of self that are assumed to be the prerogatives of the young. Because of it, even though he does not take possession of the Lady's body, he experiences *joy*. *Fin' amor* serves as a civilizing force in society, leads to a more elegant, refined social interchange, creates discipline and psychological lucidity in the lover, and derives from and contributes to a new aristocracy of the heart.

Given that these two songs, and indeed almost all courtly lyrics, elaborate the archetypal situation inherent in *fin' amor,* how does the poet create a unique work of art? One way is that the order in which the motifs are arranged, as well as the introduction of motifs in one text but not in the other, grant these poems a distinct tone, a distinct literary reality. According to the theory of reader response (here audience response), the trouvère or jongleur sings the text lineally to a listening audience, each strophe following the preceding one. In a series of stanzas n plus x, the audience's interpretation of x will be shaped by having heard n previously. The form and contents of n will influence the audience's reaction to x, and its association of n plus x will then shape its response to the y and z that eventually follow. As $x, y,$ and z are recited, each stanza should unleash an esthetic reaction, at its best a shock that would enlarge the horizon left by the preceding stanza. Therefore, the reception of the song, the audience perception, re-creation, and response to it, will be totally different whether n comes before x or x before n. Thus, while exploiting a common fund of themes and motifs, each poet, by developing them in a different way and in a different order, creates distinctive, original songs for his audience.

For example, Gace Brulé begins by emphasizing separation and obstacle: the physical obstacle of exile ("Li consirrers de mon païs . . . en estranges terres languis") establishing a version of *amor de lonh,* and social obstacle brought about by talebearers and sowers of discord ("mes anemis / Qui de moi mesdient a tort. . . . Touz ceus qui de moi mesdiront"). Given the emphasis on *losengiers,* on nefarious verbal activity *a tort* indulged in by these slanderers, the question of true love ("fine Amour") as distinguished from false love ("false . . . amours") takes on special importance. The tension, the *dolce-amar,* the dread and uncertainty, the *pensemens,* the paranoia, which mark the Speaker's psychological state and which persist through the rest of the poem, shaping our mood, are logically and psychologically valid, a legitimate outgrowth from the situation of obstacle that dominates the poem from the beginning. And sending the poem to his lady is also appropriate, in order that it bridge the gap between them, that it break the obstacle, falseness, forgetfulness, and secrecy ("ne li soit celé") and, as a verbal message, counteract verbal undermining by the tattletales.

Gui de Couci, on the contrary, opens his song by evoking the nightingale. His is a vision of beauty and gladness ("esbaudir . . . plaisir . . .
joie"), of classical myth and poetic creation (the *chant*). Fear, shyness,
and isolation in the succeeding strophes are set off against this opening
topos of sweet joy. The audience reacts to them in Gui's text in a
different way than in Gace's. Similarly, the Speaker's incapacity to
speak is set in opposition to the nightingale's blatant articulateness, and
Gui emphasizes closeness, nonparting, in contrast to Gace's separation.
He also innovates in the third stanza, at the structural center of the
lyric, with an allusion to Tristan and Isolt, a cultural motif, an archetype, that responds to and reinforces, the implicit cultural motif and
archetype of the nightingale (Philomela) in the beginning, and which
then is crowned in the last stanza by the sending of the song, again a
literary topic. Here the structure is one of reinforcement, whereas in
Gace it was one of opposition. The theme of madness, introduced by
the Tristan motif, colors the third, fourth, and fifth strophes in darker
colors, creates a tonality of irrationality, of love as violence, corresponding to the violence of the Philomela myth. At the same time Gui reasons and plays with madness, denying that he is insane while, on the
contrary, projecting the trait onto slanderers ("la fole gent ombrage").
From the perspective of reader-response they appear, in the last stanza,
as the *result* of the philtre and the nightingale, not the *cause* of dread
and misery, as in Gace Brulé.

In a highly sophisticated text the order of the stanzas becomes a
crucial esthetic factor. Witness the following song by Thibaut de
Champagne:

> Tant ai amors servies longuement
> Que dès or mès ne m'en doit nus reprendre
> Se je m'en part. Ore a Dieu les conmant,
> Qu'en ne doit pas touz jorz folie enprendre;
> Et cil est fous qui ne s'en set desfendre
> Ne n'i conoist son mal ne son torment.
> On me tendroit dès or mès por enfant,
> Car chascuns tens doit sa seson atendre.
>
> Je ne sui pas si com cele autre gent
> Qui ont amé, puis i vuelent contendre
> Et dïent mal par vilain mautalent.
> On ne doit pas seigneur servise vendre
> Ne vers Amors mesdire ne mesprendre;
> Mès qui s'en part parte s'en bonement.
> Endroit de moi vueil je que tuit amant
> Aient grant bien, quant je plus n'i puis prendre.

Amors m'a fet grant bien enjusqu'ici,
Qu'ele m'a fet amer sanz vilanie
La plus tres bele et la meilleur ausi,
Au mien cuidier, qui onques fust choisie.
Amors le veut et ma dame m'en prie
Que je m'en parte, et je mult l'en merci.
Quant par le gré ma dame m'en chasti,
Meilleur reson n'ai je a ma partie.

Autre chose ne m'a Amors meri
De tant com j'ai esté en sa baillie,
Mès bien m'a Deus par sa pitié gueri,
Quant delivré m'a de sa seignorie.
Quant eschapez li sui sanz perdre vie,
Ainz de mes euz si bone heure ne vi,
Si cuit je fere oncor maint jeu parti
Et maint sonet et mainte raverdie.

Au conmencier se doit on bien garder
D'entreprendre chose desmesuree,
Mès bone amor ne let honme apenser
Ne bien choisir ou mete sa pensee.
Plus tost aime on en estrange contree,
Ou on ne puet ne venir ne aler,
Qu'on ne fet ce qu'on puet toz jorz trouver;
Issi est bien la folie esprouvee.

Or me gart Deus et d'amor et d'amer
Fors de Celi, cui on doit aourer,
Ou on ne puet faillir a grant soudee.[11]

This piece is an example of *conjat,* a theme of Occitan origin little known in northern France, in which the Speaker quits his Lady. Thibaut's Singer creates an anticourtly situation, undermining the declarations of eternal fidelity made by woebegone lovers in the *grand chant courtois.* He questions the literary absolutes of *fin' amor,* juxtaposing them to concrete human reality, that of change in time ("chascuns tens doit sa seson atendre") and of openness and honesty ("Mès qui s'en part parte s'en bonement"). In contrast to the orthodoxy of Gace Brulé and Gui de Couci, Thibaut claims that madness is indeed to be found in *fin' amor* and that he for one prefers health to such an ill, as he prefers maturity to childishness. Part of the irony and sophistication generated in these first two strophes derives from the fact that the Singer, aware that he is espousing a heretical position, claims to defend himself from the charge of anticourtliness; he does so from within the system, by contrasting himself with false lovers, those who speak badly of *fin' amor* ("dïent mal par vilain mautalent . . . vers Amors mesdire. . . . "). However, the audience does not forget that, as Singer, he does indeed harm love ("mesprendre") through speech ("mesdire") far more subtly than if he indulged in a diatribe.

Up to now the Singer has claimed that it is he personally who has decided to avoid madness and childishness by quitting love's service. In the third stanza, however, after the traditional encomium of the Lady, he reveals to us the reason for his *conjat*: "Amors le veut et ma dame m'en prie / Que je m'en parte." It is the Lady who breaks off with him, not the other way around. With these lines, at the center, the implied audience suddenly discovers that the Singer's protestations in the first two stanzas were doubly false, that he was covering up his dismissal by the Lady. The last two stanzas and the Envoi continue the pattern of irony, the implied audience now fully aware of the Singer's predicament, able to smile at and with him. First of all, he thanks both Amor and God for having cured him and delivered him from such thraldom; yet he also promises to write new songs, some of which presumably will sing of love: He shall continue to be a trouvère and therefore a lover. (In the very first line the Speaker told of service to *amors*, "loves" in the plural. How many ladies has he served in the past? How many does he expect to serve in the future? Who is serving whom?) In the Envoi the Speaker again prays to God, previously invoked twice but in company with Amor, to keep him from loving all but one whom he ought to adore. Is she Our Lady the Blessed Virgin Mary? or, given that the capital *C* in "Celi" is an editorial option, does he refer to his secular erotic Lady, who in the third stanza just rejected him? We shall never know. The ambivalence, the ambiguity, add to the complexity of the text. Each strophe depends for its effect on the preceding one. Several levels of meaning, several degrees of complicity between implied author, speaker, and implied audience, coexist.

Another kind of verse teaches the same lesson of commonplace, continuity, and archetype and of complexity and flexibility within conventional patterns: the rose poems by Ronsard. We shall consider two of his most famous efforts in this mode:

> Mignonne, allon voir si la rose
> Qui ce matin avoit declose
> Sa robe de pourpre au soleil,
> A point perdu, cette vesprée,
> Les plis de sa robe pourprée,
> Et son teint au vostre pareil.

Las, voiés comme en peu d'espace,
Mignonne, elle a dessus la place
Las, las, ses beautés laissé cheoir!
O vraiment maratre Nature,
Puis qu'une telle fleur ne dure
Que du matin jusques au soir.

Donc, si vous me croiés, mignonne:
Tandis que vôtre âge fleuronne
En sa plus verte nouveauté,
Cueillés, cueillés vôtre jeunesse
Comme à cette fleur, la vieillesse
Fera ternir vôtre beauté.[12]

. . . .

Comme on voit sur la branche au mois de May la rose
En sa belle jeunesse, en sa premiere fleur
Rendre le ciel jaloux de sa vive couleur,
Quand l'Aube de ses pleurs au poinct du jour l'arrose:

La grace dans sa feuille, et l'amour se repose,
Embasmant les jardins et les arbres d'odeur:
Mais batue ou de pluye, ou d'excessive ardeur,
Languissante elle meurt feuille à feuille déclose:

Ainsi en ta premiere et jeune nouveauté,
Quand la terre et le ciel honoroient ta beauté,
La Parque t'a tuée, et cendre tu reposes.

Pour obseques reçoy mes larmes et mes pleurs,
Ce vase plein de laict, ce panier plein de fleurs,
Afin que vif, et mort, ton corps ne soit que roses.[13]

Both texts are based upon a simple, fundamental image or metaphor: the girl resembles a rose, and the rose resembles a girl. In "Mignonne, allon voir si la rose. . ." the metaphor is established by personification, for the rose is granted human attributes; it wears a dress, has a complexion, is sexually attractive, belongs to a family (with a stepmother). And the girl is granted flower attributes. She endures a process of "vegetalization": She flowers, is green, and plucks or will be plucked. The girl-rose identification is an old literary motif: It is to be found in Sappho, the Greek Anthology, Horace, Ovid, Propertius, Tibullus, Ausonius, Guillaume de Lorris, and Jean de Meun, to name Ronsard's most eminent predecessors. He may have consulted any and all of them; and, in chronological order, they certainly read each other. Thus we find a literary tradition, a topic of rhetoric passed from one author to another, a golden chain of rhetoric extending from Sappho to Ronsard, and from Ronsard to his successors (Desportes, d'Aubigné, Malherbe, Racan, Maynard), leading to the great rose poets of the twentieth century: Apollinaire, Jouve, and Aragon.

Yet surely there is more to the phenomenon than rhetoric and reading. The force of Ronsard's verse, as in Horace, as in Aragon, can be ascribed to its archetypal power, to the fact that, for a variety of reasons, the collective unconscious, or at least the collective male unconscious, and our culture generally assimilate women and roses. Male poets and lovers project upon their beloveds the traits they ascribe to flowers: beauty, purity, freshness, fecundity, fragility, evanescence. Their love for the rose or lily is consecrated in the "green world," the realm of nature; it is subject to the laws of time and destiny, also in nature. For the woman and the rose live but a short space, are mortal and subject to decay; and as the rose is surrounded by thorns, thus resists conquest, the lady is an ambiguous love-object embodying joy and misery, desire and repulsion. And there is a direct rapport between the physiological structure and function of the rosebud and the girl's sexual anatomy, this rapport consciously expressed in works as disparate as the *Romance of the Rose* and the classical Chinese novel *Chin P'ing Mei*. (Women readers also accept the projection and assimilation; they also are moved by the text.)

The evanescence of the rose's life, the certainty of decay and death, call forth the *carpe diem* theme, a topic as old and as universal as the woman-rose archetype itself. Here the implied author enters into the fictional fabric of the poem; as Speaker he addresses the girl-rose directly, seeking to convince her of his "wisdom." After the innocent walk comes implacable logic. And his wisdom, his logic, his message, is one of seduction. Because she is a rose, because she will wither and die, she should enjoy life ("Cueillés, cueillés vôtre jeunesse"), and she should enjoy it by granting him (the Speaker) her favors. By the mediation of the rose topic, Ronsard's *odelette* and most other rose poems are seduction poems; they belong to the same genre as songs by Gace Brulé and le Châtelain de Couci: the *requête d'amour*. Ronsard's tone is both lighter and more urgent, more sensual and more didactic than theirs. And here it is an allegedly older, wiser authority figure who instructs a mere girl. Yet his persona is fundamentally, conventionally, archetypically the same character in the same fictional world as the personae of Gace and Gui; and Cassandre, Marie, and Hélène assume the same function as the troubadour *domna*. The poem again plays a role in its own story: It generates love, it hopes to persuade and seduce a woman invented in and by itself. The exordium-topos of the *grand chant courtois*—singing of birds and the return of spring, a time of love, renewal of the year,

Easter—is evoked in new terms and on a new basis: *carpe rosam* and *nulla rosa sine spina.* But the green world is the same, reveling in natural beauty and encouraging the growth of love and the creation of poetry.

Central to the doctrinal line of *carpe diem* poems is the notion of time. In "peu d'espace," one day precisely, the rose evolves from youth to old age, from bud to withered stem. And limited time corresponds to, is confused with, limited space: temporal space (one day) occurring in the topographical space of a garden and narrated by strolling in the garden. The poem's present, in the evening, evokes the present beauty of the girl and present decay of the rose, referring backward to the past beauty of the rose (morning) and forward to the future decay of the girl. Thus the rose's progression correponds to the curve of human life: the living maiden who will grow old and die. The life and death of the girl, of the flower, of the day, of the poem—this is the archetypal kernel of existence, the ebb and flow of the universe. Hence the Speaker's allusion to three female figures: the girl and the rose, but also "maratre Nature," Nature as stepmother to the rose and to the girl, a terrible mother as well as a good one. For the reality of existence implies good and ill, life and death, the cosmic female principle of birth, nurture, and fecundity and the cosmic female principle of death.

In "Comme on voit sur la branche au mois de May la rose. . ." we find the same assimilation of girl and rose, the same personification of the one (a flower of youth, radiating grace, inciting love and jealousy) and "vegetalization" of the other (a girl newly opened, later reduced to cinders). Once again there are good feminine figures—the rose, the girl, for that matter, Dawn, who waters the former with her tears, the Earth, who honors the latter for her beauty—and terrible ones, such as the Parque or Fate who slays the maiden and the rain that beats down the flower. Time once again outlasts living creatures, and girls and roses are condemned to perish.

The Speaker plays a different role. Instead of the lover-poet hoping to seduce a live woman, he is a poet-lover consoling a dead one, consoling himself and his audience. The role of seduction is over, but the role of teaching, of didacticism, is as strong as ever. Now the lyric voice appeals not to the narratee (the girl) within the text but directly to the implied reader outside. And the Speaker's role in the fiction of the poem is as great as ever: It has simply changed emphasis. Its function is, as in other *carpe diem* works (cf. "Quand vous serez bien vieille au soir à la chandelle. . ."), to render the maiden immortal. Thus the Speaker brings to her grave his tears, milk, and flowers. His real tears for the girl parallel the metaphorical tears of Dawn (the dew on the rose). His milk, feminine image of nurture, fecundity, and life, parallels and counterbalances the destructive rain shower that slew the bud. He himself, a positive, human, creative male force, counterbalances for the girl the negative heat of the sun that destroyed the bloom. And he brings flowers to her so that she, a flower, will live anew.

The birth-death cycle of other *carpe diem* texts here becomes a birth-death-rebirth cycle. Good yields to evil but is restored by good. Nature creates and destroys, but life is re-created by a devotee-mourner and by a Speaker-poet. For the tears, milk, and flowers belong to a tradition of pastoral, in which the poet-shepherd sings and loves. It is as a poet, as an Orphic seer, that the Speaker grants metaphoric new life to the rose-girl, that he brings light to a world turned to ashes, wiped out by the heat of the sun. The priest of Apollo restores what Apollo destroyed. As a poet-priest, he performs a rite religious, erotic, and esthetic in nature. The active masculine principle reacts to a passive feminine one, not to seduce but to sing and create, to bring life in the face of death. Then the girl's dead body will nurture new flowers rising from the grave; the poem will create new flowers and girls in a universe of pure beauty; and flowers will continue to die and be reborn in an eternal cycle corresponding to the cyclical structure of the poem, which contains death at the midpoint but begins and ends with roses.

Ronsard's more sensual poetry is also grounded in tradition. He and du Bellay composed a series of noncourtly, indeed anticourtly, texts: sensual, passionate, epicurean pieces patterned after Catullus, Horace, Ovid, and Neo-Latin *basia* by Pontano and Johannes Secundus. They are conventional in their anticourtliness, as a literary repudiation of a literary code, and because in rebelling against one form of literature (vernacular Petrarchism), they turn to another (Neo-Latin epicureanism) for inspiration. It was also possible for Ronsard to fuse passion and courtliness, to integrate sensuality within the Petrarchan love-sonnet mode. His most successful text in this line is the justly famous "Je voudroy bien richement jaunissant. . ." (1584 version):

> Je voudroy bien richement jaunissant
> En pluye d'or goute à goute descendre
> Dans le giron de ma belle Cassandre,
> Lors qu'en ses yeux le somne va glissant.
>
> Puis je voudroy en toreau blanchissant
> Me transformer pour sur mon dos la prendre,
> Quand en avril par l'herbe la plus tendre
> Elle va, fleur, mille fleurs ravissant.

Je voudroy bien pour alleger ma peine,
Estre un Narcisse et elle une fontaine,
Pour m'y plonger une nuict à sejour;

Et si voudroy que ceste nuict encore
Fust eternelle, et que jamais l'Aurore
Pour m'esveiller ne rallumast le jour.[14]

Again the girl, this time "belle Cassandre," is assimilated to another girl, herself a flower, picking flowers. Again we find the seduction theme. However, in this text Ronsard voices overtly the libido, the unleashed sexual fury that in so many other poems remains veiled behind conventional rhetoric. Yet to do so he employs another veil of rhetoric, Greek mythology. For the Speaker can express unbridled passion only by comparing himself to Jupiter, who enjoyed Danaë in a shower of gold and Europa in the form of a bull, and to Narcissus, who, dazzled by his own reflection, drowned himself in the fountain. Mythology here becomes the medium for representing an erotic conceit: It serves as a metaphor for passions and a means of concretizing the courtly wish-fulfillment dream.

Male eros is embodied in the golden shower that flows drop by drop into Danaë's lap, a phallic image of male sperm and male creative power, assimilated to alchemical gold and the sun; and in the white bull, also a phallic image of male libido, who seizes the girl; and as Narcissus, who in an act of sexual aggression plunges into a fountain, a masculine figure seizing and possessing the feminine element. Libido descends from the divine to the human, from Jupiter to Narcissus, and, by implication, from myth-figures to the Speaker-lover; yet at the same time it increases from the delicate, oblique seduction of Danaë ("goute à goute"), to the gentle rape of Europa (she who plucked flowers, her flower shall be plucked), to the ravishing of the fountain. Yet, as the male figure becomes more human (gold to bull to man), the female is reified (girl to flower to fountain). Although the sexual act gives pleasure, at no time is there communication or empathy between two lovers on the same plane, in the same sphere. The ultimate fantasy for the Speaker is to plunge into the fountain for a night that shall last forever.

Here Ronsard has in mind not only the story of Narcissus. He evokes mythical suicide by water and also the possibility of sexual fulfillment, *la petite mort*, conceived as death by water, a symbolic return to the womb and tomb, at night, in the domain of the unconscious and the irrational. A high, lofty passion is assimilated to death, Eros to Thanatos, yet at the same time transgression is rewarded and mastery achieved in the cool, moist realm of the mothers—if it is achieved at all, for the text can be interpreted not as release but as eternal desire sufficient in itself, maintaining pleasure and allowing for artistic creation. Furthermore, the Speaker, who approves the unnatural metamorphoses of Jupiter, denies the natural metamorphosis of night to day and of life to death and death to life; he wishes his night of love, his return to the womb, to be eternal, himself surviving eternally as a phallic male, not what Narcissus became, neither corpse nor flower. All the rest is unstable, yet he, the image of violence, having changed thrice, craves stasis. And, figure of gold and whiteness, of male light, he denies the return of the sun. It is obvious that the realization of such a dream is impossible, that it is in fact a game, a play, an intellectual, erotic conceit within a poem grounded in convention and myth. Its strength comes from the fusion of literary libido and erotic myth, of strong masculine language of poetry and the no-less-strong wit of play.

These love poems of the Middle Ages and the Renaissance by Gace Brulé, Gui de Couci, Thibaut de Champagne, and Ronsard illustrate the points I have tried to make in the course of the chapter. A poet adopts a lyric stance or persona. The stance may or may not be derived from the author's genuine personality, and the story line inherent in the lyric may or may not be based upon real events or situations in the author's life. We do not know, and we ought not to ask. That the poet seeks to create the illusion of authenticity, to convince us that his text is based on and is evidence for an authentic experience, is simply one more convention of the trade, one additional means of winning the public's approbation. The conscious choice from among a number of conventions, genres, and modes—not the author's biography, not his power of inspiration—determines the form and content of poetry. The majority of poets, starting with Jean Bodel and Thibaut de Champagne, choose to adopt a variety of stances and to practice a variety of genres and modes, cultivating a variety of images and archetypes, in two or more of the traditional stylistic registers. This is done in response to audience expectation, to fulfill audience need. Originality and artistic success are thus achieved through skillful manipulation of the available esthetic potentialities, working within and through the tradition of one's age as it has been handed down from the past.

3

THE LANGUAGE

The distinctive mark of poetry and testimony to its greatness is originality in language and style, in other words the écart between poetry and literary prose or everyday common speech. Poetry cannot be conceived as the embellishment, ornamentation, or rhetorical amplification of literary prose or the everyday spoken idiom. It is of a different essence, just as each poet's style seeks to be different in essence from prose and from the style of his fellow poets.

The purpose of this chapter is to refute or at least to nuance the words above, to examine certain claims made on behalf of modern poetry, claims that explicitly or implicitly state the superiority of modern verse and the modern temper over the older French tradition and thereby condemn the latter. A fundamental question concerns traditional French prosody and the poetic capacities inherent in the language. This question raises the issue to what extent the modern answers to it are fair as judgments of value and are valid for all poetry. Among the points that focus on the problem are free verse, poetic musicality, French as a poetic language, multilingualism, and the *écart* between poetry and prose. The heart of the chapter discusses some older notions of poetic language, dealing with levels of style and the rhetorical tradition, with examples, and proposes an alternate thesis concerning the evolution of styles.

A first point has to do with the debate over free verse: the belief enunciated by many that for the modern poet to express himself, to create his own language, he had to be liberated from the fetters of classical meter and rhyme. This claim usually presupposes the notion that the modern is more essentially poetic than the classical or the

Romantic. It is true that for a century now poetry has evolved in directions that Machaut, Ronsard, Boileau, and even Hugo would never have predicted or understood. The percentage of rhyming alexandrines or of rhyming octosyllabic couplets or of patterns of sequential, recurrent strophes will be, without exception, much lower in anthologies of contemporary verse than in those devoted to any of the earlier centuries.

On the other hand, a case can be made that "free verse" is a contradiction in terms and a denial of itself—a case that one can deem excessive. According to this position, a demand for freedom is absurd, given that there is no freedom in art; and were the text to be totally independent from the constraints of meter, it would and could not be verse. Verse, by definition, means an audible formal pattern imposed upon language that serves to intensify its formality, or the superimposition of a metrico-rhythmic structure onto the natural linguistic structure of the language. Poetry must have an expected meter; this meter will then contrast with the actual rhythmic accent of the text when spoken aloud, comparable to a prose rhythm. The contrast thus is between the artificial convention of meter and the natural linguistic articulation of speech. The play and tension between the two—meter and rhythm—create the language of poetry. To sacrifice either is to sacrifice poetry, to exterminate it, to render its existence impossible.

A more moderate case can be made that the effects of the free-verse revolution have been exaggerated. In fact, the end result amounts to some typographical modifications and a relatively broader lexicon. The structure of the language—syntactical, grammatical, and rhetorical—remains the same. In addition, quite a few major figures have returned to one form or another of the traditional structures, including fixed meter and rhyme. The first great traditionalist, in one sense, is Valéry. Aragon and Eluard have been the most vocal in this regard, but the revisionists also include Supervielle, Audiberti, and Jean Cassou, not to speak of "semirevisionists" such as Jammes, Lanza del Vasto, and Pierre Emmanuel, who cultivate a rhymeless but metrically correct alexandrine, a French equivalent of English, German, and Italian blank verse.

Granted all this, there is still no reason to deny the prosodic significance of free verse in its European, indeed global, context and the extraordinary esthetic achievement made by poets in the new style or styles from Claudel and Apollinaire to Char, Bonnefoy, Jaccottet, and their younger contemporaries. This achievement, however, ought not to imply either that an earlier, more "regular" mode of creation is inferior to it or that regular French prosody was peculiarly, excessively constraining and had to be abandoned. The very European, global extent of the revolution ensures that it cannot be limited to France and deemed the answer to uniquely French problems. Furthermore, within France, in a French context, there is prosody and prosody, restraint and restraint. Medieval romancers, such as Chrétien de Troyes, Hue de Rotelande, and Jean Renart, wielded the octosyllabic rhyming couplet with a wit and brio, a freedom and joy, the envy of any modern. For the first century of French literary history much verse was composed in assonance, not rhyme, and it is problematic whether the Anglo-Normans counted syllables at all. The great period of order and constraint runs roughly from Malherbe to Voltaire; by 1760 poets already had begun the renewal. And at the very center of the old, ordered, constrained universe stand two of the world's greatest poets: Racine and La Fontaine. Conclusion: Chrétien, Racine, and Char are major figures, all three major each in his own way. Each man's versification is congruent to himself. None of the three is inherently superior to the others, to be elevated into a universal norm.

Another claim made on behalf of modern verse is that it has attained musicality, that it has some of the intrinsic quality of music. The Symbolists especially, citing Verlaine's "De la musique avant toute chose," stressed the ties between poetry and music, both structural (the Wagnerian *leitmotiv*) and phonological.[1] And more than one observer asserts that Baudelaire, Verlaine, Mallarmé, and Valéry are greater masters of "word music" and of a musically contrapuntal structure than were their predecessors and that the triumph of the modern is to be associated with this mastery of absolute musical incandescence.

It is true that the four poets share a style, which can perhaps be designated as one of verbal sonority. Whether they are more sonorous than early practitioners in the same line—the Châtelain de Couci, Guillaume de Machaut, Charles d'Orléans, Ronsard, Desportes, Racine, Chénier, and Lamartine, to cite the most eminent—is open to question and in any case can scarcely be proved one way or the other. Nor can it be proved that a style that pays particular attention to sound values is in fact superior to, and ought to be placed above, the sort of verse we find in some of the troubadours, Scève, Sponde, Vigny, and moderns such as Jouve and Ponge. For much of the older period *sermo rudis* was preferred to *sermo dulcis* or *mollis*. Given the phonological and intonational structure of pre-1650 French, it is possible that those poets concerned with alliteration and stress rather than vowel harmony and melody exploited with greater insight the potential of the language in those days. This also means that we are unjust to Charles d'Orléans, du Bellay, Théophile, and Corneille if we read their works aloud with a twentieth-century Parisian accent, not taking into account historical evolution. Finally, concerning that other, structural aspect of musicality, the development and modulation of theme and motif, the contrasting and balancing of moods, and transitions from one "movement" to another are techniques of the trade, common to all literary periods and to all the arts, not at all to be limited to music, modern or otherwise.

It would appear the the Symbolists—Verlaine and his followers— made an overly simplistic analogy between their own poetic practice and Wagner's reform in music, using Wagner to justify themselves. It is true, they justifiably point to an analogous contemporary development in the sister arts. However, they and their predecessors, the Romantics, also project onto music certain characteristics—emotionalism, feeling, vagueness of thought, expressivity, suggestivity, allusiveness, formlessness, loosened syntax, a more fluid structure, and the elaboration of emotionally charged sound patterns—typical of their own verse and of their age in general but which by no means correspond to or reflect the nature of musical composition over the centuries. Indeed, their exaltation of emotion and instinct over reason, of spirit over qualities of the intellect, is an absolute misreading of the essence of music. To use musical terms such as *harmony* or *melody* in a literary context results in semantic distortion so that the terms no longer refer to their original musical context.

The assimilation of poetry to music as a specifically modern phenomenon is central to the Symbolist esthetic, but, from the perspective of history and of musicology, it seems to run counter to the facts. Although much depends on one's definition of musicality, it is surely a legitimate hypothesis, and one seconded by musicologists, that poetry and music are closest to each other, are most truly sister disciplines, when verse is written to be sung and music composed in conjunction with a verbal text, when the formal structures of verse and song are almost identical. In primitive times poetry was probably created by fitting words to preexisting melodies and dance rhythms. In classical Greece the pitch accent itself contributed to melody, and the quantitative meter was both derived from music and still musical in nature.

A close, symbiotic alliance of poetry and music also occurred during the early centuries of French literature, but it most definitely did not do so at the times of the Second Empire and the Third Republic. Thus lyric verse was allied to music, and courtly lyrics were sung, were composed for the specific purpose of being sung, as a matter of course up to the end of the fourteenth century. Indeed, most trouvères composed the music for their own verse, were musicians as much as they were poets. And two great poets of the age—Adam de la Halle in the thir-

teenth century and Machaut in the fourteenth—were also two of the
greatest composers in the annals of musicology. However, toward the
end of the Middle Ages occurred the parting of the ways: Eustache
Deschamps, Christine de Pizan, Charles d'Orléans, and Villon were
supremely fine poets who did not and could not set their own texts to
music, while the leading composers of the day used literary texts sup-
plied by other hands. True, music remained a pole of attraction for
poets, and much lyric poetry, specifically in genres such as the *ballade,
rondeau, chanson,* sonnet, and ode, was susceptible of being set to music,
indeed was meant to be. The leading composers of the fifteenth and
sixteenth centuries all worked with vernacular poetic texts. Marot and
Ronsard were the authors most favored. Among the composers who
used Ronsard's verse, for example, are Certon, Jannequin, Muret,
Goudimel, Orlando di Lasso, de Monte, Cléreau, de la Grotte, and
Chardavoine. This tradition continues with the opera, the *air de cour,*
and the *vaudeville* during the ancien régime, and the romance since
1767. For that matter, Nerval, Verlaine, Apollinaire, and the Fantaisistes were strongly influenced by folksong; musicians have provided
settings for texts by the leading modern poets, from Lamartine to
Char; and Valéry, Claudel, and Cocteau worked with France's greatest
twentieth-century composers.

Nonetheless, there is something artificial, something nostalgic, about
these experiments. At various times, in various centuries, poets and
musicians have yearned for the marriage Deschamps describes between
musique naturelle (verse) and *musique artificielle* (song), have sensed the
need for a return to the old bond between the muses. Ronsard and
Baïf worked in this direction, as did the German Romantics with their
Lieder, as Aragon, Prévert, Seghers, Bérimont, and others today. A
Ronsard and an Aragon, themselves unable to compose, hoped that
some of their verse would be set to music, and they were overjoyed
when such indeed happened. Nonetheless, this is far from the auto-
matic fusion of the two media, a fusion brought about by one person,
the poet-musician trouvère, typical of the earlier time. The unique
modern equivalent of the trouvère is the *poète-parolier-interprète* à la
Brassens and Brel, Ferré and Vian; and the social, cultural, and esthetic level of Vian's songs are light-years away from those of Gace
Brulé and Thibaut de Champagne.

Especially during the Middle Ages and Renaissance, but also in the
era of Aragon and Prévert, when poetry was either composed to music
or set to music after its original verbal creation, the style tends to be
simple, limpid, and impersonal. The same is true for vernacular liturgical music: Protestant versions of the psalms by Marot and Bèze in the

sixteenth century or the traditional Catholic hymns (*cantiques*), the best of which date from the eighteenth and nineteenth centuries. The melodic line was derived from both folk art and court art: The two kinds of music, and the two kinds of verse, interacted as a matter of course. Nonetheless, setting poems to music, the norm for the early Middle Ages, has proved to be the exception since the death of Machaut. Despite heroic efforts by Debussy and Ravel, surely it is not excessive to propose that the verse of Mallarmé or Valéry, because of its willed complexity and subjectivity, its obsession with intellectuality (in this they stand apart from the main current of Symbolism), has to be situated at the farthest possible remove from the lyric impulse of Machaut, Marot, and Ronsard. This is by no means a criticism of Mallarmé and Valéry, excellent as they are in other repects. But if we say that a truly lyric impulse in the guise of musical verse implies poetry that can and ideally ought to be sung, then the wedding of poetry and music in our time is to be found in a very different current: that of the *poésie-chanson* I referred to earlier, extending from Mac Orlan to Vian and Brel, a current derived from Surrealism and seeking inspiration in part from the medieval troubadours and trouvères.

The alleged constraint of traditional French versification and the purported nonmusicality (rhetoric, didacticism) of French verse prior to Baudelaire are symptoms or manifestations of a deeper, far more serious concern focusing on the nature of the language itself. One of the more curious myths cultivated in the nineteenth century and propagated today from time to time in books on poetry and in student texts is the belief that the French language, *qua* language, is somehow less poetic, less appropriate as a medium for poetry, than are English, German, and Italian. This would account for the alleged superiority of the British or German tradition over the French, and for the fact that modern French poets, from Baudelaire on, have been obliged both to rebel against the national heritage and to struggle with as well as exploit the national tongue.

Here is a myth that I would like to demystify. One fundamental postulate of the science of linguistics concerns the equality of all languages. Black African and Native American tongues are in no sense inferior to highly developed languages of culture such as French and English, Arabic and Persian, or Chinese and Japanese. Admittedly, a speaker of Yoruba or Wolof will not be able to express certain concepts of modern Western technology; on the other hand, Americans will have difficulty expressing in English the no-less-subtle and complex theology of Islam or of African tribal religions. In a domain as all-encompassing as poetry, all languages have equal capabilities and an equal potential. Modern Indo-European tongues such as English, French, and German are so alike, relatively speaking, that, viewed from a world linguistic perspective, the divergences between them prove to be trivial. Northrop Frye has pointed out that one cannot proclaim Shakespeare to be greater than Milton and Shelley, or Milton greater than Shakespeare and Shelley, or Shelley greater than Shakespeare and Milton merely because one happens to value the peculiar domains exploited and strengths illustrated by Shakespeare, Milton, or Shelley vis-à-vis the strengths and domains of the other two.[2] So also, for the very same reasons, surely one does not have the right to assert the preeminence of poetry in English (based on meter) over, say, poetry in French (based on meter and rhyme) or in Chinese (based on meter, rhyme, and tone), nor to claim reciprocally the preeminence of either French or Chinese over English.

I have found no convincing argument why one should condemn a system of prosody based on syllabism (French, but also Chinese, Japanese, and Polish) vis-à-vis other systems of prosody such as the quantitative meter of classical Greek and Latin or the tonic meter of English, German, and Russian. Those who claim the natural superiority of English or German over French as languages of poetry often have in mind the stronger beat or accentuation and a relatively richer lexicon of the Germanic tongues vis-à-vis Romance languages. However, they neglect the fact that French attains some of its poetic effects precisely from having a less strongly accented rhythm and a less rich lexicon: from the phenomenon of vowel sonority and harmony, on the one hand, and multiple semantic overtones and the sophistication of semantic nuance from within the language, on the other. A critic or poet who prefers English to French or French to English does so on the basis of his own presuppositions concerning the nature of poetry, given that the traits he exalts in one tongue can be deemed by another critic or poet of equal renown (cf. Eliot and Saint-John Perse) to be of negative worth or typical only of prose. Or two authorities will praise the same language with dramatically opposed, mutually exclusive, indeed self-contradictory arguments.

Significantly, as distinguished a voice as Robert Champigny lauds qualities in French that so many others consider to be liabilities: homogeneity of etymological origin (Latin), phonological suppleness, absence of tonic stress, rarity of compound words, richness of vowel sonority and rhyme.[3] It is true that French poets, to some extent since Baudelaire and Rimbaud, more ostentatiously since Dada and Surrealism, rebel against a certain national tradition. However, the rebellion proves to be superficial: some typographical modifications and a relatively broader lexicon. The structure of the language—syntactical, grammatical, and rhetorical—remains the same. Furthermore, who is to say that the rebellion is "good" and the antecedent tradition "bad"? After all, an antithetical reaction occurred in Anglo-American verse, with Eliot and Pound rebelling against their heritage (the English Romantics and Milton), seeking order, control, and universal values—the "virtues of prose"—and seeking them on the Continent from Continental poets.

Even the question of richness of lexicon proves to be more complex than people realize. That in French-English dictionaries more space is given to the English than to the French proves little. Does the average middle-class Englishman or American possess a richer working vocabulary than the average French bourgeois? Does the average French peasant employ a more restricted lexicon than his Anglo-Saxon counterpart? Does the average newspaper article or popular novel in English use more words than its analogue in France? I do not have statistics one way or the other, yet were all three questions to be answered in the affirmative, it would still say nothing about *poetic language*. For poets are not average men. As I see it, a certain register of speech, characterized by a relatively restricted vocabulary and derived from neoclassicism, is associated in the popular mind with France, the French language, and Gallic culture; a more exuberant speech, with a relatively expanded vocabulary, derived from the Elizabethan Age, is associated in the popular mind with England, the English language, and Anglo-Saxon culture. Such myths may have some influence over middle-class usage, over standards and models for writing in the schools, and certainly over the compilers of dictionaries where, on the French side of the Channel, popular, peasant, dialect, and extrahexagonal terminology is consciously suppressed.

Poetry over the centuries is another matter. Shakespeare and Milton have a richer lexicon than Corneille and Racine, but Villon and d'Aubigné have a richer lexicon than Dryden and Pope. It is all a matter of period and century, of register and style. What English prose writer before Joyce can possibly equal the linguistic fecundity of Rabelais? What English poet ever can equal the linguistic variety of Saint-John Perse? The *Trésor de la langue française* and the *Französisches Etymologisches Wörterbuch*[4] prove beyond the shadow of a doubt the incredible richness of French vocabulary on all levels over the last two centuries and since the beginning. In any case, who is to say that Milton is greater than Racine or that d'Aubigné is greater than Pope? That richness or poverty of lexicon is in and of itself a poetic virtue or vice? True, richness of lexicon is often a gauge to the intensity or brilliance of metaphor. Yet some of the finest poets in literature, some of the

most honored poets in their respective tongues—Racine, Mörike, Pushkin—create largely without resorting to simile and metaphor. Are we
obliged to consider Pushkin inferior to Góngora and La Fontaine inferior to Walt Whitman?

As suggested in chapter 1, the myth goes back to the Romantics and,
before them, to Voltaire. It derives from the fact that at one time
French verse and the French language were associated with neoclassicism, and English or German verse and their tongues were associated
with Romanticism or the Renaissance-Reformation. Such distinctions
were perhaps of value in a particular historical context in the past.
They certainly helped contribute to the liberation of England and Germany from French cultural predominance. As an overall judgment on
the respective languages or poetic traditions, they are both inaccurate
in terms of history and false as a basis for esthetic judgment. After all,
the very same French tongue and poetic tradition were proclaimed
supreme throughout Europe in other periods: the thirteenth century
and the seventeenth, for instance. There is no justification for exalting
French syllabism and rhyme in the ages of Saint Louis and Louis XIV
only to condemn the same traits of prosody in the eras of Louis XV or
Bonaparte or Clemenceau.

As a final argument in favor of my thesis, I should like to cite the
phenomenon of multilingualism in literature, of writers choosing to
create in languages other than their native tongue for strictly literary
reasons, and specifically the phenomenon of poets choosing over the
centuries to write in French.[5]

The practice was common in the Middle Ages. For theoreticians such
as Dante (*De vulgari eloquentia*) and Raimon Vidal de Besalù (*Razos de
trobar*), Northern French was an appropriate medium for narrative
verse, prose, and lyric forms such as the *pastourelle,* whereas Occitan
was the right language for other lyric genres, including the *canso* (*grand
chant courtois*) and *sirventes.* From a modern historical perspective, it
would appear that because, during the formative period of the tradition, great epics and romances were first composed in French and
great courtly lyrics in Occitan, it was assumed that to write a successful
romance or lyric one ought not only to develop the intertextual themes,
motifs, and rhetorical topics inherent in the genre but also to practice
the intertextual language in which the themes and motifs did flourish.
This is in fact what took place. For a long period Italians and Cataláns
composed love songs not in their own tongues but in Occitan; similarly,
Castilians composed their lyrics in Galician-Portuguese. Quite a number of Franco-Italian epics were composed in the thirteenth century,
verse narratives written by Italians in a variety of French that could be

understood by the people of northern Italy. Similarly, Brunetto Latini composed his prose encyclopedia, *Li Livres dou Tresor,* in the Northern French *lingua franca,* the same vehicle in which Marco Polo and Carpini related their travels. And for centuries (1050–1350) almost all vital creative literature in England was composed in Norman-French. Admittedly, most Anglo-Norman writers were native speakers of French, but Chaucer's great contemporary, John Gower, was not. This Anglophone wrote *Vox clamantis* in Latin, *Mirour de l'omme* and *Cinkante balades* in French, and his *Confessio amantis* in English. For Brunetto Latini, Marco Polo, and John Gower, writing in French was not uniquely a matter of genre determination. As the international vernacular of business, war, and polite letters, the Latin of the court and battlefield, French had developed an exceptional qualitative prestige and quantitative audience. For these reasons it was cultivated by nonnative Francophones just as Latin was cultivated by a host of clerics who did not imbibe the language of Virgil at their mother's breast.

Despite the growth of national language consciousness, literary multilingualism persisted well into the Renaissance and beyond. Poets praised their prince in more than one poem, using more than one language on the same subject. Du Bellay exploited the "Heureux comme Ulysse. . ." theme first in Latin, then illustrated the same topic in French. Dutch, German, and English poets acted in much the same way, employing both Latin and French as well as their vernaculars. Jan van der Noot wrote first in French, then in Dutch (with some German). Cats wrote in French, Latin, and Dutch; Weckherlin in French, German, and even some English; Zesen in German, but also some French and Dutch. A notable French-language poet of the eighteenth century was Frederick the Great, King of Prussia!

In modern times attitudes toward multilingualism of course have changed. That Hamilton should compose his *Mémoires de la vie du comte de Grammont* (1713) and Beckford his *Vathek* (1784) in French caused no comment, whereas Wilde's *Salomé* (1894) unleashed a scandal. For with the nineteenth century came linguistic as well as personal Romanticism, the notion that languages have unique souls and that the writer has an obligation, moral and esthetic, to cultivate his own. Nonetheless, perhaps in reaction to the Romantic mentality, Symbolism proved to be an international undertaking, with a number of poets of foreign extraction—Moréas, Viélé-Griffin, Merrill, Heredia, Rodenbach, Verhaeren, Maeterlinck—living in Paris and making a major contribution to the movement in French. Then George, Rilke, and D'Annunzio composed works in French; Rilke's French texts are one of the high points in his opus. As the century progressed there appeared the polyglot verse of

Eliot and Pound, conscious bilingualism in Hans Arp, Ivan Goll, and Samuel Beckett, and the adoption of French as a primary creative tongue by Tristan Tzara and Eugène Ionesco.

It can be seen that for various reasons—historical, cultural, literary, and personal—over a period of eight or nine hundred years not only do poets choose to write in languages other than their own, but more specifically foreigners have chosen consistently and repeatedly to write in French. The number and quality of their works are unequaled by any other modern vernacular in the East or West. In this sense, as in others, French can indeed be considered a classical tongue, comparable to Greek, Latin, Arabic, Persian, Sanskrit, and Chinese. One conclusion to be drawn from the phenomenon concerns the nature of artistic creation, the fact that so many poets write not out of emotion or élan or eagerness to decipher the hieroglyphs. A second conclusion is that, for all these men, neither the French language nor French prosody is inherently unpoetical and that, for them and for us, it is absurd to cast aspersions on French or any specific century of the French tradition from one single, parochial perspective, be it the poetical practice of some of the great modern masters.

The issues raised in the preceding paragraphs all focus on and contribute to the fundamental question concerning the history of French verse: What is poetic language? The answer most congruent to modern orthodoxy and apparently most scientific in approach is the one given by Jean Cohen when, as stated in chapter 1, he observes from the seventeenth to the twentieth century an evolution toward greater and more numerous *écarts* of poetic language from the language of prose, which leads him to conclude that the essence of poetry lies in these *écarts;* that an understanding of the nature of poetry exists only with the Moderns; and that poetry becomes more poetic as it evolves in time. The same answer is given by Barthes, who claims that in the classical age verse is merely embellished prose, differing from prose in a "quantitative" manner but not in substance, whereas modern poetry *is* poetry, truly itself, pure essence.

A first objection to the Barthes-Cohen thesis is methodological. As we observed in chapter 1, specialists in linguistics, men as distinguished as A. J. Greimas, have pointed out that it is a "positivistic prejudice" to assume that everyday spoken speech and demonstrative prose are uniquely connotative, whereas poetry, differing in essence from speech-prose, is denotative. Natural speech also is poetic: It too exists for beauty and play, not just in order to facilitate communication; it is richer, more complex, and more ambiguous than people give it credit for being. Conversely, poetry proves not to be so strange or esoteric vis-à-vis common speech and written prose, whether imaginative or the more mundane journalistic or historical variety. In other words, literary prose is as artificial as verse, and verse is as "natural" as prose. Therefore, the assumption that prose—imaginative or journalistic-historical—should be taken as a connotative norm for speech and poetry defined as to how it differs from prose, as what is added to prose, in order to make the *écart*, is wrong. Furthermore, it can be claimed that any explanation based upon speech, style, language, and linguistic formalism alone is also wrong. A work of poetry or of prose must be taken as an ontological whole, and the poeticity of a verse text is contained in its themes, motifs, and ideas as well as its language.

A much greater objection can be made to Barthes and Cohen from a historical perspective. To compare three classical poets (Corneille, Molière, Racine), three Romantics (Lamartine, Vigny, Hugo), and three Symbolists (Verlaine, Rimbaud, Mallarmé), and from this comparison to posit the evolution of literary history and the ontological nature of poetry itself is a mistake. For the nine poets in question, great as they are, in no way represent or can account for French verse, either in its historical development or from the perspective of quality and value. French poetry does not begin with Malherbe. If Cohen had examined texts prior to 1650, he would have discovered a tradition of great poets—many of the troubadours, Gautier de Coinci, Rutebeuf, Villon, Jean Lemaire de Belges and other Rhétoriqueurs, Scève, du Bellay, Ronsard, Sponde, La Ceppède, Théophile de Viau, and Saint-Amant—all of whom are more "poetic" than Corneille, Molière, and Racine, some of whom are more "poetic" than Lamartine, Vigny, and Hugo: that is, using Cohen's own criteria of nonpunctuated metrical pauses, noncategorical rhymes, impertinent, redundant, and abnormal epithets, it could be ascertained that these earlier writers are closer to the Symbolists, to the norms of the late nineteenth and early twentieth centuries, than were the classical generation and even the Romantics. In both old and new poetry we find similes, metaphors, striking imagery, and the presence of rhetoric. The masters of *trobar clus* and *trobar ric*, the Rhétoriqueurs, and some very great poets of the Renaissance and Baroque consciously strove for a *stylus durus*, a harsh, ornate style in imitation of Antiquity, an artificial language, difficult, convoluted, and serious, far from prose and the spoken tongue of the mob.

At the same time, we must not forget the other style, one closer to prose and therefore purportedly less poetical, ascribed by Barthes and Cohen to the classical generation. This plainer style was prevalent throughout the Middle Ages and Renaissance as the medium for romance, pastoral, comedy, and satire, for most narrative and discursive verse. In Chrétien de Troyes, Marot, and La Fontaine it reflects a court ambience, reproduces the verve and excitement of real speech. In the erotic vein of Charles d'Orléans, Villon, du Bellay, and Ronsard, it creates the illusion of genuine love as opposed to the artifice of *fin' amor*. Thus, as we have seen, generations of critics assumed that Ronsard, using *beau stille bas* to court Marie, was more sincere, more authentic, than when he employed an ornate middle style to woo Cassandre. Scève, Sponde, and La Ceppède, comparable to the Metaphysicals in England, strove for a blend of passion and thought, expressing ontological problems in the functional imagery of everyday speech, this in contrast to the rich, sensuous language of the Pléiade. Of course, poets like Adam de la Halle, Villon, or Ronsard are consummate masters of both styles, practicing each in turn, setting one off against the other. La Fontaine, in his *Fables* and *Contes,* or within the same book of the *Fables,* or within one single fable, can be "poet" and "counter-poet." So can Boileau within one satire or epistle. The same is true in more recent times for Musset, Laforgue, and Apollinaire. Sponde and La Fontaine both cultivate the plain style. Although, obviously, there is a vast difference between Metaphysical Mannerism and the classicism of *la cour et la ville,* both poets and both schools react comparably against the High Renaissance *écart.*

La Fontaine and Boileau in no way seek the *écart.* On the contrary, theirs is a different kind of poetry, one that reproduces the rhythms and inflections of prose or the refined style of elegant, worldly conversation, that is based on convention, taste, and judgment, and that receives much of its effect from antithesis and wit. Its hallmarks are impersonality, abstraction, normalcy in syntax, rhyme, and meter, intellectual and esthetic clarity, and a quality of chaste diction, varying according to genre and mode but avoiding at all cost paradox, extravagance, and literary impropriety. This relatively simple, plain style is direct and normative; it moves within clearly defined limits and adheres to rules of decorum and of rhetoric. Although in its own way such verse is as complex, as difficult to interpret, as the most luxurious passages of Góngora or Mallarmé, this complexity derives from closeness of diction to court speech rather than from opposition and *écart.*

I have spoken of two modes or kinds of poetry: one Romantic, or Modern, the other typical of an earlier age. From a larger perspective it can be claimed that something like *trobar ric* or *trobar clus* and *trobar plan* are to be found in various forms throughout world literature. Within the French sphere, heightened diction, rich imagery, and the individual voice—the *écart*—are prevalent in the troubadours, Villon, Scève, Ronsard, the great Baroque lyricists, Hugo, the Symbolists, and such major twentieth-century figures as Saint-John Perse, Jouve, Char, and Bonnefoy. On the other hand, a plainer style, conventional imagery, and a clearly rhetorical persona are to be found in some of the trouvères, Chrétien de Troyes, Machaut, Charles d'Orléans, Marot, La Fontaine, Boileau, the eighteenth-century tradition, and, more recently, Verlaine, Supervielle, the Ecole de Rochefort, and Prévert. A case can be made for cyclical recurrence of the two styles, one dominant during certain historical periods, the other at different times. A case can also be made that, in world literature as a whole, the classical tradition, the notions of imitation, rhetoric, community, and game, prove to be more universal and are more worthy to serve as a basis for our conception of what writing verse is all about.

It is possible to chart an oscillation between the flowery style (troubadours, Renaissance and Baroque, Romanticism and Symbolism) and the plain style (much of the early and late Middle Ages, the classical age, some Moderns). If the practitioners of metaphor reacted against what they considered to be an excessively prosaic, conventional, and nonpoetic idiom, the adepts of greater simplicity repudiated what they deemed to be an excessively stilted, artificial, and rhetorical speech. At least three times in the history of French verse the devotees of plain style have asserted their claim to poetic legitimacy. Their tradition also derives from Roman practice: the Horatian voice, the Ovidian mode. Therefore, it is an error to consider one of the styles to be more poetic or more French than the other, one the rule and the other the exception. Literary history teaches us that the pattern is one of the healthy oscillation of *trobar clus* and *trobar leu*, or *sermo rudis* and *sermo dulcis*, of high style and plain style—not a case of freedom versus constraint, or poetry versus prose.

Indeed, since poetry is grounded in the vibrant, dynamic tension between meter and rhythm, it can be claimed that the language of poetry has to differ not only from the language of prose but also from the verse ideal, if such there be. One way of ensuring tension is to create a level of diction differing from but based upon the norms of elegant court speech. Leavis and Eliot criticized Milton for having wandered too far from the fount of common spoken English, for having substituted for the common style only his personal idiosyncrasies. According to Leavis, "subtlety of movement in English verse depends upon the play of the natural sense movement and intonation against the verse structure, and that 'natural,' here, involves a reference, more or less direct, to idiomatic speech."[6] Therefore, the best poets in English (Jonson, Donne, Dryden, in more recent times Eliot himself) are those who maintain a tough reasonableness, a quality of strength and "wit" that derives from their proximity to the spoken idiom, and those who for two centuries imitated the worst in Milton, took the wrong road.

Obviously, the same strictures against Milton and his English followers can be made vis-à-vis Mallarmé and Valéry in France. Fortunately for the French tradition, the Symbolist mode has come late and—given the works of Laforgue and Corbière, Aragon and Eluard, Michaux and Prévert, poets who either reacted against or simply ignored Symbolist high style—has never had a dictatorial force comparable to the Miltonic legacy across the Channel, at least not among practicing poets. The situation in the classroom and with literary reviews is another matter. However, the positive import of the Eliot-Leavis judgment, the judgment of New Criticism, is indeed applicable to and crucial for a revaluation of the history of French verse. In this light we should recognize a thousand-year tradition of plain style, of urbanity, ripeness, and wit, of strength, and of closeness to the speech of the court—in Chrétien de Troyes, Guillaume de Lorris, Guillaume de Machaut, Charles d'Orléans, Marot, Sponde, La Ceppède, La Fontaine, Voltaire, Musset, Laforgue, and Supervielle—that may well embody the best of France, its greatest contribution to literature. For Eliot in England, for Roger Caillois in France, poetry first and foremost had to possess the virtues of good prose—clarity, order, rigor—which then could be embellished by metrical constraints and the panoply of traditional verse rhetoric. To lack either the clarity and rigor or the rhetoric and metrical constraints is simply bad art.

The notion of *écart,* then, is insufficient to explain or define poetry, given that poetry contains several registers of style, all "poetic" yet some closer to prose than others. In the past the choice of register was determined by the genre the poet chose to write in and the public he chose to address. In the past the Speaker always adapted to his public, for his goal was to manipulate the implied reader, working within the latter's mental and moral framework. This permitted the traditional poet to indulge in a greater range of voices and styles than was available to Lamartine and Baudelaire or Mallarmé and Valéry. It permitted him to shift back and forth, from satire to invective to philosophical meditation to urbane wit. For even when poems seek to express universal truths or commonly held doctrine, they adhere to time-honored genres, modes, and levels of style. In other words, poetry seeks not to be original but to instruct and, in order to do so, to be "well said": Horace's "Omne tulit punctum qui miscuit utile dulci, / lectorem delectando pariterque monendo" (*Ars Poetica,* 343–44). One says *well* by imitating appropriate models, ancient and modern, by choosing one's linguistic and topical register, and by establishing an appropriate relationship with the reader. To be successful, the poem has to reflect, indeed to embody, the *urbanitas* that is the hallmark of French culture from Chrétien de Troyes to Chénier and beyond.

This manipulation of the reader, this control of the poetic voice, this choice of register, is based upon the precepts of rhetoric. And rhetoric is at the foundation of all poetic expression. From the Middle Ages to the Third Republic the poet consulted the *artes poeticae* and the *artes dictandi* available to him. His craft was one of *inventio, dispositio,* and *amplificatio,* adhering to the norms of judicial, deliberative, and demonstrative or panegyrical oratory. This is true for Chrétien de Troyes, Guillaume de Lorris, and Jean de Meun, Scève, Ronsard, and d'Aubigné, Corneille, Racine, and Boileau, Voltaire and Dorat, Lamartine and Hugo. A high or a plain style is chosen because it corresponds to or is appropriate for a particular mode of writing: epic, pastoral, satire, *fin' amor* lyricism, and so on. And such rhetoric includes, indeed fosters, panegyric and distance, flattery and parody, the illusion of freedom and the reality of self-consciousness, all at the same time.

Treatises on rhetoric tell us, as does poetic practice from the early Middle Ages well into the nineteenth century, that writers had not two but three styles to work in: *genus grande, genus medium (floridum, temperatum),* and *genus humile (tenue, submissum, extenuatum).* Classical decorum (the medieval *genera dicendi* derive from Quintilian and Cicero) determines propriety of style: Stylistic register is based upon the genre the writer wishes to practice and the dignity of the subject matter (its social standing) he chooses to exploit. The sublime is reserved for epic or tragedy or the lofty religious and secular ode; it treats of princes, of martial feats, and of the sacred. It is associated with the *Aeneid.* The middle style is appropriate for wooing a lady in the Petrarchan mode, much devotional poetry, high romance, decorous comedy, and all manner of descriptive and didactic verse. It is associated with the *Georgics.* Low style relates to pastoral, elegy, love poetry in the non-Petrarchan mode, and satire. It is also used for farce, burlesque, and invective. And it can serve as antipoetry and antiliterature, to parody, mock, and undermine the other two styles, especially the sublime. It is associated with the *Bucolics.*

Especially in the sixteenth and seventeenth centuries poetry can be understood in relation to the three levels of style.[7] Stylistic register is perhaps more helpful for elucidating poetic matters than are the notions of period style (distinctions between Mannerism, Baroque, and Classicism) or personal style (distinctions between the genius of Ronsard, d'Aubigné, and Racine). It has to be emphasized that no value judgment is presumed or implied in the hierarchy of rhetorical structure. Stylistic register concerns subject matter and genre viewed from the perspective of social class as much as it does normative esthetics. Thus a pastoral elegy in low style can be as decorous, even as ornate, certainly as prized and as beautiful, as a Petrarchan sonnet sequence or a neoclassical epic. Some of the greatest writers—Ronsard, d'Aubigné, Saint-Amant, and for that matter Voltaire—will practice all three. On the other hand, classical authors, while restricting the lexicon and metrical variety of the Baroque, while reducing metaphor and increasing abstraction, thus bringing poetic language much closer to the everyday spoken idiom of the court, at the same time contribute to the elaboration of a new high style, based on abstraction, control, and the absence of metaphor.

The poet's task was to please as well as to instruct. Often, artistic pleasure, and humor, were created by indulging in the middle or low styles or in the juxtaposition of styles. Such juxtaposition, especially in the vernacular, was far more prevalent than the *artes poeticae* would have us believe. In terms of the Christian tradition, for example, Christ as a Jew, a carpenter by trade, associated with fishermen, tax collectors, and shepherds, a man of peace and the protagonist of texts not written in Virgilian splendor, had to be associated with *sermo humilis*, yet as God, the Lord of Hosts who harrowed hell, whose military feats and family are of cosmic significance, his is also a *sermo gravissimus*.

An excellent example of *genus humile* is the style of burlesque epic in the seventeenth century: in such works as Saint-Amant's *Le Melon* (1631) and *Le Passage de Gibraltar* (1640), Scarron's *Typhon* (1644) and *Virgile travesty* (1648–52, 1659), and Dassoucy's *Le Jugement de Pâris* (1648), *Ovide en belle humeur* (1650), and *Le Ravissement de Proserpine* (1653). These men are not realists but masters of fantasy and the grotesque. Their language is not at all low class but an intentionally stylized art form; their texts are based upon other texts, and their mode, an intertextual tour de force, adheres to strictly literary norms. An artificial genre, based on *stylus humilis, a style bas et plaisant,* epic travesty was written not for the masses but for a public of "connoisseurs," for educated people familiar with the classics and with neoclassical rules. The language of *Virgile travesty* is a motley affair, a mixture of "high" and "low" expressions plus archaic, technical, invented, and foreign terms. Whatever writers normally exclude from refined poetic diction—the familiar, the vulgar, the obscene, and all forms of slang—here find a place. Classical *proprietas* is broken and the new standard grounded in dissonance and discrepancy. This rhetoric of the burlesque is the result of gratuitous, creative verbal fantasy: It is vigorous, dynamic, and can create the illusion of being natural utterance.

By having Aeneas and Apollo speak such a language, the Burlesques succeed in pulling the old gods down to the level of unheroic, undivine mortals living in the seventeenth century. In the process, not only speech is undermined but character and situation as well. The reality of modern life is substituted for handsome lies in the past. Among the techniques employed to create this effect are temporal anachronism and social leveling. The old gods wear Louis XIV clothes and wigs, hold offices appropriate only in France. They move in a bourgeois salon, or they swear, drink, and fight like the Parisian rabble. Virgil's characters are transformed into comic stereotypes worthy of Molière: Mars is depicted as a *miles gloriosus,* Minerva as a pedant, Venus as a whore, Mercury as a pander, Cassandra as a *précieuse,* Calchas as a *bigot.* Burlesque poets also emphasize concrete physical detail no less anachronistic, realistic trivia forming a part of everyday life that writers with a taste for the sublime carefully avoid. Thus we hear of Priam's binoculars, Aeneas's tobacco, and Venus's makeup. Even the sexual aspect of the old stories—Dido's lust for Aeneas, or Apollo's for Daphne—is brought into focus. Andromache's story of her life with Pyrrhus (*Virgile travesty,* Book 3) is replete with wife-beating, cuckoldry, and bottom-farce. Finally, an I-narrator, the mock-author, constantly and obtrusively intervenes in the story, breaking the fluidity of Virgil's or Ovid's style, undercutting in his own voice the *pietas, lacrymae rerum,* and *bienséances* to be found in the original.

Scarron and Dassoucy wield the light octosyllabic couplet with brio, achieving comic effect with an economy of means that never appears forced or malicious. Their verse gives an impression of unquenchable vitality, of spontaneity and nonchalance. Thus working from a classical source, suppressing passages of no interest to their contemporaries or that provide little scope for comedy, and adding developments of their own, the greatest of these poets do not merely parody a text. They grant it life in the modern world on their own terms. *Sermo humilis* in their hands is an offering of love to Virgil and Ovid, no less so than the mock-epic, low subject matter treated in *sermo gravissimus* by Boileau or Gresset. It represents the introduction into France of a current from south of the Alps; it is a legitimate artistic manifestation treating in the comic mode what others treat in the sublime. Their words manifest a spirit of independence, a refusal of pompous literary convention. Like the other Baroque writers, the Burlesques scorn measure and restraint; they seek to amuse and *far stupir* with their wit. Committed to deforming language and creating a sense of amazement in the reader, burlesque and *préciosité* can be considered the last two Baroque currents before the triumph of Classicism. This burlesque low style is no less esthetic, artistic, and poetic in its own way than the middle register of Théophile and the lofty diction of Corneille. All three are poetry. And each of the three establishes its respective distance from, and tension with, the spoken idiom of *la cour et la ville* and written prose.

Another manifestation of *genus humile* is the obscene. Obscenity, like any other trait in literature, is a conscious, willful use of traditional rhetoric, not the outpouring of a unique creative personality, not the poet creating his own language. It is to be placed within the tradition of rhetorical manipulation, not on a mythical, hypothetical scale of *écart*. In the Middle Ages and Renaissance the obscene was employed to break down barriers and to create distance, to undermine and denigrate courtly orthodoxy or heroic and esthetic norms. And long before Dante it could be introduced for esthetic and moral effect into serious, purposive works of art. This in spite of the fact that treatises on rhetoric mentioned three levels of style but showed only how to cultivate the first one. Because low style in general and the obscene in particular have received relatively little attention from scholars, compared to the academically more acceptable registers, and because I discussed the erotic middle style in chapter 2, here I should like to examine briefly four texts from the Middle Ages, from different periods and genres, which manifest distinct forms of the literary consciousness.[8]

In my first example, the *chanson de geste Raoul de Cambrai* (1180–1200), we find quite early in French literature obscenity and stylistic variety employed in a serious context.[9] The hero, Raoul, grossly insults Marsent, abbess of the Convent of Origny and mother to his squire and best friend, Bernier. He accuses the lady in the crudest possible terms of having been a prostitute, a *communax garsoniere*, of having "gone down" for a few pennies for anyone who wanted her:

> —Voir! dist R. vos estes losengiere.
> Je ne sai rien de putain chanberiere
> Qi ait esté corsaus ne maaillere,
> A toute gent communax garsoniere.
> Au conte Y. vos vi je soldoiere,
> La vostre chars ne fu onques trop chiere;
> Se nus en vost, par le baron s. Piere!
> Por poi d'avoir en fustes traite ariere.
>
> (1328–35)

The language concentrates on sexuality and social class. Terms such as *putain, chanberiere, maaillere, garsoniere, soldoiere,* indicate that Raoul insults Marsent not only for her erotic comportment but also because she allegedly sold herself for money, and for very little at that; in other words, that she was a whore of low class, the lowness as important as the whoredom.

Raoul's diatribe can be interpreted as an instance of realism: realism of speech and of subject matter. In this case *stylus humilis,* the style of *Le Roman de Renart,* intentionally undercuts the traditional *stylus gravis* of epic. Issues such as illegitimate sex, and a pillaging baron's attitude toward the nuns he pillages, do not appear in texts such as the *Song of Roland.* No less realistic is the psychological insight. Surely the trouvère has his paladin react in so irrational a way because he suddenly has to cope with the traditional class enemy, largely absent from *Roland*: (1) a representative of the Church, and (2) a woman. He, Raoul, a Carolingian warrior, a *miles dominans,* explodes with hatred, dread, and scorn, with verbal aggression before that enigma, that hidden oblique menace incarnate in the *Ewig-Weibliche.*

As if to prove the point, young Raoul acts in a comparable way toward his own mother, Aalais, insulting her when she offers him good advice, telling her to go fatten herself in the women's quarters rather than mix with men's affairs:

> Maldehait ait, je le taing por lanier,
> Le gentil homme, qant il doit tornoier,
> A gentil dame qant se va consellier!
> Dedens vos chambres vos alez aasier:
> Beveiz puison por vo pance encraissier,
> Et si pensez de boivre et de mengier;
> Car d'autre chose ne devez mais plaidier.
>   (1100–1106)

Here the male is assimilated to martial activity on the outside (*tornoier*), to asceticism in the open air; and the female to nurture, softness, and comfort within, to her idle body (*vo pance encraissier*), enclosed by four walls. For Raoul, the mother and the nun both embody illegitimate authority—that is, usurpation of authority—based upon age and engendering, which he repudiates, for in his eyes it is defiled by the flesh, by what Bakhtin, in referring to Rabelais, calls "the material bodily lower stratum": mouth, stomach, belly, and sex.[10] This feudal baron attacks both women as women, in their sex, their body, with that scorn for the body and for sex that is one manifestation of the feudal and ecclesiastical mentality.

Raoul not only repudiates the ladies verbally. He later burns down the convent of Origny, slaying one hundred nuns, and defiles the Vermandois land with flame and sword. He the orphan, embodiment of *desmesure,* of misguided *fortitudo,* lashes out at the *sapientia* figures who block his path, at the Mothers, real and surrogate, who seek to restrain his violence-oriented libido. This violence, however, is not the author's. It must be said that the count's squire and friend Bernier behaves more graciously toward his own mother and toward Raoul's; and, through subtle use of narrative technique, the trouvère indicates that Aalais's advice is good and that Marsent is a lady of high social standing and of no less high principle, moral or otherwise. Presumably, the trouvère wishes his audience to prefer the squire's more supple, resilient humanity to the master's misogynistic rage. He is condemning a fierce, virile, martial mentality—Roland's—no doubt admirable in Roland's day, but which in more recent times proves to be dangerous, a menace to social order within France. In this text the obscene, which no doubt corresponds to and reflects the spoken idiom of the precourtly aristocratic class (male), has a functional role in the narrative: It serves to reveal character, advance the plot, present a message, and contribute to a structure of parallelism and antithesis that lies at the heart of *chansons de geste.*

Branch 1 of *Le Roman de Renart,*[11] the French beast epic, dates from the 1170s. In the following passage Brun l'Ours has been tricked by Renart, and the peasants are rushing in for the kill:

> Qui lors veïst vilains venir
> et fremïer par mi la rue!
> Qui porte hache, qui maçue,
> qui flael, qui baston d'espine:
> grant poor a Bruns de s'eschine.
> Devant lui vient Hurtevilain
> et Joudoïn Trouseputain
> et Baudoïn Porteciviere,
> qui fout sa fame par derrieres,
> Girout Barbete qui l'acole
> et un des fiuz sire Nichole
> et Trosseanesse la puant,
> qui por la moche va fuiant,
> et Corberant de la Ruelle,
> le bon voideor d'escüelle,
> et Tiegerins Brisefouace
> et li fil Tieger de la Place.
>   (652–68)

This is literature mocking literature: a parody on the muster of troops, the list of epic heroes in the *Iliad* (which the Medievals did not know), the *Aeneid,* the *Song of Roland,* and other *chansons de geste,* which they did. The lofty register treating martial activity by knights of old is reduced to absurd, grotesque peasants dwelling in the present, peasants who dare to take up arms (and what arms!) in order to chase a bear already caught in a trap and whose previous exploits, enscribed for posterity in their names, are accomplished at table and in bed, or, instead, in the open field and on the dung heap. Low-class peasants, evoked in low style, are capable only of low activities, specifically Bakhtin's "material bodily lower stratum": sex, food, and the stench emanating from both. Sex is evoked in terms of sodomy and bestiality, for this is the animal half of man's nature, exemplified by animal-like people who associate with animals. Significantly, they are less noble and less courtly than the bears, wolves, and foxes—messires Brun, Isengrin, and Renart—whom they presume to hunt. Yet our beast-epic warriors are afraid of these creatures and flee them as they would the plague. The author, writing for a courtly and/or clerical public, mocks peasants and mocks earlier heroic literature at the same time. And he plays with language and has fun with writing, from the sheer joy of it.

The standard stylistic register in *Le Roman de Renart* is neither all burlesque (lofty matters recounted in low style) nor all mock-epic (humble material sung in the sublime register), but, instead, the juxtaposition of high and low. Here is part of a speech by Bruyant le Toreau at court, where Renart is accused of adultery with the she-wolf Hersent:

> Conment doit Isangrin plaidier
> de chose qui si est aperte
> et conneüe et descoverte?
> Et je sai bien, que que nus die,
> que cil qui tot le mont conchie,
> Renart, icil mavés lechierres,
> cil rous puanz, cil orz trichierres,
> eüst ma fame si baillie
> contre son cuer l'eüst saisie,
> ja Maupertuis nel garantist,
> ne forteresce qu'il feïst
> que je ne l'eüse tué
> et puis en un conpaing rué.
> Hersant, dont vos vint cist coraiges?
> Certes, ce fu mout grant damajes
> c'onques Renart, cil fel, cil rous,
> vos bati onques le velous.
>
> (86–102)

Observe, in the midst of a relatively complicated legal and moral exposition, delivered with some small command of the colors of rhetoric, the *persuasio* of the *artes dictaminis,* how Bruyant descends to insult the accused—*lechierres, rous puanz, orz trichierres*—as would never happen in the comparable court scenes of epic and romance. Observe the juxtaposition of treachery and redheadedness, placed on the same footing of moral turpitude; the double meaning of *conchie* (to trick and to shit upon), and finally the curious euphemism this great baron of the realm, *in curia regis,* employs to express the sexual act: *vos bati . . . le velous,* literally, "he beat your velvet!" Is this a common twelfth-century spoken idiom? We do not find it in polite belles-lettres. Or, more likely, is it an obscene metaphor invented by the trouvère for the occasion? Not twenty lines further on, Grimbert the Badger assures Bruyant that if the she-wolf's *vessel* has been damaged by Renart the worth of a hazelnut, he the badger is prepared to have it sown up. Sex again is mocked, and the woman as receptor and/or instigator is mocked again in her sex. We are meant to laugh at real law courts and adulterers, also at the conventional trial machinery of epic and romance and the conventional machinery of *fin' amor.* Here is what courtly love is really about, says the poet. We are never allowed to forget that, as in La Fontaine, these are beasts acting like counts and dukes, and counts and dukes acting like beasts, for Renart is denounced because (1) he seduced the consort of his colleague, Lord Isengrin, Peer of the Realm, and (2) just before leaving, he also did *pipi* on the little wolf cubs. And they talked.

In Jean de Meun's section of *Le Roman de la Rose,* at one point Dame Raison refers in passing to the castration of Saturn, "cui Jupiter coupa les coilles" (5507).[12] When the Narrator, who in fact is Guillaume de Lorris's ideal courtly lover, objects to her language, that she has uttered "une parole / si esbaulevree et si fole" (5671–72), Raison agrees to bring the matter up for discussion later. The Narrator does not forget and in due time castigates her again for uttering such filthy things improper in the mouth of a "cortaise pucele":

> Si ne vos tiegn pas a cortaise
> quant ci m'avez coilles nomees,
> qui ne sunt pas bien renomees
> en bouche a cortaise pucele.
> Vos, qui tant estes sage et bele,
> ne sai con nomer les osastes,
> au mains quant le mot ne glosastes
> par quelque cortaise parole,

si con preude fame en parole.
Sovent voi neïs ces norrices,
dom maintes sunt baudes et nices,
quant leur enfanz tienent et baignent,
qu'els les debaillent et esplaignent,
si les noment els autrement.
Vos savez or bien se ge ment.

(6898–912)

Raison presents good arguments in her defense, but in so doing she refers again to *coillons* and *viz* (6936), upon which the Narrator falls into an even greater rage at her *parleüre baude* and accuses her of being a *fole ribaude:*

—Or vaut pis, dis je, que devant,
car bien vois ore apercevant
par vostre parleüre baude
que vos estes fole ribaude,
car, tout ait Dex les choses fetes
que ci devant m'avez retretes,
les moz au mains ne fist il mie,
qu'il sunt tuit plein de vilenie.

(6949–56)

Now, in the midst of philosophical discussion, introducing an obscene term or expression, abhorrent to the courtly tradition, introducing several of them, repeating them, analyzing them, in and of itself serves to break down barriers, to open up a comic perspective. Then, a naïve, innocent, myopic lover who follows the God of Love's Ten Commandments (in Guillaume de Lorris!) to the letter (especially Commandment 4: "Aprés gardes que tu ne dies / ces órz moz ne ces ribaudies," 2097–98) brings a smile to our lips. Living up to a role, forcing love into a preconceived romantic context, and returning to his obsession—in Bergsonian terms this is symptomatic of the rigid, mechanical person who merits social correction through laughter. However, when we discover that he is obsessed only by evil talk and that he takes evil talk to be one word, *coilles,* pronounced in a clinical situation by God's daughter, then we realize that prudishness has warped the youth's character, that he has become a fanatic like Alceste or Harpagon. Raison accuses him of weeping so much that he is not a man (6351–60). Indeed, the Narrator proves to be more prudish, more virginal, than the female personification of Reason. Yet, this prudish, virginal nonman is inconsistent with himself, for, having lost his temper, he insults

Raison, using as vile a speech as she ever did to him and, in addition to errors in logic, commits the gaffe of instructing his professor in how she should deliver her own lecture. A protagonist of allegory, he vociferously denies all metaphoric dimensions to the nature of speech. And, a lover devoted to plucking the Rose, full of Sartrean bad faith, he refuses even to himself to recognize the essence of his quest, that he has *coilles,* what he hopes to do with them, what he really wants from the God of Love and from his Rose.

Raison does not remain idle during this scene, nor does she serve only as the Narrator's foil. She proves to be every bit as comic a character as he. After all, it is she who comes to the Narrator seeking to turn him from the God of Love. An inept professor and an inept psychologist, she utters words such as *coilles* in his presence, then persists in her error. This is the same teacher who, with equal disregard for elementary pedagogy, begins her lesson to the Narrator by attacking young people and youth in general. Jean de Meun is laughing at Raison's pompous philosophical jargon, her long-windedness and pedantry. Furthermore, Raison has an obsession as absurd as the Narrator's: Her insistence on philosophical love is as fanatical and perhaps as inauthentic as the Narrator's *fin' amor* for his Rose. For she wishes to seduce him and dwells upon the fact that she is beautiful, that she has a right to take a lover, and that her Father will support them financially (5765–808). Of course, in allegorical terms, asking the youth to give up the Rose for her, to become her *ami,* denotes a commitment to the philosophical life. But, *literaliter,* she is begging him to be her lover. We cannot but laugh at this confusion between the spiritual and the physical, the case of a wise virgin Goddess who uses coarse language and tries to seduce a boy, the professor who becomes a "forthputting damsel," a comic figure in romance. And, the greatest humiliation of all, Raison fails in her endeavor. The Narrator persists in preferring a flower, a plant, to her, wise and beautiful as she is.

Jean is a master of truculent speech, material detail, and picaresque naturalism. When he wants, he can wield obscenity with the same rapierlike wit that he employs for eloquence or chatty conversation. The passage in question treats of the nature of sexuality since the end of the Golden Age (the Fall); it glosses, indeed serves as literary criticism, of Guillaume de Lorris's *Roman de la Rose,* using the linguistic approach; and it is a debate on the nature of language and communication in society. Jean wrote to prove a point—the hypocrisy and bad faith of traditional courtly diction—to investigate the psychology of his characters, to stimulate comedy, and to make us realize that speech and communication lie at the heart of the world of Eros, of his representation of it, and of his public's reaction to the world and its representation: this grand *conflictus* on love. The use of the obscene serves all of these purposes and helps establish all of these points. In addition, whether proffered by the Lover or by Raison, it is in and of itself poetic: It contributes force, sparkle, and brio to the *Roman*; it makes it live. *Le Roman de la Rose,* the first work in the course of French literary history to be recognized as a classic, is poetry on all levels—sublime, mediocre, and humble.

The authors of *La Chanson de Raoul de Cambrai, Le Roman de Renart,* and *Le Roman de la Rose*—two anonymous trouvères and Jean de Meun—endow characters with obscene speech for specific psychological and doctrinal purposes: either to undermine them, their ideas, and their way of life because they are obscene, or to undermine the psychology, ideas, and way of life of their interlocutors because of how they react to obscenity. The situation is more complex still in François Villon's "Ballade de la Grosse Margot":

> Se j'ayme et sers la belle de bon het,
> M'en devez vous tenir ne vil ne sot?
> Elle a en soy des biens affin soubzhet;
> Pour son amour seins boucler et passot.
> Quant viennent gens, je cours et happe ung pot,
> Au vin m'en voys sans demener grant bruyt;
> Je leur tens eaue, froumaige, pain et fruyt.
> S'ilz paient bien, je leur diz: "*Bene stat,*
> Retournez cy, quant vous serez en ruyt,
> En ce bordeau ou tenons nostre estat."
>
> Mais adoncques, il y a grant deshet,
> Quant sans argent s'en vient coucher Mergot;
> Voir ne la puis, mon cueur a mort la het.
> Sa robe prens, demy seint et seurcot,
> Sy lui jure qu'il tendra pour l'escot.
> Par les costez se prent, c'est Antecrist,
> Crye et jure par la mort Jhesucrist
> Que non fera. Lors empoingne ung esclat,
> Dessus son nez lui en faiz ung escript,
> En ce bordeau ou tenons nostre estat.
>
> Puis paix se fait et me fait ung groz pet,
> Plus enffle qu'un velimeux escarbot.
> Riant m'assiet son poing sur mon sommet,
> Gogo me dit, et me fiert le jambot;
> Tous deux yvres dormons comme ung sabot.
> Et au resveil, quant le ventre lui bruyt,

Monte sur moy, que ne gaste son fruyt,
Soubz elle geins, plus q'un aiz me fait plat;
De paillarder tout elle me destruyt,
En ce bordeau ou tenons nostre estat.

Vente, gresle, gesle, j'ay mon pain cuyt.
Je suis paillart, la paillarde me suyt.
Lequel vault mieulx? Chacun bien s'entressuyt,
L'un vault l'autre, c'est a mau rat mau chat.
Ordure aimons, ordure nous affuyt,
Nous deffuyons honneur, il nous deffuyt,
En ce bordeau ou tenons nostre estat.[17]

However, one constant remains. As we saw in chapter 2, the Speaker of this poem, the lyrical persona that Villon adopts in composing it, is no more authentic, no more a reflection of the historical François Villon, than was the trouvère's Raoul or Jean de Meun's Narrator. Villon shapes his persona, his voice and stance, to conform to the person, real or fictional, to whom he bequeaths his text, one of many mock-heirs in *Le Testament*—in this case, Margot, a low-class prostitute. He also adheres to an anticourtly tradition in medieval letters: that of the fabliau, the *sotte chanson*, and Jean de Meun's *Roman de la Rose*, which plays an intertextual role in *Le Testament,* for one of Jean's characters, la Vieille, is the prime source and inspiration for Villon's la Belle Heaulmière and also Margot. Villon mocks courtliness as Jean de Meun did, in his image and relying upon Jean's authorial precedence. In the "Ballade," style and the obscenity it embodies are at the antipodes of courtly discretion and courtly etiquette, as are the situation, relationship, psychology, and social class of the characters inhabiting this imaginative "world." Instead of a knight-poet and his lady, we find the dregs of a bordello and her procurer; instead of his performing love service to win her favor, she sells her body to feed him; instead of tenderness and longing, they perform animal coupling. Hers is the adventure, the quest, to leave the room and discover clients. Her "superiority" to him is, in the act of intercourse, to assume the dominant position. Meanwhile, the Speaker's only act of valor, with his mock-shield and dagger, is to abuse Margot, his only heroism phallic. If anything, it is he who performs the role of cuckolded husband, for he welcomes outsiders to his domain and, unlike the *gilos* of troubadour song, even the dignified *gilos* of the *Tristan* romances and *La Mort Artu,* he himself offers his lady to the guests.

The difference between Raoul's world or Dame Raison's, on the one hand, and the Speaker's is that this one truly is obscene. Yet, as in the previous texts, we find a tension between reality and the speech used to evoke it, not obscene terms representing nonobscene reality, but in part the contrary, for the Speaker, in his refrain line, "En ce bordeau ou tenons nostre estat," juxtaposes a relatively obscene word, *bordeau,* whorehouse, with the legal, juridical, political term for one order in an ordered, hierarchical community. The purpose once again is to some extent satirical, one of undermining. Villon's is a reverse, distorted, degraded *ordo* in which the man batters the woman and the woman provides for the man, in which he exploits and reifies her (and her clients), in which their only communication is physical: beating and sex.

In spatial terms the "estate" is located in the whorehouse, at the center of which is the room (unless, as a *bordeau* or little cabin, it *is* the room), at the center of which is Margot's bed. The bed is the locus of action in the text, the fulcrum around which the action, such as it is, turns, the focus of this degraded, anticourtly court. A comparable circularity occurs in the realm of time, for the poem's action begins, let us say, in the afternoon and terminates in early morning, encompassing a typical, therefore universal, day in the life of Margot and her procurer.

Significantly, neither Margot nor her lover communicates verbally in the course of the poem. He says nothing to her. She articulates only grunts of pleasure or rough endearment ("Gogo") to him, curses, or emits wind. Her belly speaks, not her mouth. Their communication occurs through physical gesture: aggressive blows and erotic play, perhaps both at the same time, the one serving in place of the other. The Speaker-procurer as literary character also communicates with Margot's clients, but partly in a foreign language, "*bene stat.*" This use of school Latin is revealing for more than one reason. We can perhaps assume Margot's customers are members of the clergy, foreign clerics or students; thus Villon tosses an anticlerical dart. Perhaps, given the "*brulare bigot*" of the preceding stanza (an example of fifteenth-century Franglais), they are English soldiers or functionaries, thus allowing Villon to toss a political dart. In any case, the use of an artificial, scholastic, or foreign tongue renders a natural relationship between these men impossible. And the presence of Latin, the vehicle of *genus grande,* of rhetorical decorum, in such a text, juxtaposed with the reality of obscenity, serves to undermine rhetorical decorum and to make us realize the corruption and reification of this "state" even in its linguistic register, also the inadequacy of our linguistic register to cope with it.

The Speaker does communicate, not as a character with Margot the prostitute (he "writes" blows on her face), but as a Speaker, as a mock-poet and implied author, in a sense with his narratee, Margot as mock-heir (yet is she capable of understanding any poetry?), therefore above all with his public and implied readers. And here is where the obscene occurs, semiobscene speech evoking an obscene world, to undermine *fin' amor* linguistically by juxtaposing it with the distorted, corrupt, concrete physical reality of the "estate." Hence imagery of garbage, *ordure*; hence imagery of food, *pain, fruyt, froumaige*; hence imagery of low animals, *escarbot, mau chat*, and *mau rat*; hence semiargot terms referring to caresses and sex, even the sexual organs. The physical reality is one of soft earth, of rot and garbage, of corrupt viscosity. It is ugly and abject: the material bodily lower stratum again in all its force, food and sex, sex and food, the one serving as mediator, as a medium of exchange, for the other, in a reified world where the crudest forms of exchange or violence, of exploitation and domineering, replace the ordered interaction one expects in a state. Indeed, the *"bene stat,"* uttered in a sacred language, cannot but call to mind a sacred dimension that presides over all true states, images of the *civitas Dei*. The Speaker offers bread and wine—to paying fornicators. Margot seeks to protect her "fruit" (the fetus in her womb? her sexual organs?)—by assuming the dominant position. Antichrist is evoked in the same terms as the Passion, both as curses. Instead of a John the Apostle protecting the Virgin Mary, instead of a knight serving his lady, this Speaker beats, exploits, prostitutes, and enjoys Margot's flesh, she who blasphemes and curses. He, a poet, a creature of the spirit, sinks to the level of pure flesh, in which he literally wallows. Yet, says Villon, that also is a state, and theirs is an estate. Like cats or rats, nonetheless they live and keep warm; and the level of speech, the low style, *genus humile,* serves to express their world in its degradation and its haunting, concrete, authentic reality. The authenticity of the speech corresponds to the authenticity and dignity of the state as part of the human condition, horribly degraded but human all the same.

These four texts are complex, purposive, exciting works of art, worthy of the finest modern critical scrutiny. Intelligent, willed use of the obscene contributes to their greatness. In three of the texts, and also in the fourth, a male Speaker commits verbal aggression on a female interlocutor, the verbal aggression allied to a form of sexual aggression as well. The spirit takes its revenge on the body, the Clerk on the Wife of Bath. In all four, however, the male Speaker is denigrated in turn, the author presumably establishing distance between himself and his persona, the Speaker, or his literary character. The low style of the body is used to redeem the humble daughters of Eve. In three of the four poems social criticism is implied, the aristocracy mocking, satirizing the lower classes, and employing a humble register to do so. Above all, the low style does not exist alone, nor do the texts that it embodies presume to be self-referential. Low style exists in opposition to the sublime and middle registers of an earlier tradition. All four works parody literary convention, comment, criticize, and re-create it. They are truly metatexts, for their subject is in part poetry and the nature of artistic creation.

The point of this chapter is that poets choose a style or register of speech in accordance with the genre or mode they wish to cultivate, in accordance with the tradition. They do not write in order to express the deepest reaches and strivings of their soul. However, each poet, working within a traditional stylistic register, high or low, distant from or close to prose, creates a work of art in accordance with the decorum and genre expectations of his age.

In the second half of the twentieth century, as so often in the past, poetry is considered to be game, play, festivity, and an intellectual as well as emotional constraint. In this game language plays an essential part, indeed makes up the counters and the ball. As always, it serves as a means of communication between poet and reader, and as the unique medium for perpetuating the centuries-old tradition of art.

4

THE MEANING

A poem's words do not function as intellectual signs, nor are they meant to express ideas or reality as such. Instead, poetic enunciations exist for their own sake, are things, not signs, and poetry can be defined or envisaged as pure language. The nature of poetry is to be language and it represents only itself. The best poetry, the only real poetry, contains uniquely poetic value, thus is exempt from allegedly nonpoetic values such as the emotive, the moral, and the epistemological. The poem is self-reflexive, existing only for itself. Poetry creates itself, proclaims its own identity.

It is a post-Romantic notion that the goal of poetry is rapture, pure pleasure, and/or an intense psychological-emotive experience. In the words of a recent critic, "the lyric does not provide an explanation, judgment or narrative; what it does provide is feeling, alone and without histories or characters."[1] The analogous Romantic exaltation of the child or unlettered rustic leads to the inevitable conclusion that neither poet nor reader has to learn, understand, or teach when writing and reading verse. As a result, we consider poetry to be only brief lyrics, which we collect indiscriminately in anthologies, largely without gloss or commentary. And we neglect their intellectual or didactic content. From more recent times comes the idea that the poem is a self-contained entity, to be explained uniquely by infratextual, nonreferential analysis, that it pertains to what used to be called contextualism or organicism. According to this view, poems never make assertive statements about external reality. They only dramatize experience or action, specifically the experience of making statements. They cannot make assertive propositions about external reality because there is no reality outside the poem or, if there is, it is irrelevant to the poem and in any case cannot be known to us.

In response, it can be said that poems, ancient and modern, do make assertions about reality. If outside reality cannot be known to us, then neither can the reality of a poem! When modern texts deny a coherent pattern of referential mimesis, they still say something assertive and rational, even if it is only to deny assertiveness and reason. When they meditate uniquely on metaphor and on their own creation as "intransitive," self-reflexive entities, they have something to say about the functioning of metaphor and the writing of poems. And when they define themselves as pure language, signifying but not signified, words are used to comment on the nature of words, even if to negate themselves and to appeal for silence. In any case, we do not expect "true experience" from a poem but rather experience that is imaginatively conceivable, that would or could appear to be true. We expect universal truth, not facts or biographical trivia. It is wrong to say that *all* good poems are psychological, not logical, in structure. Some poems revel in irony and paradox, whereas others do not, indeed are quite straightforward. Some proclaim a mystical vision, whereas others are antivisionary and emphasize contradictions, consciously undermining a monistic view of the universe.

Much of the poetry in our culture in fact does convey significant ideas that apply to the outside world, and both the profundity and coherence of ideas are a legitimate concern of the poet. One reason why poetry occupied a central position from Homer to Goethe lies in the fact that the competing modes did not provide a greater insight into reality. Since Goethe's death, in France since the death of Vigny and the return from exile of Hugo, other notions have come into fashion: that imagination and the intellect exist in a state of conflict; that poetry is to be set apart from prose, history, philosophy, and "real life"; and that the poem itself is a mystery and an enigma, the inner sanctum of the arcane. As the claim to truth is assumed by natural science, social science, or, for that matter, the novel, the status of poetry declines.

Up to some time in the nineteenth century it was assumed that a bond existed between poetic emotion and rational understanding of the poem's subject matter. In the tradition of France, 1050 to 1856, poetry was conceived as being discursive and didactic, one of its purposes to teach universal truths, to express the common ideas of humanity, to say what all people feel. It was assumed that poetry included, contained, and subsumed unto itself all of life and all of the cosmos, that it grasped the human condition in its totality, that it was not merely one individual's idiosyncratic experience. Therefore, in a society of urbanity and a shared culture, poetry provided a medium for intellectual as well as esthetic interchange (the *dulce et utile*). Unlike the modern world, where many people believe that poets are either happily ignorant or endowed with ineffable mystical insight, the tradition demanded of its writers that they have something to teach and that they be willing and able to teach it. The *poeta doctus* is a topic dating from Antiquity and the early Middle Ages. Books were studied in the schools, and the *auctor* was by definition and by name an *auctoritas*. Jean de Meun's *Roman de la Rose* became the first vernacular classic in modern Europe more for its didactic and encyclopedic content than for its psychology, satire, and style. In the Renaissance the epic was considered the noblest, most lofty of genres in part because of the encyclopedic knowledge it was presumed to contain. During this period a genre of scientific poetry evolved, illustrated by Scève, Ronsard, and du Bartas, among others. And a tradition of philosophical verse, launched by Ronsard in his *Hymnes*, extended over the centuries, culminating in Vigny and Hugo, who were as eager to teach and had as great a claim to thought as their predecessors, including the Voltaire of *Poëme sur le désastre de Lisbonne* and *Discours en vers sur l'homme*. Of course, there is a Verlaine type of verse, evocative, incantatory, rich with sonorities and overtones, to be found in the early poets as well: Charles d'Orléans, some of Ronsard, some of Théophile, Racine, Chénier; and no one can deny the success of mood poems in the line of Verlaine, Mallarmé, Verhaeren, Valéry, and Cendrars, which mark one of the summits of French Modernism. Nonetheless, the high road of European poetry, French and foreign, remains traditional and archetypal, authentically rhetorical, concerned with ideas and intellectual commonplaces, with the appropriate choice of genre and style. This is the world of Jean de Meun, most of Ronsard, du Bartas, most of d'Aubigné, Corneille, Voltaire, Hugo, parts of Claudel, and most definitely Eluard and Aragon. This is the central focus of European verse, as poetical and as worthy of our esteem as any other.

In this chapter I shall examine six topics, six genres or modes of poetry: occasional verse, panegyric, political verse (including satire), allegory, pastoral, and the epic. Unlike the post-Romantic lyric, all six are profoundly, fundamentally concerned with meaning, indeed with a didactic message. All six depend for their effect upon reception and complicity from the public. All six are based upon rhetoric and are conventional, indeed archetypal, in essence.

One aspect of the problem, crucial to my argument, concerns the esthetic validity of what has been called "occasional verse" (*poésie de circonstance, Gelegenheitsgedicht*).[2] There are three categories of occasional verse: public celebrations connected with commemoration or festivity (the epithalamium, paean, funeral ode, coronation ode); committed political verse; and subjective, personal poetry derived from and referring explicitly to the event—the occasion—in the writer's life that gave rise to it. In modern times, under the influence of pure poetry, the first two categories were denigrated, and the third is on the point of disappearing. However, in the past the universal, not the particular, was considered the most valid basis for inspiration and the most legitimate subject of discourse, just as the role of the didactic in the functioning of poetry was considered to be at least as great as that of pleasure. The poem is created for the public, for patrons of the arts. The poet is integrated into the community, and social concerns are the bread and butter of his calling. To be successful, his verse has to reflect, indeed to embody, the *urbanitas* that is the hallmark of the times.

There is no poetry more occasional than society verse in the eighteenth century, the sort Voltaire collected under the heading "Poësies mêlées." These include epigrams, epitaphs, madrigals, and other *pièces fugitives.* They were truly fugitive in the sense that, as society pieces, they escaped their creator's control, were in fact often published anonymously and/or without his consent. As *jeux de société* they served as evidence for social life and play, were what we would call today literature of consumption for a society of consumption, art created for the pleasure of a small group, its subject matter and language adapted to and limited by the group. The most successful masters of the style are Chaulieu, Gresset, Piron, Grécourt, and, above all, Voltaire. Nothing is more rococo, more typical of the age, than the satirical-witty epigram or the sentimental-witty *stances,* and nothing more remote from our standard Mallarmé-oriented esthetic. Although many such efforts are ephemeral indeed, and meant to be so, others prove to be worthy of scrutiny.

An example of occasional verse at its best is Voltaire's "A Monsieur de La Noue, auteur de Mahomet II, tragédie, en lui envoyant celle de Mahomet le Prophète":

> Mon cher La Noue, illustre père
> De l'invincible Mahomet,
> Soyez le parrain d'un cadet
> Qui sans vous n'est point sûr de plaire.
> Votre fils est un conquérant;
> Le mien a l'honneur d'être apôtre,
> Prêtre, fripon, dévot, brigand:
> Faites-en l'aumônier du vôtre.[3]

With these lines the Speaker sends a copy of his tragedy *Mahomet* to Jean-Baptiste Sauvé La Noue. He purportedly asks for support in his literary endeavors, requesting La Noue to serve as godfather to his play. Voltaire immediately establishes a situation of paradox, of urbane irony, for everyone who peruses the epigram, including La Noue himself, knows that the "inscriber," the "sender," is more eminent a writer, more successful an author of tragedies, than the "receiver." At this point in his career, with *Œdipe* and *Zaïre* behind him and the Académie in front of him, the author of *La Henriade* is considered by friend and foe alike to be one of the greatest poets of Europe. A La Noue seeks patronage from a Voltaire, not the other way around. Yet the great man was not beneath currying favor when he needed it. And, in 1740 and 1741, he needed La Noue. La Noue, author of a moderately successful *Mahomet* (1739), was important to Voltaire in his other capacities: as director of a theater at Lille and a professional actor of repute. As it turned out, when Voltaire had nowhere else to turn, the actor did perform his play, and over the years they became friends. Still, the only priority that can be granted to La Noue is chronological. His tragedy happened to precede Voltaire's in time; it appeared first. For the rest, Voltaire's tone of supplication, of false humility, is intentionally arch: It graciously masks and unmasks his own position of superiority vis-à-vis La Noue and prepares the satire of the last two lines. The only similarity between the works is one of name: They share the same title, *Mahomet*. However, once again irony and paradox prevail, for the name refers to different characters in history, and from this perspective the chronological priority is reversed.

Voltaire's hero, Mohammed the Prophet, whose career covers the early decades of the seventh century, precedes the Turkish Sultan who conquered Byzantium in 1453. Indeed, Mohammed II and every other Mohammed in the Islamic world are named after the Prophet. By claiming that La Noue's Mohammed is older than his own, and by treating his creation as "cadet," Voltaire plays on the ambiguities of chronology, juxtaposing and confusing the time of world history and that of the French stage. He can do this because the Mohammeds exist on four levels: as historical characters, as protagonists in French plays, as titles of plays, and, by extension, as the plays. In a delightfully comic variation on the book-as-metaphor topic, Voltaire treats the two books (his tragedy and La Noue's) as people. Both the prophet Mohammed and the tragedy about him become Arouet's personal creation. Since one human creates another through the sexual act, *Mahomet* is treated as Voltaire's son and the other *Mahomet* as La Noue's offspring: hence a mock-request that La Noue, sire of the older boy, serve as godfather to

the younger one and, furthermore, as godfather help him profession-
ally. Hence also the paradoxical line two, where La Noue's Mohammed
is said to be invincible as a historical character, even though the play
proved to be only moderately successful. The play was not invincible,
he intimates, nor is its printed version, the book, a real man. They are
invincible in title only.

Voltaire thrusts the *pointe* of his epigram with a twist of anticlerical
satire. He declares that since Mohammed the Prophet is an apostle and
priest, but also *fripon, dévot* (in the Enlightenment sense of the term:
the court party hostile to the *philosophes*), and *brigand*, the latter can
serve as chaplain in Mohammed the Conqueror's army. On the one
hand, the author accuses a great spiritual leader of manifesting un-
wholesome character traits; on the other, he claims that such traits are
appropriate to a military chaplain. Since, in any case, chaplains are a
Christian institution, as in the play *Mahomet*, Voltaire overtly attacks
Islam but in fact covertly undermines the Christian church and Christian dogma. Time also is undermined, for the seventh- and fifteenth-
century Mohammeds are brought together in 1741 as characters in
French plays and, for that matter, as characters in a French epigram, as
general and chaplain in a resolutely contemporary army. The historical
past is made subordinate to contemporary reality, so that the author
can *écraser l'infâme* and *faire de l'esprit*: For it is the juxtaposition of these
levels, temporal and historical, that generates the comic wit of this
poem.

The eminently literary stance assumed in this epigram can also be
seen in a more celebrated work, Voltaire's best-known poetical epistle,
"Connue sous le nom des *vous* et des *tu*," purportedly written to a
former mistress who denied the author access to her *hôtel*.[4]

Voltaire evokes the battle between nature and culture that he had
rendered so famous in *Le Mondain*. However, in this epistle Philis's old
lover, Man of the World though he may be, sides with nature. The
artifice of the drawing room is condemned: Madame's carpets, jewelry,
plate, furniture, and vases are not worth one of Philis's kisses, "un des
baisers / Que tu donnais dans ta jeunesse." Thus, in contrast to the
stance he adopted in *Le Mondain*, Voltaire's persona prefers poverty to
riches and the past to the present (". . . qu'est devenu ce temps . . . ?"),
the traditional *ubi sunt* motif. He does so, however, for a reason the
Man of the World would understand: the priority of his personal concerns over those of mankind in the abstract, and because, in the name
of sex and the body, youth is superior to age and warm passion better
than cold respectability. *Carpe diem*, cries the Horatian speaker, insist-
ing, in a variation on the old Ronsardian topic, that flowers should be

plucked and kisses exchanged today because Philis had the good sense to do so yesterday.

The kernel of the poem lies in Voltaire's exploitation of the complementary themes of language and communication. In the same work of art, addressing the same woman, he uses alternately the *tu* and *vous* forms, to the point of giving this woman separate names: The *tu* is reserved for Philis, the past lover, and the *vous* for Madame, the unapproachable lady in the present. We laugh at the artificial, mechanical use of language by the Speaker, juxtaposing the two grammatical forms, but we also laugh at the even more artificial, rigid Madame, who has forgotten that she once was, indeed still is, Philis, and that, by refusing to accept her Philis-ness, she denies life, nature, and her very self. According to Voltaire's "fiction," since Madame has denied the Speaker access to her residence, language—the poem itself, addressed to her as a mock-epistle—becomes the only way he can communicate with her, the only mediation possible between them. It is through a work of art, the *épître* 33, and its stylistic artifice, that the Speaker seeks to denounce the artificiality of Madame's drawing room, to make her aware that she has become an *objet d'art* in her *hôtel*, a process we call reification, and thus lost her human nature. Should she fail to listen, the message will not be lost on the real addressees of the epistle, Voltaire's public, who will presumably accept his values and appreciate his art and artifice, his nature and culture.

These two poems are derived from concrete events of the day: the publication of *Mahomet* and its author's need for an actor-director; the author's snub by an old mistress. They are indeed "occasional," and there is nothing noble or significant about the occasions. Nonetheless, out of this dross is created poetry of a high order, rich, complex, capable of analysis on more than one level, full of allusion, wit, and spirit. And the gold cannot be separated from its dross. Understanding these texts depends on knowledge of the generative social event; they are not and cannot be self-referential. Indeed, complicity between the implied author and the implied reader or public (as distinguished from the narratee—La Noue and Philis-Madame) forms part and parcel of the esthetic process. The esthetic process is grounded in the author-reader relationship, a structure of reception and understanding that exists on the level of content as well as form and is inseparable from the notions of civility and urbanity as enshrined in the community.

One domain of occasional verse, an important one generally neglected in textbooks, is the encomiastic. Indeed, perhaps the aspect of past literary culture most foreign to the modern temper, and most offensive also, is the omnipresence of panegyric, the *encomium* of real or potential patrons, of great or trivial princes, by practically all poets. Yet of the three kinds of rhetoric—judicial, deliberative, and demonstrative—one of them, demonstrative, is specifically devoted to the encomiastic, to harangues, funeral dirges, epithalamia, and other genres that comprise much of occasional poetry and courtly aristocratic verse generally.

During the Middle Ages, especially the period extending from Machaut to Jean Lemaire de Belges, the aristocratic court embodied the aspirations of society (see chapter 6). Poetry served as a mirror of courtly life. It was meant to celebrate the glory of the prince, to praise great men and their accomplishments, and to commemorate events of the court year, such as weddings, births, and departures. With the advent of the Renaissance the conscious, willful praise of the prince as potential or actual patron became a literary mode in and of itself. This mode is crucial to our understanding of the literary process in early modern France. It dominates the greater part of Marot's opus, and Ronsard's also. For example, perhaps the most important single genre introduced into France by France's greatest sixteenth-century poet is the *hymne*. Ronsard's *Hymnes*, published in 1555 and 1556, with additions later, represents a milestone in his career: his first effort at narrative poetry in the sublime style, to approach the epic of classical Antiquity, and an effort to practice sublime didactic poetry, to teach the secrets of the cosmos. Each one of these poems retells a classical myth and contains scientific or philosophical lore, yet the encomiastic element is central to the functioning of the genre. For, conceived in the panegyric mode and connected to the demonstrative genre in rhetoric, each *hymne* was written with a dedicatee in mind, envisaged as a prayer to God for the dedicatee and as a gift that will grant him immortality. The learning is significant because it has been transmitted by a special act of grace from the muses to a poet in ecstasy, a *poeta doctus*, who then will transmit their message to his narratee, his public—the dedicatee. The wisdom is accompanied by, and embodied in the telling of, classical myths, which in epic style sing the deeds of gods or heroes in order to celebrate their power and, by so doing, exalt the dedicatee, himself associated with the hero-gods. These are sacred poems, celebrating, glorifying, raising up to the divine: raising up the poet, his subject matter, and his patron, the lauded dedicatee.

For example, *Hymne de la Justice* relates the myth of Astraea and the end of the Golden Age.[5] The poem concludes, however, with the return of Justice to earth: She has entered the body of Ronsard's patron, Charles Cardinal of Lorraine; and with the careers of Charles and King Henry II of France, the Golden Age will be reborn. That modern historians do not recognize the Cardinal of Lorraine to be an accomplished statesman, that modern literary people tend to view him through the prism of Agrippa d'Aubigné, in no way incriminates Ronsard's poem. What matters is neither which prince a poet praises nor whether the prince is worthy of praise, but instead how the poet expresses himself within a traditional mode, how he adapts his material to new uses while respecting the decorum of the genre or mode he has chosen. Ronsard's success is to have created a viable *literary* bond linking the philosophical idea of his hymn (Justice), the Greek myth it embodies (Astraea), and the poem's dedicatee (the Cardinal of Lorraine).

Justice, an allegory not unlike Reason or Nature in *Le Roman de la Rose*, stands as a teacher, guide, and mother within the guise of the classical virgin goddess Astraea. She appears to Charles of Lorraine as an anima-figure, the spiritual, ennobling aspects of his own personality projected onto a divine ideal. If Astraea appears to be a mother, Jupiter is depicted as a father. Indeed, Justice is his daughter, whom he gave to mankind and who returns to him seeking consolation after mankind has abandoned her ways. She is associated with milk and the flight of birds, he with fire, war, and vengeance. Flame comes forth from his male divinity's eyes, and a dagger from his mouth; his speeches contain imagery of engendering, piercing, and penetration. Their spiritual child is the Cardinal of Lorraine, a prelate, associated in the hymn with his brothers, all soldiers. The Guise family as a whole embodies Curtius's topic of *fortitudo et sapientia,* the heroic ideal that, when projected onto disparate individuals (Achilles and Patroclus, Roland and Oliver), marks one of the great flaws of the human condition. Ronsard also alludes to Charles's family in the past, to his purported ancestor Godfrey of Bouillon, one of the Nine Worthies and a protagonist of Christian holy war.

These family relations and the poem as a whole can be accounted for through the process of allegory or, more precisely, Christian typology. From a typological perspective the end of the Golden Age parallels the Fall of Man, and Jupiter stands for the Christian God. The story of the Fall implies, indeed demands, Redemption; therefore, the return of Justice to the world and the restoration of the Golden Age in the sixteenth century both postfigure the Advent of Christ and prefigure the Second Coming. Charles of Lorraine, like his ancestor Godfrey of Bouillon, is depicted as a Christ-figure, a redeemer of mankind. Such an encomium is appropriate, given Charles's status as one of Christ's vicars in the world and chancellor of France, corresponding to Christ the judge of Doomsday. From this perspective, the virgin goddess Astraea foreshadows the Virgin Mary; or as Justice, she is a Christ-figure herself, she who descends to earth, preaches the Good Word, ascends to her Father's right hand, and then returns to mankind, her second coming predicted by sibyls and prophets. Ronsard's new Golden Age will be a secular equivalent of the spiritual redemption brought about by the Messiah; thus Eden and the Age of Saturn will be restored. As Christ's birth occurred during the heyday of Roman glory, the return of the Golden Age is associated with the feats of a new French Augustus, Henry II, and a new Virgilian predestined child, the future cardinal.

Although lawyers' chicanery distorts the workings of justice, a trial scene proves to be the crowning moment of *Hymne de la Justice*. This is the judgment of mankind in heaven. There God-Jupiter tempers justice with mercy and resolves Astraea's quarrel with humans. And the secular Jupiter (Henry II) is urged by Charles of Lorraine, and the implied reader by Ronsard the implied author, to ensure that vengeance is taken on evil judges and that good ones are rewarded. A celestial trial scene ensures the survival of men and the return of the Golden Age, manifest in the birth and career of a great ecclesiastical figure, chancellor of the realm, responsible for justice in France and deserving the eventual just concord he and his line will enjoy in the *civitas Dei*.

Panegyric reaches its height not with Ronsard's generation but with Racine and La Fontaine's. It is in the age of Louis XIV that the encomiastic mode is presumed to be at the heart of literature, the unique hero and object of praise being the Sun King himself, a subordinate role reserved nonetheless for his subordinates and members of his family. Literature exists in praise of Louis XIV and in order to praise him: his glory, his military supremacy, his justice, his love of peace. As a sort of demigod, the reigning monarch is held responsible for the goodness and greatness of his age. On this everyone agrees (in print), the Ancients and Moderns alike.

As an example of the pervasive force of panegyric, integrated into texts in a subtler, wittier manner than was possible in the Renaissance, consider Boileau's delightful mock-epic *Le Lutrin* (1674, 1683).[6] The plot is based upon events of the year 1667 known to the public: Claude Auvry, Trésorier of the Sainte-Chapelle, had been quarreling with his canons and especially with their leader, Jacques Barrin, the chanter. On July 31, supported by the chaplains, Auvry had a lectern placed before Barrin's choir stall, which prevented the Chanter from being seen during the offices. Barrin and the other canons removed the lectern by force, and both sides then went to court over the issue, which was arbitrated by Boileau's patron, Guillaume de Lamoignon, Premier Président du Parlement. Much of the pleasure for Boileau's public no doubt came from the fact that the principals all correspond to real people, Boileau's friends and acquaintances on the Ile de la Cité. Readers probably enjoyed those episodes where the poet consciously deformed reality, which he did sufficiently to claim in the "Avis" that his work was largely fictional.

Le Lutrin is a charming, witty caricature of Virgilian and French epos that also derides those vices presumed to be inherent in Parisian canons and chaplains: gluttony, sloth, anger, ignorance, and pride of position. A pattern of food-bed-softness-rot imagery, the characters' obsession with position and hierarchy, their martial pretentions and clerical ineptness at real war—all is handled with precision and brio. Furthermore, the quarreling generated in the first five cantos of Le Lutrin is resolved in Canto 6, and the poem ends on a happy, moral note. The war between the chaplains and the canons is ended, peace is restored to the Sainte-Chapelle, and, although the times are recognized to be corrupt, Thémis guarantees the integrity of the Church.

In Le Lutrin Louis XIV is praised for his martial energy, in contrast to bygone rois fainéants, and for having reformed the Church. And King Louis's delegate in the world of the Saint-Chapelle, the arbiter who establishes peace and justice, is Ariste, who becomes the hero or hero-surrogate of Le Lutrin. An "homme d'un sçavoir étonnant," this embodiment of sapientia commits an intellectual exploit ("art tout-puissant") in the tradition of Solomon to reconcile the two adversaries. Through him Piété and Thémis overcome the impiety and chicanery, the false fortitudo, that dominated the action up to the moment of his intervention. Furthermore, unlike the Sainte-Chapelle's decadent clerics, Ariste lives in the world. As devout as they ought to be, his is a "piété . . . fort gaye," therefore capable of appreciating mock-epic. This "fameux Heros" and "Homme incomparable" stands for the author's patron, Guillaume de Lamoignon, who embodies forces of civilization bettering France and the Church under Louis XIV. And Lamoignon has also contributed to the betterment of the poet Despréaux.

A close relationship exists between the Narrator (implied author) and Ariste as between the Boileau and Lamoignon who really lived in the seventeenth century. Lamoignon encouraged Boileau to write L'Art poétique and Le Lutrin; in a sense responsible for the latter work ("Avis au lecteur"), he may even have been the means by which Boileau heard of the wars of the Sainte-Chapelle. In return, the author praises Lamoignon-Ariste fulsomely, and, in the last canto, this personage outside the action becomes the hero. Unlike the Aeneid, Le Lutrin is a modern poem telling a modern story. In a world of fools, of dupers and dupes, there is no place for Aeneas; but a Maecenas can deflate ridiculous *milites gloriosi* who think they are Aeneases. Since the modern poet is the contemporary of his hero and patron, by making Lamoignon the protagonist of a mock-epic Boileau renews the tradition of panegyric as well as of the heroic.

We find, often allied with panegyric, a mode of political poetry, of verse concerned with public events. This is my third facet of the tradition. Among the more notable examples in Antiquity are works by Simonides, Aeschylus, Virgil, and Horace. This mode, if commissioned by the prince or his court, will adhere closely to the encomiastic vein. It is also possible for the poet to equate politics and satire, to castigate the prince's enemies and/or his own, even to castigate the prince. Out of fashion since the rise of sensibility in the late eighteenth century, adhering neither to Arnold's notion of high seriousness nor to Symbolist pure poetry, the political-satirical mode is one of the oldest and richest in the history of French letters.

In the medieval period troubadours and trouvères wrote *sirventes* and crusade songs as well as *grands chants courtois.* Bertran de Born's exaltation of the heroic life—of making war, not love, in springtime—is no less vital than Bernart de Ventadorn's more conventional erotic alternative. However, the genre of the early Middle Ages that, above all others, treats political matters in a conscious, lucid, willful manner is the *chanson de geste.*

La Chanson de Roland calls for a united Christendom to join the crusade. In order to prosecute the holy war a powerful, authoritative central monarchy is required, a strong king to lead strong barons who have sacrificed their selfish feudal interests and pride to the cause. Other texts, which I choose to call "epics of protest," found chiefly in the Guillaume Cycle, while preaching the crusade and upholding the supremacy of the crown, also exalt the feudal baron and his family, who defend the frontier marches against Saracen encroachment while Charlemagne or Louis sits indolently in Paris. Still other poems, the "epics of revolt," accuse the king of cruelty, tyranny, stupidity, and weakness. The protagonist of epic is now a rebel, struggling not against Saracens abroad but at home against his fellow barons or the king, in order to uphold his honor, his land, and his right to bear arms. The epics of revolt probe to the depths the feudal system and the monarchy, scrutinizing the reality of flawed institutions and man's incapacity to do anything about them. They, and the other *chansons,* exalt the aristocracy, the great barons, and, even more, young landless *povres bachelers,* who assert their individual worth and give themselves to a cause in self-abnegation, in a world in which man's social existence is everything, yet where it is ever undermined by weakness, cowardice, and treachery.

The masterpiece of the thirteenth century is Jean de Meun's *Roman de la Rose,* a universal, quasi-encyclopedic text, an anatomy in Northrop Frye's sense of the term, that treats all of life and human relationships, that mirrors all love, human and divine. The mode is comic and satirical, the author mercilessly unmasking the hypocrisy, disguise, duplicity, materialism, and lust that pervade society. Jean also attacks the Franciscans and Dominicans for having undermined the secular masters in the Sorbonne and for preaching continence, either out of duplicity or out of false principle, in order to subvert the principle of fecundity, the great chain of being that supports the universe. He also scrutinizes the false, intolerable bonds of lordship that people establish one over the other, either in marriage or through the state.

As poet of the court and panegyrist of his prince, the Renaissance-Baroque-Classical poet assumes the role of spokesman, presents the court's philosophy and sociopolitical stance by his very act of singing the prince's victories on the field or in council-chamber. All great writers of the age—all those "bien en cour" at any rate—participated in this current. Indeed, quite good verse resulted when Malherbe and Le Moyne celebrated the Fall of La Rochelle, Boileau commemorated the Passage of the Rhine, and Voltaire rendered immortal the Battle of Fontenoy. The four heroic odes in question, spanning some 130 years, signal a continuity of military-political *actualité* and of an official court philosophy of patriotic, nationalistic, Catholic, and, above all, dynastic grandeur.

More interesting, especially from an esthetic perspective, is the current launched by Ronsard's *Discours des Miseres de ce tems.* Passionately satirical invectives, composed during the heat of the Wars of Religion (the early 1560s), they defend the Catholic faith of Catholic princes, attacking the Huguenots for dividing the kingdom and instituting hated innovations, for turning the world upside-down in the social, political, and religious spheres. Ronsard develops a pattern of apocalyptic and demonic imagery, assimilating the Protestants to storm, tempest, earthquake, brigands, locusts, vipers, caterpillars, pigs, foxes, hornets, wild bees, rot, and garbage. He also introduces a new epic hero: Ronsard himself as implied author, the committed poet who, an *athleta Christi,* wields a pen in place of the sword, who joins battle with his Reformist adversary, Théodore de Bèze, for the minds and hearts of his implied readers, who speaks out in these "discourses" to his countrymen, to France, to the queen, and to God.

A generation later, Agrippa d'Aubigné continues the tradition of the *Discours,* offering a thunderous response to the official Catholic position. *Les Tragiques* is a hyper-*Discours,* an anti-*Discours,* and a super-

Discours, a satirical commentary on the tragedy of the wars and of tyranny and religious persecution. These tirades are included in a sort of modern epic treating of contemporary times yet, typologically, including all of sacred and secular history and, spatially, the entire cosmos, including heaven and hell. The protagonists are the Protestant people and d'Aubigné the narrator as implied author. The theme is the triumph of a God of Love and his servants over cruel adversaries: nominally Catherine de' Medici and Henry III, but including, ultimately, Satan and Antichrist.

No religious wars divided France in the eighteenth century, and the technology of censorship had made strides during the interim. Nonetheless, Voltaire was able to disseminate *Le Mondain* (1736), a satirical-philosophical text proclaiming the value of the real world in the present, a present that manifests civilization, art, luxury, the "society of consumption," hard work, planetary exploration, and the business ethos. The author also claims the superiority of the present over the past and the real over the ideal, and that ideologies which exalt the past and denigrate the present, including official Christianity, are false and evil. After centuries of aristocratic and clerical literature, a tradition that extends from *chansons de geste* and Chrétien de Troyes to Corneille, Pascal, and Racine, Voltaire is perhaps the first great writer to cast off the old feudal-Christian myths, to exalt the modern world and concrete, material reality. In his praise of business, trade, exploration, money, and concrete material happiness, and by undermining heroic, national, and religious ideals, he appears strikingly modern, anticipating the new bourgeois myth that will become dominant in the West for the next two centuries.

The major poem of ideas in the two centuries that extend from Ronsard, du Bartas, and d'Aubigné to the Romantics is, however, the *Poëme sur le désastre de Lisbonne* (1755). In this impassioned text Voltaire does not plead a single, coherent intellectual cause. On the contrary, he compares and contrasts, questions and opposes, the various doctrines that, in his opinion, fail to account for the human condition in its totality. His one absolute point is to condemn any philosophy lacking compassion, any philosophy so rigid, artificial, and inhuman that it scorns or ignores the sufferings of the unfortunate, specifically the victims of the Lisbon Earthquake. The imagery of this text falls under the Bachelardian category of hard earth and will to power. We find collapsing walls and broken pottery, a volcano, the abyss, rocks falling, lightning blasts on trees, wounds and people drowning, killing, ripping, piercing, balls and shot, and worms in the tomb. Yet Voltaire's ultimate concern lies not with catastrophe or destruction as such but with the human condition, with men distinguished from beasts, men who are more than a conglomerate of nerves and bone. For, unlike crawling animals and broken pottery, Voltaire's people cry out, weep, and pray. Furthermore, the Narrator asks a good twenty questions. Significantly, God does not reply. No one does. The answering, if answers there be, will come from the public. Like Jean de Meun, Voltaire calls for lucidity, honesty, and truth—that his readers rip off the mask and face the terrifying reality of life, that they denounce illusion with courage. It is this call for honesty and pity, for open eyes and a warm heart, and this questioning of truth that dominate a work concerned not with a king's or a church's deeds but with God and the divinity's responsibility to man.

The militant, committed tradition does not die with the fall of the ancien régime. On the contrary, Alfred de Vigny perpetuates the heritage of Voltaire (and of the *chanson de geste*). Some of his texts, such as *Wanda* (1864), treat contemporary political events, but almost all exploit symbolic patterns of imagery to illustrate the author's major personal concerns: the injustice of God to man, the tyranny of kings toward their subjects, and the incapacity of aristocrats to guide the people or even to survive when their function is sabotaged by the weakness and viciousness of a monarch who ought to sustain them but instead permits them to be overturned.

Victor Hugo evolved from bard of the Bourbons, to celebrant of the Bonaparte cult, to poet laureate of the Republic. Whatever we think of his personal authenticity, at his best, in *Châtiments* and *La Légende des Siècles,* he recaptures the fervor and power of d'Aubigné in order to castigate wicked rulers who tyrannize the innocent. The principal tyrant-figure is of course Hugo's nemesis, Napoleon III; however, his works establish a pattern of master-slave and torturer-victim valid for all history.

In spite of the apolitical, *poésie pure* stance of Symbolism and post-Symbolism, committed verse has not disappeared in the twentieth century. The Surrealists were profoundly, passionately drawn to the Left; *Le Procès de Maurice Barrès* (1921), *Un Cadavre* (1924), and *Le Premier Manifeste* (1924) evidence their desire to change people's lives as well as their art. Former Surrealists—Aragon, Eluard, Char, Desnos—were to contribute a nucleus of Resistance poetry, to launch the current that dominated French verse during the 1940s and also included Jouve, Pierre Emmanuel, Loys Masson, and, in the wings, Supervielle and Saint-John Perse. When Benjamin Péret refers to their production as "Le Déshonneur des poètes," he expresses indeed post-Symbolist orthodoxy but condemns not only the best verse of the decade but also one of the most startling esthetic phenomena of the century, the resurgence of a mode powerful and pervasive in world literature.

Although Aragon is no doubt the greatest poet in his line, he is not the only one, nor should we consider his work to be an anomaly. In the socialist camp, which now makes up a good portion of the globe, the Aragon-Eluard-Mayakovsky-Brecht approach to art is the dominant mode by far. Third World poets like Césaire, Damas, Senghor, Diop, Glissant, and Tchikaya U Tam'si prove to be as close to the author of *Le Paysan de Paris, Hourra l'Oural,* and *Le Musée Grévin* as to Valéry and Char, not to speak of experimenters associated with *Tel Quel* and *Change*. At poetry conferences throughout the world political commitment is either extolled or at least tolerated, and participants often arrive at a consensus that *poésie engagée* should not be rejected out of hand. On the contrary, all great verse is deemed great for the same reasons, for greatness can descend upon a politically engaged writer as easily as upon the esthete in his tower. Indeed, when a committed person turns out to be an artist, it is because, not in spite of, that commitment which gave him the inspiration to create.

The Western heritage has developed modes of writing specially designed to treat occasional verse and the didactic spirit, modes neglected by some specialists of poetry in the twentieth century. One of these, the fourth topic of discussion in this chapter, is allegory.

Like comedy or tragedy, the Baroque and the classical, "allegory" is an illusive term. The medieval formulations are extremely vague—Isidore of Seville: "Allegoria est alieniloquium. Aliud enim sonat, et aliud intellegitur"; Augustine: "Allegoria dicitur, cum aliquid aliud videtur sonare in verbis, et aliud in intellectu significare"; Aquinas: "Allegoria est tropus seu modus loquendi quo aliquid dicitur et aliud intellegitur." Perhaps the vagueness and all-inclusiveness of such definitions—in essence, "allegory is to say one thing and mean another"—has led some scholars, who quite legitimately defend allegory from the neglect or scorn of the Romantics, to confuse the term with or to extend it to include symbolism, thus, for example, to define allegory as any "twice-told tale written in rhetorical, or figurative language and expressing a vital belief."[7] As a result, it is then conceived as a mode to be found throughout world literature, corresponding to the comic or the tragic, evidenced in writers as disparate as Virgil, Dante, Spenser, Swift, Hawthorne, Melville, Zola, Kafka, Orwell, Camus, Michaux, detective stories, and Westerns.

Allegory can also designate a technique of writing: a structure of extended metaphors, figures, or personifications that functions as a trope on at least two levels of meaning or that includes a pattern of relationship in both tenor and vehicle, signified and signifier. Here we have to distinguish, for the Middle Ages and Renaissance, between the personification allegory to be found in the *Romance of the Rose* and the allegorical or typological interpretation of Scripture and of classical myth, no less prevalent, which was to culminate in Dante's *Commedia*. In both cases we are dealing with a text that contains multiple simultaneous meanings, that calls for a self-conscious commentary on itself. The allegorist or the reader of allegory is an exegete who reads in function of a nonliteral interpretation; the reader learns to read the text while reading it and thus plays a central role in interpreting and re-creating the author's intended structure.

Finally, the mode was so prevalent during the early centuries of our literature that one can designate as "allegory" a particular genre or subgenre of the late Middle Ages, comparable to and no less important than epic and romance. Around the year 1190 or 1200 it ceased to be a mere ornament or didactic element and became instead the fictional cadre for an entire work of art. In this sense allegory can be defined as a narrative poem, often in the form of a dream or vision, pseudoautobiographical (told in the first person), the subject of which is often love or religion and the majority of whose characters are personified abstractions. The master of philosophical or religious allegory in French is Guillaume de Degulleville, author of *Le Pèlerinage de la Vie humaine* (1330–31) and *Le Pèlerinage de l'Ame* (1355–58). The first great vernacular love allegory is of course *Le Roman de la Rose* by Guillaume de Lorris and Jean de Meun, perhaps *the* masterpiece of the Middle Ages, followed by witty, sophisticated *dits amoureux* from the hands of Guillaume de Machaut (*Le Jugement dou Roy de Behaingne, Le Jugement dou Roy de Navarre, Le Dit dou Lÿon, La Fonteinne amoureuse*), Jean Froissart, and Christine de Pizan.

The tradition of allegory persisted into the Renaissance, indeed well into the Splendid Century. True, personification allegory in the erotic sphere—virtues and vices inhabiting a Garden of Love and/or the psyche of Guillaume de Lorris and Charles d'Orléans—yielded to the vogue of classical myth. In the Middle Ages Jean de Meun and Guillaume de Machaut retold Ovid in their own guise and for their own purposes, didactic and comic. In the sixteenth century a Greco-Roman Délie (Scève), Olive (du Bellay), Cassandre or Hélène (Ronsard), and Diane (d'Aubigné) replaced once and for all the medieval Rose and the anonymous Dame embodied in Pitié, Danger, Franchise, Peur, Honte, and Bel Accueil. However, the allegories fleeing the Garden of Love take refuge in the Temple of Honor. They are to be found in Ronsard's *Hymnes,* in d'Aubigné's *Tragiques,* and in moral, political, and satirical verse throughout the period. The battle of vices and virtues, the satire of the court, the mirror of princes—these themes based on the old allegories persist and abide. In the late Baroque period Pierre Le Moyne composed a series of *Lettres morales et poëtiques* or *Entretiens et lettres poëtiques*, which include titles such as "La Carte de Paris," "Le Palais de la Fortune," "Le Theatre du sage," "De la cour," and "Carte de la cour." They are relatively long didactic, satirical poems, powerful in their rhetoric and with dynamic, archetypal patterns of imagery.

On the other hand, allegory of the typological Christian variety, if anything, increases during the period that extends from Jean Lemaire de Belges and Marot to Le Moyne. The "allegorical theology" of the Renaissance was based on the assumption that pagan poets, like the Old Testament prophets, were in a state of grace, and that their utterances, perhaps influenced by Scripture, prefigured the New Testament in much the same way that the Old Testament does. Ronsard himself learned from Dorat an allegorical, typological interpretation of classical myth and how to harmonize the statements of the poets with Christian doctrine. He and Dorat both believed in syncretism, in a mystical Christianity that subsumed unto itself the best of the Greco-Roman cultural world. He speaks of how Dorat taught him how to hide truth behind a veil of poetry. This is presumed to be the correct method, whether the writer's goal is to initiate the masses and teach them by pleasant fables the truth they are too gross to understand directly (*Hymne de l'Autonne, Art poëtique*), or whether, following in the tradition of Petrarch and Boccaccio, he claims that the rabble are unable to understand his work, which must be reserved for an elite (*Hymne de l'Hyver, Elegie à Jacques Grevin*). In the seventeenth century Pascal, Bossuet, Godeau, Desmarets, Marolles, and a host of Baroque lyricists all favored and/or practiced figurative readings of the Bible; and figurative allegory forms the basis of the best Renaissance-Baroque epics: specifically *Les Tragiques* (d'Aubigné), *Moyse sauvé* (Saint-Amant), and *Saint Louis* (Le Moyne).

A good example of the functioning of allegory, in texts sufficiently brief for close reading, can be found in the *ballades* and *rondeaux* by Charles d'Orléans:

> En la forest d'Ennuyeuse Tristesse,
> Un jour m'avint qu'a par moy cheminoye,
> Si rencontray l'Amoureuse Deesse
> Qui m'appella, demandant ou j'aloye.
> Je respondy que, par Fortune, estoye
> Mis en exil en ce bois, long temps a,
> Et qu'a bon droit appeller me povoye
> L'omme esgaré qui ne scet ou il va.

En sousriant, par sa tresgrant humblesse,
Me respondy: "Amy, se je savoye
Pourquoy tu es mis en ceste destresse,
A mon povair voulentiers t'ayderoye;
Car, ja pieça, je mis ton cueur en voye
De tout plaisir, ne sçay qui l'en osta;
Or me desplaist qu'a present je te voye
L'omme esgaré qui ne scet ou il va.

—Helas! dis je, souverainne Princesse,
Mon fait savés, pourquoy le vous diroye?
C'est par la Mort qui fait a tous rudesse,
Qui m'a tollu celle que tant amoye,
En qui estoit tout l'espoir que j'avoye,
Qui me guidoit, si bien m'acompaigna
En son vivant, que point ne me trouvoye
L'omme esgaré qui ne scet ou il va.

"Aveugle suy, ne sçay ou aler doye;
De mon baston, affin que ne forvoye,
Je vois tastant mon chemin ça et la;
C'est grant pitié qu'il couvient que je soye
L'omme esgaré qui ne scet ou il va!"[8]

On the literal level the poem tells a story. The plot concerns a voyager, presumably a knight on horseback, the Speaker, who, riding through a forest, encounters a lady, with whom he engages in a dialogue. They discuss the Speaker's plight, his exile caused by two other characters, one of whom has seized the Speaker's beloved. As a result, he finds himself lost in the woods.

The various personifications (Ennuyeuse Tristesse, Amoureuse Deesse, Fortune, Mort) signal that the "story" forms part of a metaphorical structure that demands interpretation on another level. This other level, the tenor as distinguished from the vehicle and the signified from the signifier, concerns the Speaker's inner life, his psyche. We realize that the beloved is dead; because of her death, the Speaker suffers from mental torture and melancholia, from psychic depression that verges on madness. On still another plane, exile in the forest of "Ennuyeuse Tristesse" caused by Fortune can allude to the author Charles d'Orléans's imprisonment in England after the Battle of Agincourt. The deceased beloved can refer to Charles's late wife, Bonne d'Armagnac, or to someone else, or to the invaded, ravaged motherland, France.

In large measure the strength and beauty of the text derives from the appropriateness of the personifications, the clarity and precision of the allegorical equivalents. At the same time, the *ballade*'s imagery, whether interpreted on a literal or allegorical plane, contains powerful symbolic overtones, archetypal overtones, that derive from the literature of romance as well as of didactic allegory.

The Speaker as wanderer recalls centuries of knights-errant proceeding on martial quests: all the Lancelots, Percevals, and Gauvains of Arthurian romance at odds with their *gaste forest* and *gaste terre,* the forest and wasteland of danger, dread, and adventure. The "Amoureuse deesse" he encounters, Venus, plays the role of *mediatrix* and *consolatrix,* a late version of Boethius's Philosophia, Jean de Meun's Raison, or Guillaume de Machaut's Esperence. Centuries of culture bring intertextual overtones to the banal but poetic motifs of the quest and the encounter. Charles innovates vis-à-vis his predecessors, his "pre-texts," by having the quest end in failure and the consolation in uncertainty. The Speaker learns, he grows in the course of the *ballade,* but his is a tale of exclusion and alienation. Indeed, it is he who informs Venus, who communicates with her; she has nothing to tell him. There is no solution to his problem, no answer to his dilemma. Female authority figures either fail to console him or, like Fortune and Mort, prove to be hostile. The Speaker's confusion, helplessness, and inner loss are given expression in the final metaphor: A voyager in the forest, he is transformed from an Arthurian knight into a blind beggar groping his way, his horse metamorphosed into the blind man's *baston.* He who fails to know also cannot see, for his world becomes as dark as the black forest. This is, metaphorically, a case of social degradation—the prince-poet Charles d'Orléans as implied author reduced to an excluded, marginal, estate-less mendicant, a man without community—and of sexual impotence, the horse gone, the groping stick and blindness.

The implications were as clear to Charles's public as to our post-Freudian, post-Marxist generation. This poem of quest and desire, of *militia* and *amor,* ends in frustration, near immobility, and collapse. The only triumph the knight-Speaker can attain is insight, his knowledge of self and the world, the prophetic force granted to a blind and asexual Tiresias, and presumably the knowledge and creative force that enable him to compose the story of his misfortune, the poem, Ballade 63.

> Je fu en fleur ou temps passé d'enfance,
> Et puis aprés devins fruit en jeunesse;
> Lors m'abaty de l'arbre de Plaisance,
> Vert et non meur, Folie, ma maistresse.
> Et pour cela, Raison qui tout redresse
> A son plaisir, sans tort ou mesprison,
> M'a a bon droit, par sa tresgrant sagesse,
> Mis pour meurir ou feurre de prison.

En ce j'ay fait longue continuance,
Sans estre mis a l'essor de Largesse;
J'en suy contant et tiens que, sans doubtance,
C'est pour le mieulx, combien que par peresse
Deviens fletry et tire vers vieillesse.
Assez estaint est en moy le tison
De sot desir, puis qu'ay esté en presse
Mis pour meurir ou feurre de prison.

Dieu nous doint paix, car c'est ma desirance!
Adonc seray en l'eaue de Liesse
Tost refreschi, et au souleil de France
Bien nettié du moisy de Tristesse;
J'attens Bon Temps, endurant en humblesse.
Car j'ay espoir que Dieu ma guerison
Ordonnera; pour ce, m'a sa haultesse
Mis pour meurir ou feurre de prison.

Fruit suis d'yver qui a meins de tendresse
Que fruit d'esté; si suis en garnison,
Pour amolir ma trop verde duresse,
Mis pour meurir ou feurre de prison![9]

This text deals explicitly with the prison motif. *Literaliter,* we are told of the life of a flower become fruit, picked green from the tree and stored for winter. *Allegorice,* the implied author Charles d'Orléans evokes his insouciant youth, then years of imprisonment in England waiting, his life cut off in its prime, placed inside parentheses as it were. The personifications allude not only to the flower-fruit-life allegory but also to the problem of responsibility. Folie and Raison are responsible for the Speaker's plight, or, since they are aspects of his psyche, it is he who is morally responsible (he committed *fol' amor*) for his fate, just as France has suffered defeat in the wars as punishment for her sins. As in the previous text, the theme is one of exclusion, reification, and symbolic mutilation; the Speaker, "fletry," his "estaint . . . tison," is acted upon, rendered passive and immobile. Denied his basic humanity, transformed into a flower and fruit, he is forced to play a quasi-feminine role in a masculine world. The image pattern evoking the "green world" brings overtones from the *locus amoenus* of medieval love books, especially *Le Roman de la Rose.* Nothing can be more appropriate than to assimilate man's life, especially his amorous career, to the cycle of nature. However, when the imprisonment of a prince is concretized as the withering of an unripe apple or pear in a *buanderie,* and he wishes someone to wipe off his mold and take him out to dry in the sun, the implied reader-audience has to smile. The same is true for the Speaker's seeming acceptance of his imprisonment, or rather the pear's acceptance of its plucking. Charles d'Orléans is playing a game with himself—as Speaker-hero and unripe pear—and with his public. This is a poem of gentle irony and mannered wit, *sub specie ludi*, worthy of the Baroque.

Finally, the hoped-for outcome includes a religious dimension, contains typological as well as personification allegory. The Speaker is associated with a tree, the genealogical tree of the House of France, but also the biblical *Arbor vitae*, the Tree of Knowledge of Good and Evil, and various medieval trees of the virtues and vices. He admits having committed sin (Folie), of having been rightly punished (by Raison) for misdeeds. Then in the third stanza God himself is invoked twice. The sun that will burn off the fruit's mold is the light of Christ's grace as well as the physical warmth of Touraine or the Beauce country; the Speaker calls for rebirth in the baptism of the spirit, in the water and fire of divine Charity, as well as a return to erotic activity beyond the range of British castle walls. No longer a child, no longer subject to Folie or to sot desir, he has attained maturity and will be reborn as a child in a better, newer world. The cycle of life, whether of apple blossoms and apples or of princes and poets, goes beyond existence to eternity, to the only life, food, and peace that shall endure. Christ the King suffered for us; the prince-poet also suffers, imitates his King, and hopes to follow him to his reward.

Even Charles's briefest poems, his *rondeaux*, which, perhaps more than any other texts in the West, approximate the Japanese tanka and haiku, even these briefest of jewels attain density, complexity, and richness through allegory and through the archetypal tradition.

> Ou puis parfont de ma merencolie
> L'eaue d'Espoir que ne cesse tirer,
> Soif de Confort la me fait desirer,
> Quoy que souvent je la treuve tarie.
>
> Necte la voy ung temps et esclercie,
> Et puis aprés troubler et empirer,
> Ou puis [parfont de ma merencolie
> L'eaue d'Espoir que ne cesse tirer.]
>
> D'elle trempe mon ancre d'estudie,
> Quant j'en escrips, mais pour mon cueur irer,
> Fortune vient mon pappier dessirer,
> Et tout gecte par sa grant felonnie
> Ou puis [parfont de ma merencolie.][10]

On the literal level Charles d'Orléans again recounts a narrative. He tells how the Speaker, suffering from thirst, seeks to draw water from a well; the water proves to be troubled; the Speaker then uses the troubled water for ink, but someone rips up his paper and casts it back into the well. Allegorically, the text again refers to the Speaker's psyche, his inner state. The personifications inform us that he is in need of comfort, that he desires hope but only succeeds in attaining depression and anxiety. Merencolie at least could serve as inspiration for his poetry or for creative meditation were it not for external events, the course of the world, chance, the mutability of existence (Fortune), which disrupt the creative process as well.

In Western literature water evokes connotations of purity, goodness, fertility, health, the mother's milk and womb. In Guillaume de Lorris and in Guillaume de Machaut it symbolized love and the Eternal Feminine. The well establishes a spatial configuration of enclosure, depth, and moist darkness, which also are symbols of the feminine, the irrational, the unconscious. The Speaker's thirst, his repeated efforts to draw up water, allude to desire as well as anxiety, desire never satisfied, for the water proves to be troubled and he does not slake his thirst. Enclosed in a feminine world (the well, the room), relatively passive and immobile, unable to attain his ends or influence his destiny, the Speaker at least can think and write. The very feminine qualities of his being—his melancholia, passions, and desire—open to him the realm of art. However, tragically for the Speaker, a hostile feminine authority figure, Dame Fortune, instead of consoling or rewarding him, assumes a masculine role, breaks into the Speaker's enclosed space and tears his paper, thus destroying his precarious peace and violating his art. Her throwing the fragments of art into the well indicates that the Speaker's meditative-poetic endeavors have proved fruitless, that he returns to a state of anxiety and frustrated desire, that he again thirsts for water that will not come and for ink that dries up. The Speaker's torment runs a cyclical course, its circularity corresponding to the circular form of the *rondeau*.

The well is associated with Merencolie; the Speaker suffers from melancholia. This is a condition linked to an excess of black bile in the body, under the influence of the Greater Infortune, the planet Saturn, matching autumn or winter in the life of the year and old age in man's life. Clerics and scholars, poets and lovers, are peculiarly prone to melancholia and the capital sin of *acedia*. How appropriate it is, then, that the state of melancholia be allotted to a literary projection, a persona, of Charles d'Orléans, the aging prince, leading court poet of his day, former apostle of love and present disciple of Nonchaloir. How appropriate also, in terms of consistency of imagery, that melancholia, embodied in black bile, should be concretized as a well from which the Speaker draws a troubled black fluid that serves as ink for his quill. The metamorphosis of water to bile to ink corresponds to the transformation of the Speaker from lover to sufferer to poet. Or, rather, it corresponds to our changing perception of him. For in the process of audience-reader response, in the course of the *rondeau,* the implied reader-audience discovers that the well's water is bile and that it is writer's ink, that the speaking poetic voice is that of a poet, and that the subject of the poem, in the last analysis, is its own creation. The reader-audience also realizes one fact that escapes the Speaker, though not of course Charles d'Orléans the author. For the Speaker fails as a man and a poet: His page is ripped into fragments, and his fragmented psyche returns to the well. This, however, is not the case for the real author, Charles d'Orléans. About his psyche we know nothing. But we do know that he succeeded where his lyric voice-persona-Speaker failed: because the poem was written; the page survived intact or the text was copied later from memory; it was stronger and denser than torn paper and has come down to us, as the symbol for and analysis of a psychic state and of a unique, privileged moment of artistic consciousness and esthetic creation.

Another esthetic mode of the court, especially prevalent during the ancien régime, is the pastoral. Pastoral is not a manner of writing like allegory, nor is it specifically didactic in nature, automatically contributing to the *utile* as well as the *dulce.* However, it is a mode, a network of themes, images, and motifs that cut across genre lines—they can be found in lyrics, in novels, in epics, and on the stage—and across the centuries. Pastoral conventions, pastoral archetypes, dominate poetry for three centuries, from the Renaissance to pre-Romanticism, from Marot to Chénier, inclusively.

In the Middle Ages the leading genre anticipating this mode was the *pastourelle,* a noncourtly or anticourtly lyric in which, instead of adoring a lady in fear and trembling, the Speaker-knight-poet tries to seduce a shepherd girl. His success in this endeavor, a form of idealized rape (she is a virgin, she is overjoyed to have her flower plucked by a knight, she begs him to return), confirms that the genre embodies male wish-fulfillment fantasy no less flagrantly than the *grand chant courtois,* indeed that it proposes a counterideal to the courtly lyric and the ideology it represents. Furthermore, in such poems, whether we think of them as aristocratic ("aristocratisants"), or pseudopopular ("popularisants"), the direct influence of Antiquity proves to be all but nil.

Such is not the case in the Renaissance. Marot, Scève, Ronsard, Baïf, and Belleau knew their classics well. Inspired by Virgil, Ovid, Petrarch, and Sannazaro, they staked out the kingdom of Arcadia in Gaul. The bucolic epithalamium, the funereal eclogue, the political court pastoral, the pageant and entry, the narrative idyll, are among the genres they discovered or rediscovered. By the time of the Baroque a pastoral tonality suffuses, frames, embellishes, and contributes structure to love poetry. It encourages the vogue of descriptive verse and a concomitant interest in nature (Théophile de Viau and Tristan l'Hermite). The dramatic pastoral dominates the stage from 1625 to 1635. And Saint-Amant introduces into France the "idyle heroïque" with his epic of peace, *Moyse sauvé* (1653), a subgenre developed further by La Fontaine in *Adonis* (1659). The century of the rococo maintained the pastoral tradition in dramatic, lyric, descriptive, erotic, and mythological verse, the leading practitioners being Fontenelle, J.-B. Rousseau, Piron, Gresset, Dorat, Saint-Lambert, Bertin, Léonard, Parny, and André Chénier. Finally, despite the inevitable transformations that came with Romanticism, two poets of pastoral—Lamartine in *Jocelyn* and Mistral in *Mirèio*—maintain the archetypes well into the age of Balzac and Flaubert.

It is obvious that the pastoral mode expresses man's desire to return to the womb, to Eden, to a world of happiness and innocence, far from the madding crowd, far from the court. Whether in fiction (*l'Astrée*), the epic (*Les Tragiques*), or the lyric (Ronsard, Théophile, and La Fontaine), positing Arcadia presupposes, indeed calls forth an attack upon its antonym, the evil, corrupt capital. Arcadia is a place without riches and ambition, where the virtues of idleness (Virgil's "Deus nobis haec otia fecit") contribute to a *vita contemplativa,* to reflection in solitude (Théophile, Saint-Amant, Le Moyne). Self-conscious city and court poets exalt an artificial world of sheep and shepherdesses, a Golden Age without gold, a primitivistic Utopia where all men are equal and renounce the vanity of human wishes. Central to the Arcadian vision is the notion of a love that is chaste, pure, without sin and without children, giving voice to the gentle or passionate encomium by the Speaker-poet of his Philis, Sylvie, and Aminte.

Christian pastoral, present in the Mystery plays and in pieces by Marguerite de Navarre, receives its finest literary treatment in d'Aubigné's *Tragiques.* Here the little people, the *pauperi* of Scripture, are assimilated to persecuted Huguenots, isolated in the Alps and the Pyrénées, disciples of the Agnus Dei, the flock that Christ the Shepherd sacrificed himself to the Wolf in order to save. These are a collective, passive hero whose deeds of sacrifice replace the active prowess performed by their heroic forebears. Abel, slain by Cain, is redeemed by the Shepherd of

Man, born like a lamb in a stable, his birth predicted by shepherds in Virgil's Fourth Eclogue and revealed to shepherds lying in the fields, a wonder child restoring to the world a *pax christiana* that shall supersede the false, Satanic *pax romana,* the Babylonian tyranny of popes and emperors. Finally, these amorous, reflective, ecstatic shepherds are poets, and poets are shepherds. The singer's voice is assimilated to the oaten flute and the pipes of Pan. It is in the guise of a shepherd and amorous swain that the artist conventionally, archetypally, speaks as artist to a public that not only accepts his conventions but also could not and would not listen to him otherwise.

The sixth and last element of literature to be treated in this chapter is the most conventional of genres, the one that most blatantly denies the precepts of Symbolist and post-Symbolist poetics: the epic.[11] Because of post-Symbolist bias, the tradition in France of epic or narrative verse has largely been ignored. Yet, both in quantity and quality, the life of the epic is as strong, as rich, and as varied in France as in any other European country.

It is a fact that the epic was central to the preoccupations, theoretical and practical, of French poets from the earliest singers of *geste* (end of the eleventh century) to the generation of Lamartine, Vigny, and Hugo, indeed to the age of Leconte de Lisle and Sully Prudhomme. One reason for the centrality of the epic was the assumption that this genre was hierarchically the highest, finest, and noblest, including all others. It is ample in scope, contains vast practical and theoretical knowledge, and is worthy of being interpreted on one or more allegorical levels. Therefore, it has to be morally exemplary, didactic, capable of instructing princes. Some of the greatest writers in French literature—Turold, Chrétien de Troyes, Guillaume de Lorris, Jean de Meun, Machaut, Froissart, Ronsard, d'Aubigné, Saint-Amant, Boileau, Voltaire, Lamartine, Hugo, for that matter Saint-John Perse, Aragon, and Pierre Emmanuel—have cultivated the long poem, whether in the serious or comic vein, with outstanding success. Indeed, what is most amazing about the evolution of the long poem in France is its continuity.

Although individual decades or generations can be unproductive and some are less rich than others, and despite Romantic pronouncements that each nation shall be represented by one and only one epic, nonetheless we find a surge of masterpieces over the ages. In fact, all centuries, with the possible exception of the fifteenth, make a significant contribution. In this respect, France is unique among the European nations, and the fortunes of epos, as of political verse, allegory, and panegyric, do correspond to the development of French literature as a whole: a steady, homogeneous stream of masterpieces launched by the

Saint-Alexis in the middle of the eleventh century and never interrupted since. Indeed, with the contribution of Saint-John Perse, Aragon, and Pierre Emmanuel, the long poem continues its career in our own century, despite stricture, despite neglect, oblivious to chic Parisian circles and their manifestos. In its adherence to tradition and to a didactic, encyclopedic, all-encompassing purposiveness, the epic, like the occasional poem, panegyric, political text, allegory, and pastoral, represents the Great Tradition of French and European verse.

5

THE CREED

The poet discovers, then transmits to his reader, secrets of the universe. His spiritual adventures grant him the right to create myths, to elaborate a poetic theology based upon atheistic mysticism. He is or becomes a seer (Rimbaud's voyant), a prophet, a modern Orpheus, who discovers poetic truth: the sacred, the unknown, the unsayable, superhuman knowledge, divine mysteries. He seizes the ineffable and the transcendent, then reveals them to his readers as poetic, secular scripture.

Since Hugo, Gautier, Baudelaire, and Nerval, since Shelley, Poe, Arnold, Swinburne, and Wilde, poetry is said to have replaced religion, to have become the secular religion of modern man. For Shelley, there is a knowledge to which only the imagination has access and to which only poets can give voice. For Mallarmé, the poet himself creates reality, *le Grand Œuvre*, an alchemical transmutation of prose that arrives at a mystical, quasi-religious quintessence. According to this thesis, poetry is sacred, an object of religious adoration, and the poet, whether he conceives himself to be God (*Deus artifex*) or his priest (*sacer vates*), is the practitioner and embodiment of the new cult.[1]

The *poeta sacer vates* is hardly an invention of the nineteenth century. Plato underscored the poet's enthusiasm and his role as a divine mediator. Certain of the troubadours, the Rhétoriqueurs, Scève, and Ronsard make a claim for visionary poetry and for the sacred, mystical vocation of the visionary poet. Nonetheless, they form a minority in the tradition of French verse as a whole, whereas since 1789, and especially in the last one hundred years, the Orphic voice has become the predominant one, at times the only one to be heard. It is no coincidence that the myth of Orpheus is the most distinctive theme in poetry of the last two centuries, forming a chain that includes works by Goethe, Hölderlin, Novalis, Hoffmann, Ballanche, Nerval, Rimbaud, Valéry, Rilke, Segalen, Cocteau, Anouilh, Jouve, and Emmanuel. And the Orphic current, the notion that the poet seeks after metaphysical truth, predominates in major contemporary reviews such as *L'Ephémère* and *Argile* and inspires the major contemporary poets, including Char, Bonnefoy, du Bouchet, and Dupin.

It can be said that the Orphic stance is a conception of poetry and the poet's calling that has come into prominence during the modern era largely for historical reasons: the decline of religion, the decline of the status and prestige of humane letters, and the corresponding rise in favor of science, technology, and the materialistic life in general. It is in order to compete with science and technology, to compete with prose fiction for that matter, that poets have established the claim that they are magi who attain metaphysical truths, that as priest-alchemists they discover the Mysteries, in this case a quintessence of poetry or myth, then reveal them to the world. And it is in order to compete with creative writers that professors today claim for literary criticism or the theory of literature the same quasi-religious reverence that the Symbolists accorded to poetry, the new sacred texts being Derrida, Lacan, and Foucault alongside of Rimbaud, Mallarmé, and Lautréamont.

One of the truths revealed by modern criticism—by all major schools of criticism—is that the poem is an ontological whole, a structural entity of literariness, consequently that the poet is not a seer or prophet, not a saint or hero, but uniquely a maker of poems. From this perspective, poetry is a craft, "an art or skill—a trained habit of using certain instruments to certain ends."[2] Some versifiers, in the Wordsworthian, Lamartinian, and Hugolian sense, possess enthusiasm, sensitivity, and compassion; others do not. And we must not forget the mass of enthusiastic, sensitive, and compassionate men who never write a line. Poets can be great persons or scoundrels; they can use their gifts to teach the truth or to lie or to be neutral and withdraw; they can expend their talent on universals or on trivia. It is surely an error to substitute art for morality or religion. Art can cause harm as well as good. Neither poets nor their readers are inherently better than anyone else. These are the lessons to be inferred from the number of S.S. officers or concentration-camp commandants who had been nurtured on Goethe and Beethoven and who, throughout the war, remained loyal to the classics.[3] Finally, there are any number of writers who, as they became better thinkers and men, declined as artists, such as Racine, Wordsworth, Tolstoy, Pound, and many another.

It is also clear that much great poetry, ancient and modern, is nonvisionary, indeed antivisionary: verse based on wit and satire, on paradox and ambiguity, or in which a monistic, universal message is undermined and logical or doctrinal contradictions are revealed. This is the case with Horace, Villon, La Fontaine, and Pushkin, among the most eminent. Furthermore, it has been said that pretentions to magus status during the Romantic and Symbolist age sometimes gave rise to pompous didacticism and cheap sentimentality. Surely the artists who have claimed to be thinkers—Wordsworth, Shelley, Browning, Lamartine, Vigny, Hugo, for that matter Mallarmé and Valéry—are inferior to professional philosophers in terms of depth, rigor, and originality of intellect. They express the generally accepted values of their society or of a social class in their society with the same acuity that we find in, say, Jean de Meun, Ronsard, d'Aubigné, and Voltaire. In the last analysis the poet does not think deep thoughts or discover mysterious truths; he does not express his personality or his experiences. He provides us with instruction and pleasure. He expresses the common experience: the secular, world-oriented preoccupations of all men, what all people feel but which he can say the best.

But what of the sacred? What of revelation? Are there no Mysteries? Is the artist forbidden to touch them? The most pertinent answer to the poetry-as-a-new-religion thesis states that other men are better equipped to wrestle with the Mysteries: philosophers, theologians, even (*mirabile dictu*) scientists. In historical terms the *sacer vates'* existence is predicated upon a debatable presupposition: the death of God, the end of real priests and of real faith. In other words, the nineteenth century assumed and perhaps was mistaken in assuming the need for a new religion of art that was supposed to replace the old one. It is true that the Symbolists elaborated patterns of symbolism, allegory, and psychology with little reference to the traditional classical-Christian typology. Indeed, it can be said that their tragic vision was predicated upon the death of Christianity. However, in the long run poetry could hardly replace Christianity, since Christianity had never disappeared. Despite Sartre, despite Nietzsche, despite Marx, despite Robespierre, God was not dead, nor were his believers asleep. And throughout the Western tradition, for century after century, from *La Chanson de Saint-Alexis* to the present, poets have served as spokesmen for the faith of their fathers, for the Church Militant and Triumphant. It goes without saying that they and their society would have been incapable of comprehending the notion of poetry as prophecy or scripture apart from Prophecy and Scripture, or that verse could in any way be sacred other than as Sacred Verse. They believed in divine inspiration, but that it comes indeed from God and that the poet does not receive grace other than the one accorded to mystics or, for that matter, all members of Christ's body, the Church.

In other words, the poets presumed as a matter of course that a bond existed between themselves and the divine mysteries. They were not gods; they were men revealing God's truth to others. For the great Christian poets, whether of the past or the present, whether they speak as prophets or as humble sinners, never construct a religion out of art, never dream of making a new creed. Their faith is taken for granted, at least in the past, and their culture is based upon commonly accepted beliefs. Nonetheless, it is they who are indirectly the precursors, the fathers, of more recent artists who indeed claim to be divine or to be priests of the cult of art, the new faith in which their own verse is both the object of the cult and its means of mediation to the world. Modern poetry does not replace religion. It continues to seek and to teach the unsayable and the superhuman.

In academia and in the outside literary world the tradition of Christian letters, especially in France, has been neglected.[4] The renascence of sacred poetry in the twentieth century, extending from Claudel and Péguy to Jouve, Emmanuel, and Jean Grosjean, is termed the Catholic school or the Catholic poets and considered to be no more and no less than one among a dozen currents or developments on the contemporary scene. As for the past, medieval secular genres such as the *chanson de geste,* courtly romance, courtly lyric, and the allegory of love have generally received far more attention than, say, hagiography and the mystery plays. Until recently the Protestant-Catholic Baroque was neglected in favor of the allegedly more secular, more "modern" classicism of the Age of Louis XIV; among the classics, the specifically Christian texts of La Fontaine and Boileau were also neglected. Outside of the university the general educated reader assumes as a matter of course that French literature is more secular, less Christian, than the literatures of England, Germany, Italy, and Spain. Yet the Christian tradition, which posits a radically divergent conception of poetry and the poet's calling from the post-Symbolist esthetic, is crucial to our understanding of the nature of poetry in its totality. It will therefore be of some interest to explore what poetry as religion, that is, poetry serving the Christian faith, really meant for almost all of our history.

The Middle Ages was a time of belief, also a time of war, love, satire, feudal honor, and verbal obscenity. However, whatever the variety of vernacular literature, it is certain that the intellectual and pedagogical establishment was ecclesiastical and no less certain that the principal vernacular genres to some extent originated in the Church. They came into existence because of and in conjunction with Christian faith inspired by a Christian worldview. This is true obviously for the saint's life, the oldest genre in the Middle Ages, which, with the *Vie de Saint-Alexis,* gave to France its first literary masterpiece. Two *vitae* and a miracle play were composed by one of the leading poets of the thirteenth century, Rutebeuf; narrative miracles of the virgin were the specialty of another thirteenth-century master, Gautier de Coinci. Christianity also inspired mystery plays that derive from liturgical drama originating within the church and forming part of the sacred office. The great mystery plays and cycles of miracle plays were to form a high point of late-medieval literature and one of the summits of world drama; they also were, for all intents and purposes, the only serious theater the Middle Ages was to know.

Other genres—the epic, for example, or the courtly lyric—although not specifically Christian in orientation, were of clerical origin and owed much of their form and structure to the Church. *La Chanson de Roland,* the oldest of French epics, preaches crusade against the infidel and urges, for that purpose, that divisive feudal interests yield to the authority of the crown. It also explores problems of personal pride, strength, wisdom, heroism, and compassion within the framework of an eschatological battle between France and Spain, Christianity and pagandom, good and evil, Christ and Antichrist, projected into a figural universe that contains all of sacred and secular history, from Creation to Doomsday, and in which Roland and Ganelon recall, for example, Adam and Satan, Christ and Judas, even Christ and Antichrist. Although the *chanson de geste* is soon secularized, many late texts, among these some of the most beautiful, still preach the crusade and a sentiment of personal abnegation as the only road to fulfillment in war and personal salvation. Even epics of revolt, concerned with secular problems inside France, with loyalty, treason, tyranny, and feudal honor at court, end with the rebel yielding to the tyrant and then proceeding on a pilgrimage or crusade, attaining fulfillment in an eschatological experience that brings him close to sainthood (*Girart de Roussillon, Renaud de Montauban*).

Courtly love, *fin' amor,* can be thought of as a Christian heresy, a new secular religion in which the lady, the *domna,* replaces Christ or the Virgin Mary, the lover-poet replaces the priest or good Christian soul, and the *joy* of the troubadours replaces an earlier, sacred *gaudium.* It is probable that the troubadour songs owe much of their vocabulary and their formal structure to hymns of the Church, as they owe some erotic motifs to the Song of Songs and to commentaries on it. And for three centuries courtly texts—Chrétien's *Lancelot,* the *Flamenca,* Guillaume de

Lorris's *Roman de la Rose,* and Machaut's *Voir Dit*—exalt and illustrate the new passion, their protagonist a priest of *fin' amor* who adores his lady and follows the Ten Commandments of the god of love.

We also have reason to believe that secular passion influenced *caritas* in turn. *Fin' amor* can and often does return to its source. Under these conditions sacred love then comes to embody structures that originally were the province of the courtly. Gautier de Coinci composed songs in praise of the Virgin, *contrafactum* pastiches of secular erotic lyrics. Courtly romancers, who at first exalt the new Eros and valorize the quest for glory and human love in an Arthurian setting, eventually turn to a greater, higher quest. The grail romances, beginning with Chrétien's *Perceval,* propose a striving for perfection and salvation and designate a new, Christian hero, Perceval or Galahad, as an alternative to Tristan and Lancelot. Perhaps the greatest of all medieval texts, the *Lancelot-Grail Cycle* (here I allude to a work in prose), depicts the rise and fall of the Arthurian kingdom *sub specie aeternitatis,* the disintegration of the secular world balanced and crowned by the realization that Galahad's is a better way than Lancelot's or Gauvain's and that charity proves to be the only love that can endure.

One myth imposed by the Third Republic establishment represents the Renaissance as a denial of the Middle Ages and of medieval Christianity, a denial embodied in a humanism that proclaimed the return to classical Antiquity and the exaltation of love, life, and the dignity of man. Nothing could be further from the truth. On the one hand, love, life, and the dignity of man were the products of the High Middle Ages. On the other, the succeeding epoch continued medieval beliefs and practices, including fervor for the sacred. Thus Clément Marot, who wrote delicious epigrams and epistles, also translated the Psalms; his version, continued by Théodore de Bèze, became a rallying cry for the new Huguenot church. Similarly, Marguerite de Navarre composed sacred lyrics and dramas as well as the *Heptameron.* Du Bellay juxtaposed throughout his career the sacred and the profane, was influenced by and contributed to both currents. The same is true for Belleau and Baïf, who composed a significant religious corpus, including paraphrases of Job, Ecclesiastes, the Canticles, and the Psalms. And Ronsard, author of so much splendid erotic verse and poetry of wine and roses, also composed Christian philosophical and meditative *hymnes* and passionate, politically committed Christian *discours,* attacking the Huguenots and upholding, by divine right, the position of a Catholic monarch and church.

These *discours,* which develop patterns of magnificent demonic imagery and play with narrative point of view and voice, are the finest

French example of the sublime in the period that extends from Jean de Meun to d'Aubigné. Ronsard is typical of his age as a great classical and Christian poet, singing of roses and of his king, of women and of Christ. As we saw in chapter 4, like the other members of the Pléiade, like all men of his century, he interpreted myth in allegorical terms. The allegorical-typological interpretation of myth granted it fervor, numen, and didactic weight; it also revealed accrued meaning, inculcated virtue, and celebrated glory. Indeed, the *hymnes* were composed in order to "recuperate" pagan myth by Christianizing it. The result, a splendid monument of syncretism, enabled Ronsard to be classical and Christian at the same time, to cherish Greece and Rome while exalting the God of his homeland.

The Baroque period, extending roughly from 1570 to 1650, represents a return to religion, a revival of the faith second to none in the history of our culture. Sacred lyrics, Protestant and Catholic, inspired by new Jesuitical forms of devotion or of other provenance, form the richest single component of the age; and great masters—Sponde, La Ceppède, Chassignet, Favre in the first generation; Lazare de Selve, du Bois-Hus, Martial de Brives, and Pierre Le Moyne in the second— contribute to a flowering of poetry the equal of the Metaphysical school in England and the *góngoristas* in Spain. Christianity also dominates the epic, for the most successful long poems of the Baroque—du Bartas's *La Sepmaine;* d'Aubigné's *Les Tragiques,* Saint-Amant's *Moyse sauvé,* and Le Moyne's *Saint Louis*—are Christian texts, based upon the Old and New Testaments. It is no accident that epicists are given to one form or another of Christian commitment. These four poems, two Protestant and two Catholic, are more descriptive, pathetic, and elegiac than comparable epics were in the Renaissance, and all four preach a new heroism based upon suffering and martyrdom, passive innocence, and endurance as well as and in place of achievement.

Derived from the Protestant Reformation and the Catholic Counter-Reformation, the Baroque has to be seen as a modern style, which in many respects repudiates Renaissance classicism. Baroque poets are less beholden to Antiquity, less concerned with rules and convention; their language is often either harsh or casually chatty; and they are obsessed with doctrinal truth, with expressing commitment in faith. Statements of dogma, figurative language, heroism, paradox, and sensuality are juxtaposed, if not fused. Even the motif of solitude in nature is set off in antithesis to the worldly corruption of city and court. The reader is told that the only true peace comes from God, indeed that the beauty of nature *proves* the existence and goodness of God. In many respects the Catholic Renaissance can be thought of as a return to the Middle

Ages, to a world of crusade militancy and feudal-aristocratic splendor, where the will, the senses, and worldly glory all serve the living Christ and His Church.

Neoclassicism represents the first break, the first sliding away from the old Christian-feudal synthesis. The new, bourgeois, Parisian-oriented culture is less ostentatiously Catholic than the old, provincial, aristocratic one. Molière and Voltaire are children of Paris, as later on will be Anatole France and Aragon. On the other hand, viewing the ancien régime through a Third Republic prism veils the fact that La Fontaine set down the *Captivité de saint Malc* and a plethora of Christian verse, some of it translated from citations in Saint Augustine; that Corneille wrote *Polyeucte* and *Théodore, vierge et martyre,* and translated the *Imitatio Christi;* that Racine composed *Esther* and *Athalie;* that two of Boileau's greatest poems, his last satire and epistle, are Christian texts that treat avowedly Christian subjects.

The eighteenth century in prose is the age of Montesquieu, Voltaire, and Diderot. Curiously, however, the old beliefs retain their sway over the realm of the muses. Bernis's *La Religion vengée* and Louis Racine's *La Grâce* and *La Religion* are among the most important long poems of the century, dealing, especially in Racine's case, with the inner life of a new epic hero, the poet speaking as a Christian. These are theological epics by men who, reacting against the Philosophes, reject pagan epic machinery in favor of what they consider to be the only Truth. Some of the finer, more vibrant lyrics of the century are to be found in collections of sacred odes by Jean-Baptiste Rousseau and Jean-Jacques Lefranc de Pompignan. Inspired by the Psalms, they brought to these texts a concreteness of imagery, nobility of diction, and authenticity of belief lacking in the secular sphere. Voltaire in Paris ridiculed Lefranc, destroyed his career, and prevented him from sitting permanently in the Académie; nonetheless, back home in Montauban the petty aristocrat proved to be not only a genuine Christian but a genuine Christian poet of the first order. Voltaire also is a first-rate poet, as much in need of rehabilitation today as is Lefranc. There is room for both of them in the eighteenth-century pantheon and in the annals of French verse.

This coexistence of the sacred and the profane, of Lefranc and Voltaire, does not cease with the Revolution. Lamartine and Brizeux are two Catholic poets of Romanticism who exalt God and the faith of the centuries with as much fervor as that manifested by Vigny or Musset on the opposite side. It is hardly necessary to recall in more recent times how Verlaine, Claudel, Péguy, Jammes, and Jacob contribute to a Catholic Renaissance, the most striking in all of Europe, or the revival of the sacred carried on by Jouve, La Tour du Pin, Emmanuel, Grosjean, Renard, and others in our time. The "Catholic school" is one of the vital and dynamic currents since the Liberation.

Christian tradition is a certainty; it persists throughout the history of French verse. Indeed, what perhaps surprises the modern reader is the concentration of French religious poets, the quantity and quality of works that illuminate each century. Eliot remarked on the lack, since Chaucer's day, of truly great religious poets in England, in contrast to France;[5] and Eliot, who had in mind Villon, Corneille, Racine, and Baudelaire, knew nothing of Gautier de Coinci, Rutebeuf, the mystery plays, d'Aubigné, La Ceppède, and of course the most recent Catholic school.

What I call the Christian tradition forms part of our culture, provides a pattern of images and archetypes that all writers, even Sartre and Aragon, use automatically, perhaps unconsciously. It *is* Western culture, in the same sense that Islam *is* Middle Eastern culture. Of course, from the medieval trouvère who tells stories—miracles, *exempla*—serenely confident that the seed will sprout, to the Baroque lyricist who exhorts his readers to live the good life, on to the Romantic or modern Catholic who questions himself and God in a state of perpetual anguish, the tradition has evolved over the ages. Nonetheless, one thing is certain: These poets do not presume to create a religion or even to modify one. They do not exalt themselves as artists, nor do they overemphasize the value of art. Their Christianity is traditional; so is their culture. As prophets, they bear witness to a given faith—that of their fathers, their nation, and their king. Above all, their purpose is didactic: to preach the Word, to teach prevalent values in the community. As much as any reader of Virgil and Ovid, they are imitators, dependent on Scripture, the Fathers, and a more recent Magisterium. The role of personal creativity and originality is slim indeed. The Christian brings with him a structure, a mind-set of ways of viewing reality and expressing it in literary terms. One of these, surely the most important, is the allegorical or typological reading of the Scripture, also applicable to Greco-Roman myth and, ultimately, to all serious literature (cf. chapter 4). According to this view, allegorically, a literary hero prefigures or postfigures Christ (hence the modern term, often misused, of Christ-figure); on the tropological level his action refers to the individual Christian or to the Church in the present, *hic et nunc*; anagogically, he anticipates Doomsday and the end of the world. This pattern is not only of exegetical value: It provides a philosophy of history and a pattern of symbolism, esthetic as well as intellectual in nature. Typology has dominated sacred writing in France from the *Song of Roland* to the most recent work of Pierre Emmanuel and Jean Grosjean.

Even in their notion of style Christian poets are traditional. On the one hand, adhering to a brand of Neoplatonism that goes back to the twelfth century and before, an assimilation is made between the good, the beautiful, and the true, and between the false, the wicked, and the ugly. From this perspective *sermo gravis* is considered appropriate for sacred lyric, drama, and epic because, as religion is the loftiest, most beautiful of subjects, it demands the loftiest, most beautiful of styles. On this point the Christian writer rejoins his pagan forebears, recognizing a hierarchy of styles and, as a normal matter of course, giving preference to the highest.

There is another current in Christian esthetics, however, one that exalts *sermo humilis*. As we saw in chapter 3, because Christ came into the world incarnate as a Jew and the apparent son of a carpenter, because he consorted with publicans and fishermen, because he preached a doctrine of peace, not war, and was crucified in a public execution, because he claimed to be a shepherd of men and the Lamb of God, the events of his life are "low" and were recounted in demotic Greek, translated into demotic Latin, the lowest of languages. His is the humblest of stories yet also at the center of history and the cosmos, humble yet revealing more significance and sublimity than any other. *Sermo humilis* is transformed into *sermo gravissimus,* and the language of the people can and ought to be exploited to tell these sublime, earth-shattering truths. Hence rough vernacular in the mystery plays, hence the proliferation of shepherd and sheep imagery in Baroque lyrics and the convention of Christian pastoral. Nonetheless, even here the Christian poet, when reversing, juxtaposing, or mixing styles, is conscious of tradition, is partaking in and contributing to it. Whether he exalts the sublime or the low style, he is aware of rhetoric; he works within stylistic and rhetorical norms. He speaks in Virgil's register or Saint Jerome's, he imitates Aeneas's or Saint Paul's, but he never presumes to invent his own.

Last of all, bearing witness to the Word of God forms part of the Christian writer's everyday life. He is not a magus, a genius, an inspired demigod possessed by the muses; he is simply a poet and a craftsman. Some consecrate their entire production *ad majorem Dei gloriam:* Such are the example of Gautier de Coinci, Arnoul Greban, Jean de La Ceppède, Antoine Favre, Pierre Le Moyne, and Louis Racine. It is the way of the modern Catholic poet, whose persona as a writer is often Catholic and nothing else. Yet in their everyday work La Ceppède and Favre were magistrates, and Le Moyne a Jesuit priest

with pastoral and pedagogical duties. These men lived a normal existence in the world, their verse serving as part of their lives, but not as a
unique mystical vocation. For the majority of Christian poets, however,
the story is different. It is more often the case that Chrétien de Troyes
devote his fifth romance to a semi-Christian theme, Perceval's quest of
the grail, whereas the first four are of largely secular inspiration, and
that Desportes, d'Aubigné, and Sponde begin their careers with erotic
verse, then turn to the sacred in middle age. It is much more common
for Rutebeuf, Villon, Marot, Ronsard, and La Fontaine to alternate the
sacred and the profane, to praise their ladies and Our Lady, to sing of
themselves as lovers, poets, and Christians, to tell of men and of the
Son of Man. These themes are juxtaposed in an author's opus, juxtaposed, not fused, because the sacred is one concern among many; it is
perhaps the most important, but it is not unique. Such men wrote in a
classical-Christian culture where no one theme, motif, conviction, or
esthetic eliminated all others. In this sense even the fiery Huguenot
captain d'Aubigné and no-less-fanatical Jesuit propagandist Le Moyne
are brothers. Religion forms an organic entity in the lives of these poets
and is no less organically joined to all other facets of their poetic opus:
love, war, nature, satire, and the state. In this sense they are less exclusive, less narrow, perhaps even less partisan than their descendants
today.

Given the force of this tradition and its significance for the subsequent evolution of French verse, it would be helpful to see Christian
poets at work, to examine in a more precise, concrete manner the kind
of texts they write and the goals they seek. Here, then, are representative texts from the two most important periods of French religious
writing: the High Middle Ages and the Baroque. I have chosen a song
by the leading vernacular poet of the sacred in the century of Saint
Louis—Gautier de Coinci—and sonnets by two among the more
prominent lyricists of the age of Henry IV, one Protestant and one
Catholic: Jean de Sponde and Jean de La Ceppède. All three poets
have been rehabilitated in our generation.

> Quant ces floretes florir voi
> Et chanter oi ces chanteürs,
> Pour la flor chant qui a en soi
> Toutes biautés, toutes valeurs.
> Ele est et mere et fille a roi,
> Rose des roses, fleurs des fleurs.
> Certes mout l'aim: Diex doinst qu'aint moi
> Et qu'ele i mece bones meurs.

La fleurs dont chant est fleurs roiaus.
De nule flor tant de biens n'ist.
C'est li vergiers, c'est li prealz
Ou Sainz Espirs s'aümbre et gist.
C'est la pucele emperïalz
Qu'apelons mere Jesu Crist,
Ou li fix Dieu, qui tant fu biaus,
Pour nous sauver char et sanc prist.

Mere Dieu, trop a le cuer vain
Qui ne te sert par grant deduit,
Car tu portas en ten douz saim
La douce espece et le dous fruit
De quoi nos sommes soir et main
Rasazïé et peü tuit.
Sacrares fu dou sacré pain
Qui les angles paist jor et nuit.

Dame, seur toz nons est li tienz
Dous et piteus, dignes et hauz.
Tu iez la dois de tous les biens,
Tu iez dou ciel pons et portaus.
Dame, tu iez de toutes riens
Tous li confors, tous li consaus.
Par tes preces tous nous soustiens,
Car seur tous sainz pués tu et vaus.

Dame d'aval, dame d'amont,
Dame de quanque Diex a fait,
Ta grans douceurs bien nous semont
Que te servommes tuit affait.
Dame, bien ont monté le mont,
Bien sunt gari, bien sunt refait
Cil qui te servent en cest mont,
Car ja leur lit ou ciel sunt fait.[6]

Gautier de Coinci composed *chansons* in honor of the Blessed Virgin Mary in conjunction with his collection of miracles, *Les Miracles de Nostre Dame.* The *chansons* are songs of praise in the lyrical mode that imitate the form and manner of the *grand chant courtois,* the genre examined in chapter 2. Gautier is aware of the similarity between the two literary kinds. His texts, especially this one, partake of the technique known as *contrafactum,* or sacred parody:[7] the conscious, willful imitation of a well-known, fashionable genre, in this case the courtly lyric, but with the purpose of transforming the secular genre into a sacred one, thus of transforming secular into sacred love. In the thirteenth century, the

Golden Age of *contrafactum* in France, the vernacular religious song is a parasite register, totally dependent upon the secular lyric; for, lacking an autonomous typology, it exists in reference to preceding secular works, by imitating and refuting them. In such a text the poet retains the meter, rhyme, and much of the imagery and lexicon of the profane register, substituting or adding the spiritual to it. The poet "converts" the source poem or genre in order to convert his reader.

Thus Gautier exploits the themes and motifs of *fin' amor,* applying them to *caritas,* the love of God for man, of man for God, of God for Mary, and of the speaker, spokesman of mankind, for the Mother of God. The spring topos that opens the poem, the poet presented as lover and singer, the Speaker who loves a lady and begs her to love him in return, his exaltation of her, the comfort and sweetness she manifests, the notion that she can make him a better person and that it is good for him to serve her—these are standard courtly motifs, to be found in hundreds of lyrics. Similarly, the lexicon of Gautier's text— *chanter, aim, flor, sauver, deduit, sert, Dame, confors, preces, douceurs*—has a courtly patina and is redolent with courtly overtones. This is possible because Christian literature in Latin evolved over the centuries, and the nascent literature of the court owes a great deal to the Christian tradition. Its language, its semantic register, its imagery are based upon and derive from those of the Church. They conserve a clerical patina and, in their own right, oscillate back and forth from the sacred to the secular. Hence *aim* or *aor* contains overtones of erotic passion and Christian charity, of secular and sacred adoration. Hence *preces* evokes entreaty and prayer, *dous* sweetness and humility, *sert* martial or feudal and devotional or liturgical service. Gautier then takes the courtly lexicon, with its religious connotations, and brings it home as it were, exploiting the Christian elements inherent in these words yet also retaining their more profane overtones. The language remains ambivalent or, rather, attains a new ambivalence in conjunction with the old.

The poet introduces all these motifs into his universe, adapting, undercutting, and redeeming them as he applies them to the Virgin. His poem refutes *fin' amor,* showing it to be narrow, shallow, petty, and distorted; and at the same time he exalts it: For he indicates that the themes of secular Eros, petty and shallow as they are, open the gate and construct the bridge to a higher, better, and nobler love, *caritas,* of which *fin' amor* can be considered at best a pale simulacrum, truth in a glass darkly, *sicut in aenigmate.* Charity is superior to secular Eros as the City of God is superior to cities of men. But the one leads to the other, as the Song of Songs, interpreted allegorically, conducts us as brides to our divine Spouse.

From the perspective of reader response, the first four lines of the first stanza are in the pure courtly style and can be envisaged as coming from a *grand chant courtois;* indeed they call for such a reading. The implied audience has no way of knowing that the song is to be interpreted *a lo divino* until the fifth line, "Ele est et mere et fille a roi," corrects possible false expectations and shocks the audience into comprehension. And it is only in the second stanza, with an allusion to the Holy Spirit, that the ambiguity is suppressed once and for all. However, for the remainder of the song the audience is expected to keep in mind the registers of secular and sacred love, to keep in mind that Gautier is using secular themes and images to praise the Mother of God, that courtly motifs are present and at the same time refuted, transformed, and surpassed in the name of Christ.

The courtly world in its totality, based upon the conventions of *fin' amor,* is integrated into a Christian context and sublimated from a Christian perspective. Thus the lady, referred to as *dame,* is of course Notre Dame, Our Lady; she is "married" to God and has received the embraces of the Holy Ghost. Differing from the secular tradition, the Speaker's devotion to her is spiritual and chaste. Above all, Gautier emphasizes her power and nobility. As *dame,* Our Lady is a *domina,* the archetypal feudal mistress; she is also a royal flower (*fleurs roiaus*), an imperial maiden (*pucele emperïalz*), mother and daughter to a king, more worthy than all the saints, *domina* over all that is high and below. She is truly the queen of heaven, *regina coeli,* and earth, the dominant female presence in the universe. For this reason her lordship deserves praise, for it renders the temporal and/or spiritual greatness of a mere fleshly mistress trivial in comparison.

Mary's power lies in her closeness to God, *Dominus tecum,* her capacity to influence the divinity, therefore her ability to facilitate salvation for her devotees. This is the principal theme of the *Miracles.* She is, for these devotees, for the Speaker, and, by implication, for the implied audience, the bridge and gate to heaven. In other texts Gautier develops the Christian commonplace according to which the Mother of God, *Ave,* redeems the Mother of Men, *Eva,* reversing the course of history, in the same way that the New Adam, Christ, redeems and transforms the Old Adam. In contrast to the adulterous frame of the courtly universe, the Speaker adores his lady without offending her Husband, without insult to a *gilos.* On the contrary, she can intercede with Him as *mediatrix* on the lover's behalf. Nor does he love her uniquely by himself in his own voice. The *je* is transformed into a *nous* of collective devotion, for the Speaker seeks to join his audience, mankind, in reverence to Mary, who is *Nostre Dame,* not *ma dame.* The

Speaker and his fellows will perform love service on her behalf; they will serve her. However, the service will be spiritual, not martial. As a result, they will have conquered the world (*monté le mont*) not by winning it, but by overcoming it, and their reward will be a bed: not one of erotic pleasure on earth (for they now deny the world, the flesh, and the devil), but *leur lit ou ciel,* a couch in heaven, where they will lie in eternal bliss, reborn after death, reawakened to a spiritual life after lusts have disappeared in the first bed of the tomb.

In courtly texts the spring *Eingangsmotiv* emphasizes the rebirth of love in April or May, the season of renewal in nature (birds and flowers) and of the New Year. According to medieval science, this was the sanguine period, favorable to the young, warm and moist, associated with the astrological sign of Taurus in the House of Venus, a time appropriate to the flowering of Eros. By alluding to flowers and birds, Gautier de Coinci reminds us that springtime also marks the flowering of the liturgical year, Annunciation and Easter, that it stands for the renewal of life here and now and for the commemoration of the most important events in history, the renewal of history caused by the conception, crucifixion, and resurrection of Christ. He tells us that the flower imagery of courtly lyrics is misused, exploited in a trivial context, for what are these roses and gardens of *fin' amor* compared to the Rose of Sharon, the bride of Christ prefigured in the Canticles: "Rose des roses, fleurs des fleurs . . . fleurs roiaus," a woman indeed but unique among mothers in that her flower remains intact, uniquely blessed among women (*benedicta tu in mulieribus*) to be God's consort.

Needless to say, the qualities ascribed to women and roses in the trouvères and in Ronsard—freshness, youth, beauty, purity, goodness, spirituality—those qualities inherent in nature, unsullied by man, are magnified a thousandfold when applied to the Mother of God. The rose in turn evokes visions of the garden, the *locus amoenus* of eternal spring, the "green world" in nature, a décor of innocence and joy. Gautier de Coinci expands his pattern of floral imagery to include the grove and the meadow, "li vergiers . . . li prealz," Mary assimilated to a *locus amoenus* where the Holy Ghost lies and literally takes his shade (rests, is incarnate). On the one hand, the *locus amoenus,* which can be traced back to Homer, to Virgil (Elysium, the Golden Age), and to the earthly paradise of Genesis and the gardens of the Canticles and the Apocalypse, is conceived as a place of perpetual spring and eternal joy, a "dignus amore locus" that encourages the growth of love, secular or sacred, is in fact the only décor where it can properly flourish. We also find in Gautier de Coinci the metaphor of the male plowing a field or planting his seed and the female assimilated to Mother Earth, earth being one of the four elements, feminine in essence, as opposed to masculine fire and air, the flame and breath of the Spirit. The imagery is explicit, the sexual reality of the Incarnation unambiguous. Mary is flower and field, ever Virgin yet plucked and impregnated by the Holy Ghost in order to become the Mother of God.

It is as mother that Mary plays her most important role. She is a flower, but one from whom so many good things flow, "De nule flor tant de biens n'ist." She is a flower who produces fruit and fecunds the world. Hence the notion that Christ took his flesh and blood from her, that she is the duct containing all good things; she is represented again in terms of feminine imagery, this time water, the second feminine element. Finally, Gautier praises her for bearing in her womb the spice (perhaps spiced wine) and fruit that nourish us, and for being the sanctuary containing the holy vessels and, more specifically, bread that feeds the angels. The poet tells us that his flower of flowers gives birth to fruit, the *fructus ventris tui* nourished by her body and blood, her flesh and mother's milk. This spiritual food satisfies more than physical passion; we are satiated, "Rasazïé," by it in a way that joy of the court can never do. The infant Jesus become the living Christ sacrifices his body and blood on the Cross and, in the sacrament of the Mass, feeds us spiritually ever after with bread and wine. Lovely as they are, flowers prove to be only decorative in a courtly universe. From a Christian perspective, they give birth to fruit, and it is the spiritual nourishment offered by such fruit that changes the universe. The Mother of God nurtures her son; he nurtures us in turn. Her flesh and her milk are necessary preconditions for his body and blood, for the bread and wine of the Mass that nourish us the implied audience and the Speaker, who together comprise the Church, the body of Christ, for we are children in need of food as was the Infant Jesus.

Last of all, there is the question of art and communication. Gautier de Coinci exploits the traditional courtly motif of the Speaker who proclaims himself to be a lover and poet, amorous because he is a poet and making songs because he loves. He sings to the lady, praising her, adoring her in verse, thus performing service, but not as knight or crusader. He sings as the birds sing, who love and who herald the renewal of the seasons. He sings like the nightingale, bird of love, embodiment of the ravished Philomela. He also sings as a Christian poet for a Marian Rose, as a Christian nightingale weeping for the Crucifixion and heralding the coming Resurrection. And his song is reciprocated. In the courtly tradition, the lady does not answer, she stands impassively on her pedestal, and the Speaker never pierces her mask or divines her sentiments. But this lady is different. We can be assured of her empathy and response. The Speaker prays, and so also does the Lady. She speaks to God, her prayers (*preces*) intercede on our behalf, for she is *imperatrix* and *mediatrix*. Her relationship with God and with the Speaker is more genuine, more responsive, more recipro-cal than courtly passion, more real because it deals with the only Reality and the only Love.

It is significant that the singer-narrator, the implied author Gautier de Coinci, speaks directly to the Virgin Mary. She is the narratee. Implicitly, of course, Gautier also appeals to his public, but indirectly. Although his text is a *contrafactum*, a refutation of secular *fin' amor*, his tone is serene. He has full confidence in the Mother of God and in the audience. The situation is somewhat different in the Renaissance, where religious lyrics are derived from the devotional or homiletic tradition, and exhortation is directed to the public. The public or im-plied reader becomes the narratee. Consider my second text, a "sonnet de la mort" by Jean de Sponde.

> Qui sont, qui sont ceux là, dont le coeur idolatre
> Se jette aux pieds du Monde, et flatte ses honneurs?
> Et qui sont ces Valets, et qui sont ces Seigneurs?
> Et ces ames d'Ebene, et ces faces d'Albastre?
>
> Ces masques desguisez, dont la troupe folastre
> S'amuse à carresser je ne sçay quels donneurs
> De fumees de Court, et ces entrepreneurs
> De vaincre encor le Ciel qu'ils ne peuvent combatre?
>
> Qui sont ces louvoyeurs qui s'esloignent du Port?
> Hommagers à la Vie, et felons à la Mort,
> Dont l'estoille est leur Bien, le vent leur Fantasie?
>
> Je vogue en mesme mer, et craindrois de perir
> Si ce n'est que je sçay que ceste mesme vie
> N'est rien que le fanal qui me guide au mourir.[8]

At first reading the quatrains partake of the satirical mode. In part under the influence of du Bellay's *Regrets*, devotional poets such as Sponde composed a number of texts illustrating the topic of *vanitas vanitatum*. The Speaker, by his interrogations, signals to his implied reader the evils of the court. Those who seek worldly riches and power are excoriated in imagery evoking precious materials (ebony and ala-baster) and are said to humiliate themselves in a lord-lackey relation-ship. Courtiers, evil men of the world, even though they yearn for victory over heaven, cannot forthrightly indulge in their vile practices;

they are not strong enough to fight God or man in the open. Instead, theirs is a universe of hypocrisy, secrecy, and manipulation, hence masquerades, "masques desguisez," souls of ebony hidden behind alabaster faces, and indecision as to who are the masters and who are the slaves. Sponde characterizes the ambiance of the court with the verbs *flatte* and *s'amuse à carresser:* These courtiers are vile, their practices are low, and we are meant to see in them a hint of perverse eroticism, of oblique, misdirected sexuality. By alluding to the "fumees de Court," does the Huguenot poet seek to denigrate Catholic liturgy, specifically the incense used in High Mass? In that case, does his evocation of masquerades and masks, of spectacle and splendor, refer to Catholic liturgical splendor as well as to Catholic-sanctioned royal pastimes, both anathema to Calvinists? It is true that secular corruption is assimilated, in the very first line, to idolatry, for the idolatrous heart prostrates itself at the feet of the world, adoring the world, placing the century before eternity, the court before the city of the Just, and a symbolic calf of gold before God. These men of ebony and alabaster, supremely wealthy yet reified in their wealth, cannot be the *pauperi* who will win the Kingdom of Heaven. Thus natural harmony and the proper functioning of man, society, and nature are distorted.

In this Baroque *verkehrte Welt* the master-lackey relationship has replaced the more decorous and appropriate feudal bond between lord and vassal; and people, mere created beings, dare to think of conquering heaven, home of their Creator. The corruption is such that it is impossible to distinguish masters from their lackeys, and the heaven-conquerors are cowards, mere *entrepreneurs* unworthy of *militia* and of *caritas*. Christian love is subverted by vile caresses, human dignity by idolatrous prostration, and reason by the antics of carnival. The vanity and inconstancy of the world, the corruption and stench (*fumee*) of the court, are made manifest. Illusion and reality are indistinguishable in a world spectacle, a masked ball in which the characters themselves, reified, dehumanized, play roles in their own mad play of appearance and illusion.

The implied reader imagines of necessity a locus of antithesis, a universe other than corrupt idolatry and obscene masquerade. In the sixteenth century the obvious foil to the court is the pure, innocent, amorous poetic realm of pastoral, idyllic shepherds plying their idyllic trades in the countryside. Pastoral innocence would have occurred to the sixteenth-century reader, would have provided the "horizon of expectations," the implicit backdrop to the satirical court spectacle stage center. And perhaps the quatrains do contain an implicit pastoral motif. However, in the tercets Sponde does not fulfill readers' expectations with pastoral, implicit or explicit. Instead, he evokes a sea motif, voyagers on boats quitting the port. This is a version of the *peregrinatio* topic, the notion that all men are pilgrims and our life a pilgrimage, by land or sea, from birth to death, from time to eternity. Sponde restates the feudal analogy: The courtiers become sailors who offer homage to life instead of to death, the afterlife, and, by so doing, are treacherous to the afterlife; for, in biblical terms, no man can have two masters, and the Lord our God is a jealous God. He repeats the themes of illusion and reality, of men who know not what they do and who they are, and of evanescence, change, fragility, and falseness, depicting a people who put their good into an unattainable, uncontrollable star, their fantasy and fantasm into a no less unattainable, uncontrollable wind. Once again flesh is opposed to spirit and blackness to light.

Here the role of the Speaker becomes paramount. In the quatrains he was a spectator, a free spirit who distinguished himself from the worldlings. He assumed the voice of a prophet, a witness to evil, a righteous man who questions the wickedness and wrongness of his brothers at court and seeks to convince his other brothers, the implied readers, to mend their ways, to heed his condemnation of the world, the flesh, and the devil. In the last tercet we find that his role changes. Now, for the first time, he admits solidarity, even identity, with the worldlings. He who watched their idolatry and masquerade now claims to be, like them, a sea voyager in his boat. Like them, he is a *peregrinus;* like them he crosses the sea of life. The difference of course lies in the fact that his values are true, not false. He is lucid while they are blind, he is firm while they are changeable, he is loyal while they are treacherous, he knows truth while they only masquerade. He follows a better light, his *fanal* is *ceste mesme vie* that guides him to Christ the Way, the Truth, and the Life. In an example of paradox typically Baroque and archetypically Christian, unlike the others who will perish because they treasure only life, the Speaker will not perish; he will live because he is loyal to death, the afterlife, because he scorns the century in favor of true Life and the living Truth that come with eternity.

The Speaker preaches to his public, the average Christian reader of his age. Like a preacher, he addresses an imaginary congregation, arguing, persuading, making a point; for this kind of poem is closely allied to and in part derived from the sermon literature of the day. Thus he appeals to the reader, seeks to mold his norms in a sort of *captatio benevolentiae,* by admitting his own mortality and weakness— that he also is tossed on the sea of life. Affected modesty helps bridge the gap between himself and the reader. However, another implied reader or narratee can also be presumed, one for whom modesty is an even more crucial argument. This is the Way, the Truth, and the Life. For God also listens to the Speaker, and surely the Speaker seeks to justify himself to God, to excuse his weakness and mortality, to justify his humanness, to plead for a guiding light in the darkness, as much as he seeks to convince the public to follow him and not the courtiers. He begs the divinity to distinguish him from the others, to help him, to hear him, to reward his humility. Sponde's text is a satire, a sermon, and a prayer.

As a satire, sermon, and prayer the text adheres to the tradition of the evening meditation: a devotional convention of penitence, introspection, and concern over the vanity of human wishes, inspired by the Old Testament. This sort of verse was especially congenial to the Huguenots. Quite different is the mode cultivated more usually by Catholics: the morning meditation, poetry of incarnation and redemption, derived from the New Testament and treating the life of Christ. I offer the following text by La Ceppède:

> Aux Monarques vaincueurs la rouge cotte-d'armes
> Appartient justement. Ce Roy victorieux
> Est justement vestu par ces mocqueurs gens-d'armes
> D'un manteau, qui le marque et Prince, et glorieux.
>
> O pourpre emplis mon test de ton jus precieux
> Et luy fay distiller mille pourprines larmes,
> A tant que meditant ton sens mysterieux,
> Du sang trait de mes yeux j'ensanglante ces Carmes.
>
> Ta sanglante couleur figure nos pechez
> Au dos de cet Agneau par le Pere attachez:
> Et ce Christ t'endossant se charge de nos crimes.
>
> O Christ, ô sainct Agneau, daigne toy de cacher
> Tous mes rouges pechez (brindelles des abysmes)
> Dans les sanglans replis du manteau de ta chair.[9]

This poem is one of Jean de La Ceppède's *Théorèmes,* a sequence of several hundred sonnets that makes up a recital of, and meditation on, Christ's Passion and Resurrection. La Ceppède, Favre, Gabrielle de Coignard, and Anne de Marguets all composed integral, unified sonnet sequences on the life of Christ. The event referred to in the text is the moment when Jesus' persecutors forced him to don a crown of thorns and a purple robe. The Romans force Christ to wear purple (crimson) in mockery. They laugh at him, crying "Hail! King of the Jews!" He was accused of having fomented political as well as religious disorder, and it is the charge of political subversion that brought Pilate to agree to the rabbis' demand for his execution. The soldiers mock Jesus ("ces mocqueurs gens-d'armes"), indulge in ironic sport, because it is obvious to them that the poor, persecuted, abandoned wretch handed over to their keeping is the lowest of mortals; he, of all men, is king of nobody, his kingship a figment of his crazed imagination. The Speaker, however, is aware of a double irony, a second level of meaning. Unknown to themselves, the soldiers are right to grant Jesus a crimson robe, he who is indeed of noble blood and a victor in war, a monarch triumphant and glorious. For he is the Son of God, Christus Rex, Dominus Deus Sabaoth, ruler of the universe. It is he, the Lord God of Hosts, who led the army of victorious angels against Satan's legions at the beginning of time. It is he who will in the next twenty-four hours harrow hell and liberate the Patriarchs of the Old Testament, defeating Satan a second time. And he will vanquish Satan and Antichrist a third time, then at Doomsday, in majesty, he shall come to judge the quick and the dead. Thus Christ is not only a ruler, a prince of the noblest blood; he is also a military commander, the most victorious of all soldiers. And it is because of his aristocratic, military heritage that, more than any king in the universe, he deserves to wear royal crimson. The irony, the paradox, of the Christian faith derives from the situation that God becomes incarnate to save man, that a seeming carpenter's son in Palestine is that God, and that his obscure life and works, recounted in demotic Greek, are the most important, noble exploits of all time.

Red is also the color of Christ's blood, shed for us, which becomes the wine of the Eucharist, "ton jus precieux." The Speaker begs that the royal purple fill his head (make him drunk with love) and distill a thousand purple winelike tears. His tears will be purple (red) in that they reflect the purple of Christ's robe, for the Speaker is a witness to the Passion. They will be red because in his passion the Speaker imitates Christ's Passion; he also suffers and in his suffering shall weep tears of blood. Thus also his tears of imitative passion will physically reflect, as in a mirror, Christ's physical blood, the blood dripping down his face from the crown of thorns. And, last of all, red is associated with poetry, for, according to the Speaker, "Du sang trait de mes yeux j'ensanglante ces Carmes." This means that his songs are bloodied by the blood-tears he sheds and that, literally, his weeping disfigures the paper on which he writes. Also blood from his eyes and the Holy Blood of the Savior provide inspiration, indeed are the subject of this meditation. For ink on paper can symbolize the congealed blood on Christ's sweet white flesh. So purple juice shall be the ink the Speaker as poet, as implied author, uses to compose his songs.

La Ceppède's tercets develop the motif of *Agnus Dei*. Since Christ is the Lamb of God, who takest away the sins of the world, *qui tollis peccata mundi*, his red cloak can be imagined as sins that Jesus literally carries away, bearing them (it) on his back. Red, again, is the appropriate color, especially for sins of passion—violence or lust—hence in English the figure of the "scarlet woman" and the title of Hawthorne's *The Scarlet Letter*. Sins of passion derive from the flame of violence or lust in the heart; therefore, the Speaker refers to his own "rouges pechez" and their flamelike aspects, "brindelles des abysmes," sins that, as sparks of fire, can launch a conflagration, burning his own soul and casting it into hell, his sins envisaged as the cause of the suffering by fire—by violence and lust—that he will endure for eternity.

However, Christ is not only the Lord of Hosts, the general of heaven who conquers violence; he is the gentle Lamb of God, whose charity, *caritas*, conquers our lust, *concupiscentia*. His love for us is red, the color of divine charity. Red is the color of his body and blood, the body and blood of the lamb willingly sacrificed to save mankind. Thus he offers us in the sacrament of the Mass his body and blood (*Hic est corpus meum . . . hoc est calix sanguinis mei . . .*), in order to grant us his peace (*Dona nobis pacem*). The Speaker evokes in poetic terms Christ's absolute incarnation and redemption, that man's sins are not only borne by Christ, but that he, as man, takes them unto himself: The robe and his flesh are one; the robe becomes his flesh, just as his flesh becomes our flesh, because he is God-Man, the Son of Man, and because we devour his divine Lamb's flesh and blood in the Eucharist.

Christ is an epic warrior and a god of love, the Lord of Hosts and the Prince of Peace. In this text he is mocked and humiliated, yet he conquers the powers of the world, the flesh, and the devil through the red flame of charity. Red is his victory in war and love, in *militia* and *amor*. The formal envelope of the text is a sonnet, a genre of Italian origin that replaced the older, indigenous lyric forms (*ballade, rondeau,* for that matter the *grand chant courtois*) but, like them, was associated with the poetry of love, specifically *fin' amor*. Since this is a song of divine love, Christ's charity, it also assumes heroic status and is worthy of *sermo gravis*. Indeed, *Les Théorèmes* as a total work of art proves to be an epic, sublime recounting of the sublimest events in the history of the universe. However, because these sublime events are also humble, having occurred to an alleged carpenter's son in Palestine, it is appropriate that they take the form of a sonnet sequence, not the *poème heroïque*, a sonnet sequence where charity replaces lechery and the poet's own imitation of the Passion replaces other versions of desire.

As in the text by Sponde, the Speaker plays a role; as with Sponde, his role is as stylized, as universal, as the matter he recounts. He is of course the implied author, in this case a lyric and epic poet offering his talent to the cause. On the one hand, he purports to be an eye-witness to the Crucifixion in the year A.D. 33; he is also the contemporary of his implied readers, his public in the early seventeenth century. Thus in his own voice the Speaker participates in the typological process: Typologically or allegorically he witnesses Christ's passion and at the same time he exists centuries later, morally or tropologically, as a Baroque French Christian. He imitates Christ's passion in that he suffers with and for Jesus, he suffers emotionally and in his flesh, he seeks salvation by imitating the Savior in pain as well as joy. And by so doing, he serves as a bridge between Christ and his implied readers. He is a witness, a prophet, a Christ-sufferer, and a mortal like the rest of us. His persona can mediate between us and the Savior; his physical tears inscribe God's physical and spiritual ones. By and through his rhetoric, focalization, and privileged voice, the mysteries of the Passion are filtered. Thus, as mind and senses, as reasoner and sufferer, as preacher and man, he speaks to Christ, to the Holy Blood, and to us, manipulating us, molding our responses and beliefs, causing us to relive the Passion. Following the Ignation pattern of devotion,[10] this highly skilled preacher brings us to composition of place by imagination (first quatrain), to analysis and reflection by intellect (first tercet), and to colloquy (affective prayer) and resolve by the will (second quatrain and second tercet). His is an intellectual and emotional text, a poem of war and love, whose purpose, within the tradition of Christian apologetics and classical rhetoric, is to please and instruct us, to create poetry and to create in our soul the desire to lead a truly Christian life.

All three texts illustrate the functioning of Christian verse prior to the Romantic age and the coming of Symbolism. Such verse is profoundly intertextual: permeated with textual and thematic references to the Bible and to writings of the Church. Typological and allegorical structures predominate. This poetry stakes out a claim against the secular tradition, setting itself in antithesis to or proclaiming its superiority over the secular. The figure of the author plays a central role as lover, preacher, and witness, appealing to the reader-audience and to God or Mary, acting as a voice and bridge or bond from the secular to the sacred, from the reader-audience to God. Last of all, the mood is largely one of self-confidence, of complicity with the public, for writer and reader exist within a common culture and share common values: the faith of their land, the faith of the Ages.

One final question: Is it necessary for the reader to share the poet's beliefs, to accept what he says? In other words, for Christian verse to be appreciated today, must the reader be Christian? What is the exact relationship between the poet and his public concerning doctrine, those passionately held ideas that the committed poet wishes to inculcate?

On the one hand, it is certain that Turold, Rutebeuf, and Gautier de Coinci, Sponde, Chassignet, and La Ceppède, Corneille, Boileau, and Racine, assumed as a matter of course that their audience was Christian. As Christian poets, to the extent that they were Christian poets, they sought to illustrate and propagate Christian doctrine. It would never have occurred to them that atheists or infidels might enjoy their work for esthetic reasons only, and they would probably be abashed at the thought that their teachings failed, that the specifically didactic aspect of their work, for them the most important, is the one of least interest to posterity.

On the other hand, it is a truth of modern criticism that the author's intentions determine neither our reading of a specific text nor, even more, our understanding of a genre, period, or mode. Eliot himself distinguishes between philosophical belief and poetic assent, between Dante's faith as a man and as a poet.[11] We can surely indulge in temporary poetic suspension of disbelief, captivated by the text, acting within its poetic universe, whatever our personal philosophical commitments happen to be. A traditional faith demands sympathetic understanding and a form of assent even when we do not accept it in confessional terms. It is as much a question of knowledge and ignorance as of faith and disbelief. As for the Christian tradition in the West, for one to reject it merely because one happens not to be Christian is to reject the foundations of our culture out of hand.

From this perspective, can we not put on the same footing all passionately committed writing, whether religious or political in nature, sacred or secular, divinely or humanly inspired? It is an error for critics to condemn authors because they do not share their philosophy: for Communists or atheists to denigrate Claudel, for Catholics or monarchists to reject Aragon. The ideal, in a civilized society, is for readers to read, enjoy, profit from, and exalt Protestants (d'Aubigné, Gerhardt, Milton), Catholics (Turold, Dante, Calderón), and atheists (Lucretius, Neruda, Aragon), poets on the Left (Jean de Meun, Voltaire, Hugo, Mayakovsky, Eluard, Aimé Césaire) and on the Right (the singers of *geste*, Dante, Ronsard, Claudel, George, and Pound). One does not have to be Florentine and Catholic to understand the *Commedia* or a member of the Party to love Brecht and Gorky.

This does not mean that the writer's ideology is to be considered irrelevant to our appreciation of his work or that we prize it for its form alone. Great committed poets are great because of, not in spite of, their commitment. Faith provides them with the inspiration to be great. Because of it they arrive at a super-truth, a super-reality, at insights into the human condition and the divine essence that transcend their own immediate conscious reasons for writing and ours for reading.

6

THE PUBLIC

The poet himself is seen as a sublime and/or pathetic creator, alone, standing in opposition to society. He is an outsider, alienated, persecuted, misunderstood.

The above words express the Romantic and Symbolist attitude concerning the poet's relationship to society in general and to his public, readers of poetry, in particular. A number of publications insist upon the "crise de la poésie" in contemporary France, that, at this moment, even though a good fifty thousand individuals in the Hexagon write verse, it is verse for an elite; it is not popular; above all, it is not published, not sold, and not read. Despite efforts from radio, television, the major presses, newspapers, literary reviews, and the schools, despite encouragement from public figures and critics, poetry appears to be a lost art. Verse does not sell in a manner comparable to novels and nonfictional prose. With the exception of a few names—Char and Bonnefoy, Aragon and Guillevic, Emmanuel and Grosjean—poets are obligated to publish at their own expense, in the equivalent of vanity presses, and their readers turn out to be largely other poets.[1]

Given this context, experts compare the contemporary scene to the age of Romanticism, underscoring the thousands and thousands of copies regularly sold by Byron, Lamartine, and Hugo. An authority on English verse claims that, for the first time, after 1830 the importance of poetry was inferior to that of prose in terms of quantity and quality of production, size and diversity of audience, and appeal to literary talent; the unique domain reserved to the muses was prestige.[2] It is probable that the identical situation occurred in France, although perhaps at a later date, after the publication of *Jocelyn* and *La Légende des*

Siècles. And, as anyone can observe upon perusing reviews in which the term *roman* encompasses that of *littérature* as a whole, today even the husk of prestige is gone. A thousand years ago, two hundred years ago, it was an honor to be a poet, and poets, along with philosophers, stood at the summit of Mount Parnassus, at the top of the esthetic or "communications" hierarchy. Today the summit has been taken over by novelists, filmmakers, actors, political journalists. Contemporary poets have slid down to the valley, if they are recognized at all.

Perhaps more significantly still, the relative scope of verse has declined over the years, a process begun long before Dickens and Balzac. At one time verse included all that was written and known, all that people sought to remember: myths, magic, prayers, ritual, legends, tales of heroism, annals, chronicles, wisdom literature, and *textes de circonstance;* that is, all that was scientific, didactic, and sacred, all that dealt with birth, marriage, death, praise, blame, victory, defeat, genealogy, and the divine. In the course of the ages much of the poetic domain was handed over to prose. Slowly but surely the latter occupied subjects, genres, areas, and modes at one time exclusively poetic. In France great prose fictions (the *Lancelot-Grail Cycle,* the *Prose Tristan*), the first encyclopedist in the vernacular (Brunetto Latini), the prose chroniclers (Villehardouin, Robert de Clari), date from the thirteenth century. Prose biography dates from the beginning of the fourteenth century (Joinville), as does the first great travel literature (Marco Polo). In the sixteenth century we find great writers of ideas in prose (Calvin and Montaigne, preceded, it is true, by Gerson, c. 1400). In the seventeenth and eighteenth centuries appear truly great prose comedy (Molière, Marivaux, Beaumarchais) and *moraliste* satire (Cyrano, La Bruyère, La Rochefoucauld, Voltaire, Diderot); in the eighteenth century, bourgeois drama (Diderot); in the nineteenth century, prose tragedy (Hugo, Musset), the epic in prose (Ballanche, Quinet), and "prose poems" (A. Bertrand, Baudelaire, Rimbaud). Thus the entire range of medieval-Renaissance verse—encompassing epic and romance, tragedy and comedy, the didactic, meditative, satirical, and pastoral—has been invaded by prose, with a result that, today, for the general reader, for most professors, and for most poets, poetry means only the brief personal lyric, a genre of secondary importance in the history of verse.

In addition—and this is perhaps the major difference between the poet-public nexus of the past and that of the present—the tradition of French and European verse extending from the *Song of Roland* to Goethe or, at the latest, Hugo assumes a natural, organic relationship between the poet and his public, just as poetry itself is rooted in and grows from the lexicon, syntax, diction, and intonation of courtly idiomatic speech. The poet and his public are in intimate contact, and the traditional classical-Christian culture presupposes a symbiotic bond, indeed a fusion, that includes the poet, his public, a common language, and a literary tradition shared by poet and public alike. In this context the tradition, nourished by study of the classics and by the propagation of Christian belief, both performed in the schools and including, among other things, a common fund of theme, motif, topic, and myth, a common heritage of metaphor, allegory, typology, and rhetoric, contributes the frame for literary production, dissemination, and consumption.

Therefore, people are mistaken when they claim that a hiatus has always existed between great poets and the readers of their own generation, or when they posit that critics have always failed to appreciate contemporary authors.[3] These are modern phenomena and modern problems. Similarly, it is a historical error that literature enjoyed a mass public prior to the invention of printing, then lost its public with the shift from an oral to a written culture heralded by the Renaissance. This theory is similar to the one according to which the very notion of literature came into being with the bourgeoisie in the fourteenth century; therefore, pre-fourteenth-century texts such as the *Song of Roland* ought not to be considered literature at all.[4]

In point of fact, medieval letters are no more and no less rhetorical, artistic, literary, and "elitist" than is French literature as a whole. Certain genres, especially the *chanson de geste,* derive from an earlier oral-vernacular tradition, and popular legend no doubt contributed to Arthurian romance and the *Roman de Renart* beast epic. The formulaic style of *chansons de geste* indicates that these texts are the reworking of material once composed and transmitted orally, which retains the archaic style of the original and serves as an aid to recitation. In other words, the epic is a highly stylized, self-conscious genre that in the past derived from an oral style and still willfully imitates it. Furthermore, all medieval literature is oral in its "consumption"; it was meant to be sung, chanted, or read aloud. Aside from this, the *chanson de geste,* like the romance, the beast epic, the fabliau, and the lyric, was composed by a trouvère or a minstrel. Although based on legend and imitating what was recognized to be an oral style from the past, it appears in the form that has come down to us, in the manuscript collections, as a structured, composed, esthetic work of art in the highest sense of the term, a work of art consigned to parchment, with a unique structure, psychology, thought, even imagery and tone. And highly stylized or hermetic verse, whether it be the *trobar ric* and *trobar clus* of the troubadours or the formalism and aureate diction of the Rhétoriqueurs, is as prevalent in the Middle Ages as in all more recent epochs prior to Mallarmé.

Trouvères must be distinguished from the jongleurs who recited their works, even though some trouvères were also jongleurs and vice-versa. We know next to nothing about the lives of early masters such as Chrétien de Troyes, Gautier d'Arras, Jean Renart, and Guillaume de Lorris. What little we do know, however, confirms that they had a clerical education and were influenced by classical *auctores* (the twelfth century is the *aetas ovidiana*) and contemporary treatises on rhetoric, and that they often dedicated their works to the leading provincial nobility, sometimes to kings and queens. In the later Middle Ages we find striking cases such as Guillaume de Machaut, friend and confidant of princes, offered a series of ecclesiastical livings culminating in a canonry at Reims, and Alain Chartier, royal functionary and ambassador extraordinary—both men either adulated or attacked within their lifetime as *poëtes,* in their function as men of letters.

In the Middle Ages the various genres, modes, and styles, composed for divergent publics, embody or give voice to divergent mentalities and ideologies. A text expresses less the trouvère's personal bias than the attitudes of a social group. One such mentality, the best known perhaps, is clerical: It is to be found in saints' lives, in sermons, in scriptural commentary and didactic literature generally; it is present in the religious theater, in the *Song of Roland,* and in grail romances. There is no doubt that religious orders in the cloisters, and the secular clergy outside, were responsible for the greater quantity of Anglo-Norman literature; the situation on the Continent differs in degree, not in essence. However, the clerical is not the only medieval attitude or, in vernacular letters, necessarily the dominant one. No one truly familiar with medieval France can claim that all serious medieval literature praises *caritas* and condemns *concupiscentia.*

The normal situation was for a clerical or clerically trained trouvère to write for the feudal aristocracy, giving expression to and reflecting its worldview. The feudal-aristocratic ideology is to be found, first of all, in the *chanson de geste,* where the primary concern is to exalt martial glory and the concept of lineage, and to scorn monks, merchants, and councillors of peasant extraction. Epics belonging to the Cycle of Rebel Barons reflect intracultural tensions within medieval society, specifically a *crise de conscience* in the aristocracy. A commonplace of sociological criticism states that, in the words of Lukács, "the division between the personal individual and the class individual, the accidental nature of the conditions of life for the individual, appears only with the emergence of class, which is itself a product of the *bourgeoisie.*"[5] It is my

belief that consciousness of class and objective class struggle first appeared in the vernacular much earlier than Lukács imagines, and that
its concrete manifestation, although brought about partially by the emergence of a middle class, occurred within the aristocracy. In the course
of the twelfth century the Capetian monarch, always suzerain and ultimate master of his realm *de jure*, began to establish de facto control as
well. He seized the land of feuding barons, imposed the king's justice in
regional disputes, and sent his *familiares* throughout the realm. For the
nobility, the increase in royal power was a hated innovation and viola-
tion of long-standing rights, a misuse of authority placing society in
jeopardy. Meanwhile, for the first time the rising bourgeoisie strove to
obtain a measure of sovereignty in its affairs. Most important towns in
northern France were declared independent communes in the twelfth
and thirteenth centuries. Often the king and burghers worked together, allies in their common struggle against the barons. The nobility's influence went into a relative eclipse. This second feudal period
represents a moment of crisis in the ranks of the aristocracy, a time
when they consciously or unconsciously sensed that for the first time
since Charlemagne they were no longer the dominant force in society.

Certain poets, those who composed the epics of revolt (*Girart de Roussillon, Raoul de Cambrai, Garin le Lorrain, La Chevalerie Ogier, Renaud de
Montauban*), strove to come to grips with the malaise of their society.
They portray a situation in which a king is weak, cowardly, tyrannical,
and readily swayed by traitors. He prefers his favorites to the barons of
the realm. Disinherited, insulted, with no place to go, no crusade to
distract their energies, the nobles are forced into rebellion or civil war.
Although selfish, vindictive barons are criticized as much as the king,
the author does take the side of the aristocracy; and the poor, exiled
count, who in the end wins (back) prerogatives and land, is perhaps a
projection of the landless petty nobility, the *povres bachelers*, whose aspirations are not at all the same as those of the great barons and the king.
The enthusiasm and spontaneity that it was possible to idealize in *La
Chanson de Roland* become dangerous, if not irresponsible, in the context of a more complex national society. The valor, so prized in older
texts, can only be exercised against one's own people. And good in the
individual becomes a social curse; indeed, individual and group interests enter into conflict.

The solutions arrived at by the trouvères are more than a little ambiguous. In most of these texts the rebel yields to the king even though he
is in the right, then sets out on a crusade or pilgrimage to the Holy
Land. He fails because the ultimate lesson of the *chanson de geste* is one
of order and harmony, an all-inclusive peace that goes beyond individ-

ual, family, and feudal honor to preach submission to authority. Perhaps the trouvères understood that an ideal past is neither the present nor the future, and that reality and history lay with the king, not with the barons. Even in *Raoul de Cambrai* and the *Lorrains* cycle, although the emperor is humiliated, his life and office remain sacrosanct. None of the rebels could have dreamed of abolishing the kingship, assassinating the reigning monarch or even forcing him to abdicate. Rebellion results in no program for reform. The barons' alienation is stated as a fact; the trouvère provides no easy answers because there are none.

Another response to the barons' dilemma occurs with the rise of *fin' amor*, in the lyric and, above all, in Arthurian romance. For example, fictions by Chrétien de Troyes depict a world of escape, of wish-fulfillment different from that of *chansons de geste*. However, Chrétien, Béroul, Thomas, and their followers wrote for approximately the same public as did the epic trouvères, and they provide a no less significant perspective on the problems of the age. Arthurian romance probably expressed the aspirations of the Angevin rulers of England, was meant to serve as a counterweight to epics that proclaimed the glory of the reigning Capetian House of France. And we have reason to believe that the *roman* also supported the petty nobility, young, landless knights and squires (*bachelers*) alienated from the feudal world. In these poems we find a generous but inactive King Arthur who, bursting with largesse, delegates power and glory to his barons. These are relatively poor but gently born knights-errant who set out alone on quests, right wrongs, and triumph over obstacles. In this fundamentally reactionary vision of life, the knights destroy wicked new *costumes*, marry heiresses, and become kings or princes in turn. Because of the young men, unattached *juvenes* free for a life of adventure, the realm achieves spiritual and moral splendor. They are responsible for and are integrated into a new aristocratic class, an *ordo* created by God in which all knights, rich and poor, participate as equals. Chrétien glorifies the Arthurian myth, projecting onto it the aspirations of a threatened social class. He resolves intracultural tensions by creating a world of fantasy.

Thus ritualized action and popular myth are exploited by poets who exalt the nobility, who help it claim status on the basis of a highly ornate code of chivalry founded on artificial distinctions of birth and breeding, enforced by law, and nourished by a literature of escape and wish-fulfillment. However, whereas Chrétien arrives at a kind of synthesis, wherein love and prowess reinforce each other, in which the private life (*fin' amor*) and the public life (chivalry) contribute to the establishment of the ideal *ordo*, in succeeding generations the synthesis breaks down, and the *ordo* loses its ideological hold on the public. Two new responses are offered: either another pattern of escape, this time elaborated in terms of religious abnegation and mysticism (the various grail romances), or a more optimistic fiction no less "fantaisiste" (the *roman d'aventures*), in which the public and private domains are largely separate and the protagonist undergoes no inner development. Among the characteristics of such fiction are an imposed series of happy endings, an idealized Oepidal pattern of displaced wish-fulfillment (the *juvenis* triumphing over the *senior*), and a preference for marriage at court as opposed to adulterous trysts with a fay.

These thirteenth-century romances are in no way problematic: They avoid posing serious ideological or ethical questions, and idealism and abnegation are significant by their absence. On the contrary, they revel in marvels and adventures, rapidity of incident, a reasonable dosage of sex, and, once again, the happy ending. In the late *chansons de geste* also, neither king nor rebel baron is now to be blamed, since guilt is projected onto scapegoats: inner scapegoats, the lineage of traitors, who play the role of evil councillors; or external scapegoats, the Saracens. Epic action, launched by these embodiments of evil, permits the innocent protagonist to lead a life of adventure and to acquire the highest reputation for prowess. In both epic and romance the ultimate is to tell a story, to entertain the public, not to instruct it. Thirteenth-century literature has become the recounting of adventures, and the best recounting often implies an interlace pattern with two, three, five, or a dozen heroes, where favorite plot increments are repeated again and again for the sheer pleasure of storytelling and indulging in the formal pattern of narrative. At best we find the charm, elegance, sociability, and serenity typical of Adenet le Roi; at its worst, it is what Curtius has called *Unterhaltungsliteratur* in the manner of Dumas and Sardou (for our generation, say, television serials and science fiction in the cinema), produced to satisfy the public's craving for distraction.[6]

But whether we deal with fearless, probing works of art such as *Raoul de Cambrai* and *La Mort le roi Artu* or a more superficial, trivial *Unterhaltungsliteratur,* whether it be the classical perfection of Chrétien de Troyes or the exuberantly baroque *Prose Lancelot,* the public is the same: the feudal aristocracy. The patronage system, which extends well into the nineteenth century, began in the twelfth and was the most pervasive means of subsidization for writers in the Middle Ages. The influence of provincial courts and the aristocratic-clerical dominance in literary matters extended into the reign of Louis XIV. In the beginning the new vernacular literature—epic, romance, historiography, the lyric, satire—was encouraged not by the kings of France or, for the most part, the great ecclesiastical figures, secular and monastic, but by the counts of Poitiers, Blois, Champagne, and, above all, the dukes of Normandy, counts of Anjou, and Francophone kings of England and their entourage. Such literature was designed for those members of the aristocratic class who strove for culture and were eager to learn. First the troubadours and trouvères, then later poets such as Jean de Meun, contributed to the raft of translations from Latin, to the dissemination of lay wisdom, to the development of a rhetorical, even philosophical use of the vernacular. They even vulgarized classical myth and a certain Greco-Roman attitude toward life, death, and nature. Chrétien, Guillaume de Lorris, and Jean de Meun embody that awakening of humanism, rebirth of interest in Antiquity, and joyful lust for life that mark so much of the twelfth and thirteenth centuries.

As one ideal, poets proposed the *miles clericus,* a master of *fortitudo* and *sapientia,* the sort of ideal warrior and lawgiver or judge capable of benefiting from the *translatio imperii et studii* from Antiquity, the transferal from Greece and Rome to France of political power and of culture, poetry, and the life of the spirit. The *miles clericus* serves in turn to enhance the court, the ideal community of good people, refuge of an elite, that embodies the aspirations of society. The court thus contains the epitome of chivalry, learning, and martial glory, is a community where heroes are rendered immortal through fame and honor.

Although literature of the court evolves over the succeeding centuries, its essence remains unchanged. For example, the great seventeenth-century pastoral romance, *l'Astrée,* presents affinities with its thirteenth-century counterparts. The nobility renounces political life and social ambition in order to obtain an illusive, intangible aristocracy of the heart, based upon the capacity to love, embodied in and reinforced by sublimation and moral-ethical constraint. Similarly, the plays of the Baroque illustrate the last flowering of a feudal mentality, the striving of aristocrats to defy fate, to exalt their egos at the expense of others, to express their pride, authority, and rebellion in the face of central authority. In Corneille's best-known dramas Eros is joined to reason and harmonized with the will; as in the courtly romance, love and honor stand together, each impossible without the other. Like Lancelot and Gauvain, like Roland and Girart, Corneille's heroes believe in the values of duty, sacrifice, and chivalry. They shine with glory. These aristocrats are profoundly *généreux,* that is, of noble blood and caste. Their *vertu* can be defined as manliness, grandeur of heart, and the resolution to become and remain masters, not slaves.

Therefore, we can say that the aristocrat-oriented court situation is not peculiarly medieval but a universal mode of literature and life that was to dominate classical-Christian Western culture up to the age of

Louis XIV and Saint-Simon, even, in its way, up to the age of the Prince of Wales and Charles Swann. Indeed, it was granted supreme legitimacy when the primary function of patronage was assumed by the crown. Among patrons of the arts in general and of French poetry especially, we find, under the ancien régime, the Valois kings from Louis XII to Henry III inclusive, Marguerite de Navarre, Marguerite de Valois, the Bourbon line from Louis XIV to Louis XVI, and foreign potentates such as Maximilian of Austria, Charles V, Philip II, Mary, Queen of Scots, Elizabeth, Catherine the Great, and Frederick the Great. For centuries the court was considered a center for the arts and for love, the latter envisaged as art, game, and spectacle, as compliment, pretext for speech, and literary convention. Literature celebrates the court's feasts and festivities, its rites and rituals, its births, marriages, and deaths, its departures and homecomings. It is a mirror that reflects the ideals that men wished to live up to. It proclaims the glory of the Prince and his lieutenants, his ladies and their suitors; it commemorates the natural rhythm of the year and the social rhythm of "the World."

The place of the poet—as likely as not low-born and of clerical formation—in this courtly world remains problematic, full of tension and ambiguity. In texts from the late Middle Ages to the fall of the ancien régime the Speaker will often adopt a stance of Horatian friendship, and his poem will, overtly or implicitly, be concerned with class relations, specifically those of the implied author with his aristocratic patron. A situation is created in which the Speaker, often an obtrusive narrator-witness or even narrator-protagonist, is admitted into the company of the high nobility and, because of his tact and wisdom and their graciousness, permitted to become their friend. This convention includes Guillaume de Machaut, Froissart, Jean Lemaire de Belges, Marot, Ronsard, Saint-Amant, La Fontaine, and Voltaire, to cite some of the most eminent figures who span the period from 1300 to 1789. The artist—a real or metaphoric cleric—seeks to establish a bond with his secular aristocratic master, the *miles dominans,* through flattery and self-denigration, thus to achieve through rhetorical manipulation that synthesis of *fortitudo et sapientia,* Mars and Apollo, *chevaliers et clercs,* which served as a courtly ideal. Such a stance demands an unusually complex and sophisticated modulation of voice and manipulation of the reader-audience.

One way of attaining, or hoping to attain, the desired complicity between Speaker and implied reader-audience was for the poet to adopt an aristocratic stance, to praise, not denigrate, his projected authorial self and to denigrate, not praise, the audience, a *profanum vulgus* incapable of appreciating the works of art set before it. In order to do this, he has to divide the public into two categories, the genuine *vulgus,* which includes rivals and immediate predecessors, and the elite audience of princes and high court officers, those capable of appreciating his art and willing to patronize it. Such was the attitude of certain troubadours and of the Rhétoriqueurs. It became a dominant motif in the Renaissance, with du Bellay and Ronsard making a claim to high style, a *sermo gravis et durus* in opposition to the *sermo mollis* of their purportedly less-gifted predecessors. For the Pléiade, poetry was conceived as difficult, serious, and committed, derived from lofty classical models and adhering to stern classical precept. The poet sets himself in opposition to his public, the *vates* against the *vulgus.*

A divergent stance exhibits the "esthetics of negligence" (see chapter 2) to be found in prose masters such as Rabelais and Montaigne, and in Ronsard (for the *Discours*), du Bellay, d'Aubigné, Théophile de Viau, Saint-Amant, and La Fontaine. According to this notion, the aristocrat partakes of life and creates in a spirit of enthusiasm, in contrast to the dull, low-class, pedantic court poetaster, whose work can only be the result of labor and adherence to rigid, artificial rules. The "negligent poet" is spontaneous (he breaks the rules), consubstantial (form matches content), and irresponsible. In the case of d'Aubigné, writing *Les Tragiques,* the narrating persona makes a special truth-claim by declaring that the poem was composed on the field of battle. Feigning to apologize for the text's rough exterior, in fact d'Aubigné establishes a bond with the implied reader, claiming the author-narrator to be a captain as well as a poet, therefore an epic hero in his own right, who struggles against the world, the flesh, and the devil and who therefore becomes one of the heroes, perhaps *the* hero, of his own story. Significantly, the Romantics—Lamartine, Hugo, and Musset especially— adopted the negligent persona, took it seriously, and presented it to their public as the quintessence of personal sincerity and authenticity.

In spite of a current of scorn for the nobleman who wields the pen, not the sword, complementing the esthetics of negligence is a third category: a tradition of the aristocratic poet writing for his peers, his own aristocratic public. As with all writers, such literary activity is determined by considerations of rhetorical and social decorum. The Medievals and the men of the Renaissance distinguished between genres, establishing a hierarchy according to level of style and subject matter. In *De Vulgari eloquentia* the courtly lyric is attributed the highest place in the hierarchy, perhaps because, unlike *chansons de geste* and *romans courtois,* it had indeed been cultivated by the high nobility. The genuinely aristocratic literary kinds, those practiced by writers of gentle birth, were the *grand chant courtois* and the prose chronicle or memoirs, the latter deriving from the nobleman's career as warrior and lawgiver. Among the troubadours writing in Oc and trouvères in the north, we find a host of lesser nobility too numerous to list, and some of the very highest figures: Guilhem, Count of Poitou and Duke of Aquitaine; Thibaut, Count of Champagne and King of Navarre; King Richard the Lion-Hearted; Geoffroy, Count of Brittany; and several kings of Aragon; also Jaufre Rudel, Lord of Blaye; Rambaut, Lord of Orange; Beatritz, Countess of Die; Raimon Jordan, Huon d'Oisy, Conon de Béthune, Hugues de Berzé, the Chastellan of Couci, the Vidame de Chartres, Beaumanoir, and others. The two greatest court poets of the fifteenth century were Charles, Duke of Orléans, and René d'Anjou, Count of Provence and titular King of the Two Sicilies. Among lyric poets of gentle blood in the Renaissance-Baroque period we can name, to cite the more notable, Marguerite de Navarre, Pontus de Tyard, du Bellay, Ronsard, Baïf, Belleau, du Bartas, d'Aubigné, Sponde, La Ceppède, Mage de Fiefmelin, d'Urfé, Malherbe, Racan, Brébeuf, Scudéry, and du Bois-Hus; in the eighteenth century, Grécourt, Lefranc de Pompignan, Bernis, Saint-Lambert, Rulhière, Boufflers, Florian, Fontanes, and Parny. And with Romanticism the motif of the poet-aristocrat endures, in the persons of Lamartine, Vigny, and Musset, followed by Maurice de Guérin, Laprade, Banville, Heredia, and André de Guerne. In this category should also be included princes of the Church. Some ecclesiastics turned out to be poets; some poets were rewarded by their secular patrons with livings and rose in the hierarchy. Among leading writers in French we must cite cardinals du Perron and Bernis; bishops Héroët, Pontus de Tyard, Amyot, Bertaut, and Godeau; and, among those rewarded with canonries or other important benefices, from the fourteenth century on, Machaut, Froissart, Molinet, Lemaire de Belges, du Bellay, Ronsard, Baïf, Desportes, Vauquelin des Yveteaux, Régnier, Boisrobert, Chapelain, Boileau, Chaulieu, and Delille.

This aristocratic literature was a literature of the provinces, patronized by and produced for the provincial courts. As we have seen, in the early northern French Middle Ages the preponderant lines of force focus on the counts of Anjou, Blois, Champagne, and Flanders, the Dukes of Normandy, and of course the Anglo-Norman and Angevin kings of England. Central to the flowering of verse in Occitan are the courts of Poitou, the Limousin, Auvergne, Toulouse, Narbonne, Montpellier, Provence, and Montferrat, and the royal patronage of Aragon and Castile. In the later Middle Ages the Valois dynasty plays an important role—Charles V especially was a patron of the arts—but provincial centers remain strong. The courts of Jean de Luxembourg, King of Bohemia, his son Wenceslas of Brabant, Philippa of Hainaut, Louis and Charles d'Orléans, Jean de Berry, Gui de Blois, Gaston Phébus, comte de Foix, and René d'Anjou, comte de Provence—for that matter the two-centuries'-long existence of Burgundy as an independent state—testify to the role of provincial centers in supporting creativity in the arts. The heart of French literature in the fifteenth century beats in Dijon and Blois, not Paris, just as in the twelfth and thirteenth centuries it flourished in Troyes, Arras, Angers, Poitiers, and London, not the Ile de France.

The Renaissance-Baroque era accentuates the pattern. French writers take pride in their provincial origins and connections: Rabelais from near Chinon in Touraine; Marot from Cahors in Quercy; Scève and Louise Labé from Lyon; Ronsard the Vendômois; du Bellay the Angevin; Montaigne the one-time mayor of Bordeaux from Périgord; du Bartas, Monluc, and Théophile de Viau from Gascony; Sponde from the Basque country; Rapin, d'Aubigné, and Mage de Fiefmelin from Poitou; La Ceppède, Laugier de Porchères, and Lortigue from Provence; Lazare de Selve and Schelandre from Lorraine; Chassignet from Besançon; Saint-Amant, Rotrou, and Corneille from Rouen. From the region of Caen (la Basse-Normandie) alone we find Gringore, Lefèvre de la Boderie, Desportes, du Perron, Bertaut, Montchrestien, Vauquelin de La Fresnaye, Vauquelin des Yveteaux, Malherbe, Boisrobert, Brébeuf, Sarasin, and Segrais, although most of these did move on to the capital. The Occitan Renaissance occurred at Pau and Nérac—the court of Henry of Navarre—and in Aix, Marseille, and Toulouse. During Malherbe's period of glory, from 1600 on, poetry witnessed an extraordinary resurgence, much of the best coming from the provinces, with important verse collections published in Rouen, Caen, Poitiers, Toulouse, and Lyon.[7]

It is in the seventeenth century, during the reigns of Louis XIII and above all Louis XIV, that we discover for the first time a number of Parisian bourgeois authors, the most notable being Cyrano de Bergerac, Molière, and Boileau, working alongside their colleagues from Normandy, Champagne, and Provence, the latter obliged to quit their native regions for the capital in order to succeed in the world of letters. In Louis XIV's world the poet writes not for a provincial aristocratic court but for *la cour et la ville,* that is, for the Sun King himself and for the high Parisian bourgeoisie. Literature and culture are centralized. Louis XIV shimmers at the center. Because of a system of pensions and esthetic control exercised by the Académie, he alone dispenses literary success, and all literature celebrates his glory. As the chosen deputy of

God on earth, responsible for the prestige of his century and his people, as a sort of demigod in his own right, Louis becomes the ultimate hero in literature. The seventeenth century, then, and specifically the reign of Louis XIV mark the dividing line between the old classical-Christian world, literature written by provincials for aristocratic provincial courts, and the modern world, centered in Paris, where, Parisian by birth or adoption, the writer has to please either the central government or the bourgeoisie.

The reign of Paris is ensured by the rise of the *salon,* an ubiquitous institution extending from the time of Madame de Rambouillet to that of Madame Necker. With the *salon,* control of literary and cultural matters is assumed by *le monde,* a high society of ladies and courtiers. This opening-out of the public, which now includes the middle class—a literate middle class becoming slowly but surely the dominant force in society—explains in part the success of enlightened ideas in the Age of Voltaire and the rise of the novel, which replaces epic, tragedy, and the high lyric as *the* genre to embody literariness. Thus Pierre de Ronsard, Vendômois, yields to Jean-Marie Arouet, Parisien, *dit* Voltaire. Admittedly, Monsieur de Voltaire and, for that matter, the son of Bonaparte's General Hugo desperately, agonizingly wanted to be treated like nobility, to be noble. Regardless of the objective situation in the world of letters and in French politics, an aristocratic, provincial Catholic such as Alphonse de Lamartine remained the archetypal figure of the poet until the end of his century.

Nonetheless, underlying the rise of Romantic and post-Romantic verse we find, perhaps for the first time since the Germanic invasions, an essential change in society and therefore in the public. Voltaire and Balzac write for different worlds. In literature the nineteenth century, especially in France, is marked by the triumph of bourgeois ideology or a reaction against it. A number of writers accepted, indeed exalted, bourgeois ideals, including the myth of progress and the myth of the close, hardworking, virtuous nuclear family, what Jauss calls *la douceur du foyer.*[8] However, the majority of poets, whether of gentle blood or sons of the middle class, attacked the new bourgeoisie with ferocity, especially after 1850. Writers depended entirely upon sales, upon pleasing a relatively vast bourgeois public that had replaced the old aristocratic or royal patron. No longer grounded in a worldview based upon hierarchy, order, reason, harmony, stasis, and Christian moral and cosmological certitude, the poet turns inward, exalts the emotions, instinct, the lone individual, change, rebellion, and himself as artist. Although the public has been enlarged, the poet senses he has no public or is torn between divergent, conflicting minipublics. He exalts the past or the future while consistently downgrading the present. He no longer recognizes a social or intellectual community, common standards, classics, a canon, and rules or models. Hence *l'enfant du siècle,* followed by *le poète maudit,* myths that replace the notions of chivalry, heroism, *fin' amor,* and the poet of princes who renders his prince immortal.

Before Romanticism authors knew for whom they were writing: in the early Middle Ages, for provincial courts (Poitou, Anjou, Blois, Champagne, Flanders, Normandy); in the late Middle Ages and Renaissance, for the royal courts of France and Navarre, for Burgundy, Savoy, and Ferrara. They wrote for "persons of quality," they knew who they were, they shared their patrons' taste and beliefs, and they assumed that public acceptance was the gauge of their success. This despite censorship and the persecution of individual poets—Marot, Théophile, and Voltaire, among others—for their ideas. The object of writing verse was not to revel in private emotion but to scrutinize the human condition in its social context. This was the case in part because the creator and his reader shared a common social, intellectual, and esthetic background. Writing, reciting, and reading were social acts, the natural function of man as a political and social animal. This state of affairs stands in antithesis to that of Romanticism and the modern world, in which the poet deems himself not to be one member of the community but uniquely an individual, not a spokesman for society but an exile, martyr, or prisoner, a creator allegedly without a public, one not sure for whom he is supposed to be creating: for himself, for a few friends, or for posterity (the Happy Few).[9]

The traditional poet-public bond provides the ideal condition for the functioning of what we now call the "esthetics of reception." Although no genre, mode, or single work of art can or ought to be considered a norm, a prescriptive model to be followed at all costs, it is true that the past tradition in any genre—epic or lyric, tragedy or comedy, pastoral or satire—persists over the centuries and, in so doing, provides a complex of directives for the reader and for the author himself. All poets, however "primitive," are aware of the tradition and work within it. It is an invitation to writing within a conventional pattern that inevitably helps shape a work in progress and its interpretation by the public. Each work of art is thus perceived by author and audience alike against its generic background, adhering to a form or reacting against it. The public has a "horizon of expectations" for literary works that attract its attention. A mediocre poem, play, or novel will fulfill the public's expectations in as natural, as inoffensive a manner possible, without causing change or disturbing the public in any way. Such is the case for late epics and romances in the Middle Ages, for sonnet sequences by Desportes, for plays by Pradon and Campistron. An excessively innovative, revolutionary work will violate or disregard audience expectations so brutally that communication between the creator and his patrons proves to be impossible and the work of art disappears from purview. This is the case for much of the avant-garde, for experimental writing in the twentieth century.

The true masterpiece fulfills public expectation and stimulates and disturbs the public at the same time; it challenges and creates distance, it enlarges the public's *Erwartungshorizont* for all works that come after, so that readers' and poets' sense of the genre can never be the same, will forever have been expanded and enlarged. Examples of such successful mutations in the domain of narrative verse are *La Chanson de Roland, Tristan et Iseut,* Chrétien de Troyes' romances, the first and second *Roman de la Rose,* the *dits* of Machaut, *La Franciade, Le Lutrin, La Henriade, Jocelyn,* and *La Légende des Siècles*; for the lyric, the works of Guillaume d'Aquitaine, Bernart de Ventadorn, Thibaut de Champagne, Guillaume de Machaut, Villon, Marot, Ronsard, Malherbe, La Fontaine, Voltaire, Lamartine, Vigny, and Hugo. It is also true that, after a successful mutation, a new style will coexist with the old one, in competition for public favor: romance alongside the *chanson de geste,* Desportes alongside Ronsard, Malherbe alongside the Baroque, for that matter the *Ecole romane* alongside *Symbolisme.*

All poetry echoes older poetry, and each poet bases his work upon, derives it from, and "contains" preceding masterpieces. All poetry is more or less intertextual, and it is this intertextuality that enables the writer to interact with his public, a public familiar with the classics, whatever they may be, however we interpret them, and capable, because of that familiarity, of appreciating the new texts generated by them. Furthermore, because of these new texts, under their influence, the public also reads the classics in a reinvigorated, renewed manner. We see the troubadours through the eyes of Pound and Aragon, or Virgil through the eyes of Valéry and Broch. This is "creative misreading." We cannot avoid it, nor should we try to avoid it.

A striking example of such intertextual creation, dependent upon understanding and complicity from the public, is the phenomenon of burlesque and mock-epic endemic to France in the seventeenth and eighteenth centuries (see chapter 3). Burlesque and mock-epic do not represent a reaction against classicism or the Greco-Roman masters; on the contrary, they are an offering of love to Virgil and Ovid, Ariosto and Tasso, and can even serve to renew interest in them. Scarron, Dassoucy, Boileau, Gresset, Voltaire, and Parny are masters of literature. Their language is an intentionally stylized art form, their texts are based upon other texts, and their chosen mode adheres to strictly literary norms. An artificial genre, mock-epic was written for a public of connoisseurs, for educated people familiar with the classics and with neoclassical rules.

Thus, to take the example of *Le Lutrin,* in the age of Louis XIV Boileau mocks real people, social forces, and books. He deforms contemporary reality, viewing it from the perspective of literary convention, and deflates literary ideals by juxtaposing them with the tawdriness of ordinary people living in seventeenth-century Paris. Unlike that of Scarron and Dassoucy, his parody is not limited to any one classic, however preeminent; instead, he borrows traits from epic ancient and modern and from contemporary tragedy. *Le Lutrin* undercuts grand sentiments wherever they are to be found: in Homer, Virgil, Tasso, Chapelain, Scudéry, Corneille, and Racine. Boileau begins with a mock proposition ("Je chante les combats, et ce Prelat terrible . . .") and invocation; he writes in an appropriately elevated, chaste style, with Homeric similes; and he tells of a full-fledged, miniature War of Troy, "un second Ilion" (p. 222). More than one of Curtius's topics finds a place here, *in risu:* something never said before, inexpressibility, *fortitudo et sapientia,* the book as symbol, poetry as perpetuation and entertainment, and brevity as a stylistic ideal.

Part of the charm for well-educated readers comes from recognizing traditional epic motifs when they appear in the most unexpected places, from Boileau's ingenuity at disguising his canons and chaplains in classical dress. Council scenes take place at the refectory table, where imprecation barely triumphs over the call of the stomach. Epic heroes are reduced to the level of types in Roman comedy: the parasite (the Prelate), the *senex iratus* (the Chanter), the pedant (Alain), and the churl (Evrard). The wise counselor, say Achates or the aged Nestor, is transformed into a *dolosus servus* or *gracioso:* a valet ("le zelé Gilotin," p. 194: "le vigilant Girot," p. 206) and an old habitué of law courts. The voyage to the Underworld, to consult a sacred oracle in a no less sacred grotto (*Odyssey* 11, *Aeneid* 6), becomes a tour of the Palais de Justice. And the heroes are assailed by monsters, by hideous shadow figures from the Other World, which turn out to be an owl (a delightful reincarnation of the Bird of Athene) and the lectern itself, when, in the form of an oneiric dragon, it terrifies the sleeping Chanter (Canto 4). Although warriors undertake a night sortie, as in the *Iliad,* the *Aeneid,* the *Orlando furioso,* and the *Gerusalemme liberata,* they are armed with saw, hammer, and nails, their purpose is to move a lectern, and they are routed by the screeching of an owl. Finally, a pitched battle does occur, next to Barbin's bookshop, where the only casualties are felled with weighty romances or tomes on canon law and put to sleep by the soporific verse of Louis Le Laboureur. Thus the *fortitudo et sapientia* of ancient epic ceases to function in a modern nonaristocratic world; thus *pius Aeneas* is reembodied in selfish, materialistic clerics obsessed with the most petty of ecclesiastical prerogatives.

Like *Le Lutrin,* Voltaire's *Pucelle d'Orléans* deflates literature as well as real life.[10] *La Pucelle* undercuts traits associated with heroism and romance and the more specific epic motifs: a host of scenes, characters, and images to be found in Homer, Virgil, Honoré d'Urfé, Milton, Fénelon, Voltaire's own *Henriade* and *Temple du Goût,* and, most of all, Tasso and Chapelain. Joan of Arc and Agnes Sorel are antiheroes in the full modern sense of the term, even more so than Candide and the Huron. However, unlike his predecessors, Voltaire has in mind a particular comic model and therefore imitates Ariosto and, to a lesser extent, Tassoni and Boileau even more than he undercuts serious epic. Thus any given motif derives from and evokes to the cultivated reader sources both sublime and ridiculous, serves as parody and travesty at the same time. For example, the timid, fleeing Agnes Sorel serves as a variation both on Angelica and Erminia, while Chandos's arrogance has precedents in Rodomonte and Argante. For this reason *La Pucelle* must not be considered a mere pastiche of the *Furioso.* Unlike Ariosto, Voltaire comes at the end rather than at the beginning of a rich period of national culture. Consciously aware of his heritage, he exalts some aspects of it (Ariosto, La Fontaine) while deriding others (Tasso and Chapelain). And that which he loves is recast in a new form. He delights in demystifying a comic motif in Ariosto, exploring the reality of rape or the nefarious consequences of wearing a mask; and he scrutinizes aspects of life—sodomy, pillage—largely absent from Ariosto's world, true conditions of existence in a distant, barbaric past and hardly more glorious present. Although he retains the Italian's understanding and humane refinement, Voltaire's vision of woman, of chivalry, of the Middle Ages and its Church, are far different from Ariosto's. He uses the great Italian and honors him but for his own purposes—to create his own, uniquely Voltairean world.

Only the centuries of the past, the era of French civilization at its highest, provided the requisite conditions for travesty, burlesque, and mock-epic. In the modern period a number of writers view the masters of Antiquity with good-humored irony (Giraudoux and Anouilh, for instance), but the modern public is neither sufficiently grounded in the classics nor obsessed with classical doings, no longer possesses a homogeneous cultural tradition, to permit full-fledged parody or pastiche.

Only during the ancien régime, and to a lesser extent in the Middle Ages, do we find a relatively sizable audience of well-educated people, an elite grounded in a common culture based on Latin school texts, with a keen sense of genre, literary norms, levels of style, and decorum. Theirs was a literature of imitation and of convention, also of modernist revolt, for people were sufficiently independent to laugh at the classics yet sufficiently under their sway to love and honor them. Finally, the period that extends from Chrétien de Troyes, *Le Roman de Renart,* and Guillaume de Lorris to the age of the Rococo gave rise to a society of wit and paradox, of fashion and refinement, in which literature was a major subject of discussion, taken seriously yet, like the rest of life, considered to be a game.

It is hardly necessary to point out that the organic relationship between poet and public, the shared culture grounded in the classics, and the social game have ceased to exist for well over a century. Although the overall number of readers has increased enormously, it is divided into an elite public and a mass public. Dislocation of form corresponds to the dislocation of the modern community, the court having given way to the city. Disintegration of character, alienation, exaltation of the pathological, and a static sense of the outside world—these traits or symptoms proclaim modern man's alienation from society, even from objective reality, his loss of faith in our culture and in himself. One aspect of the problem lies in the *écart* between poet and public (and, in the case of the *nouveau roman,* between novelist and public), the fact that the public and the poet (novelist, musician, painter, sculptor) no longer share a common language, common assumptions, a common mentality. Indeed, since World War II there is some doubt as to whether Western man consciously possesses a culture at all, except in the anthropological sense of the term, that he considers superior to or the equal of other cultures. This gap between author and audience, this cultural inferiority complex, is perhaps at the same time the cause of, and the chief evidence for, *la crise de la poésie.* The *crise* then helps shape the kind of literature that is written.

A case can be made that the organic poet-public relationship of the twelfth or seventeenth centuries was also an elite phenomenon. The vast majority of Frenchmen, peasants who tilled the soil, were not oriented toward high culture. And those individuals who appreciate poetry always form a minority. In this sense today's scholars and students are not all that different from yesterday's courtiers. In addition, it is perhaps true that the pervasiveness of topical allusions in Villon and Boileau—for that matter the pervasiveness of classical myth in du Bellay and Ronsard—made these matters as hermetic for some of their readers as Rimbaud, Valéry, and Char appear to be for a number of readers today. Still, the modern writer, unlike his forebears, is torn between publics—the elite audience, the mass audience—and often financially dependent upon the mass, a vaster, more powerful force than used to be the case. Whatever the objective situation, the modern writer's anguish is real and not at all congruent with those sentiments displayed by the medieval trouvère or the Louis XIV *poète de cour*.

However one answers these questions, whatever one's prognostic or hopes for the future, it is clear that the clock cannot be turned back, that to swim against the current of history is futile, and that nostalgia for the twelfth or seventeenth centuries can never bring about a world in which Chrétien de Troyes or Jean de La Fontaine will live again or in which contemporary or future poets will function in the way that Chrétien and La Fontaine did. Nor, as Mounin and his followers have demonstrated, does it help to single out one facet of contemporary literary culture—the public, the schools, the publishers, the mass media, the poets themselves, the critics, or the spirit of the age—and blame it for our problems. Such schematization will always be wrong. Furthermore, there are many who claim that all literature, including the novel, is receding to the periphery of the "communications world," replaced by radio, television, and film, the dominant media in a McLuhan Age.

Nonetheless, several of the postulates generally held by poets, critics, and professors concerning the poet's unique genius, his authenticity, his creating a new language, his expressing a new consciousness, his insights into the ineffable, his solitude and alienation, are historically determined by and limited to the modern, not universal to the poetic experience or to culture as a whole. These postulates are related to the scorn of the elite writer for his bourgeois or mass public, one that he refuses to accept or that refuses to accept him, and to the *écart* between poet and public, the concrete manifestations of *la crise de la poésie*. That authors should write solely for other authors, that they should be unknown to all but a handful of professors or critics, is a pity. That they should intentionally cultivate obscurity for its own sake is a pity. Today's common reader does not accept the alexandrianism, allusiveness, and eccentric speech patterns and diction that since Mallarmé characterize so much of our verse. If Leavis experienced frustration over the Auden–Spender–Mac-Neice–Day Lewis–Isherwood coterie that for decades dominated the production and distribution of poetry in England, in his opinion a clique that permitted no criticism of itself,[11] what would he think of the Parisian *chapelles* that many deem responsible for *nouveau roman, nouveau nouveau roman*, structuralism, deconstructionism, and Freudian Maoism? Here the university professor, French and foreign, must bear a share of the responsibility, to the extent that criticism no longer serves as the handmaiden of artistic creation but often claims to be the mistress, and the critic or pundit influences poets, young and not so young, more than they can hope to influence him. It has been suggested that today's critics encourage, patronize, even demand a literature sufficiently abstruse that their function as exegetes will not become redundant. (This is one of the leitmotivs in Nathalie Sarraute's *Les Fruits d'Or!*) They also exalt the function of criticism to heights of prestige such that it can claim to suffice in and of itself, as a primary act of creation, no longer dependent on poems and novels. Or, as Marxists, they claim that all art is commodity and exploitation, that all culture inculcates the dominant ideology, therefore is bad. They scorn high culture as elitism and, while denying the greatness and "relevance" of the past, propose in its place the study of literary theory (their own) or of nonliterary communication (comic books, posters, film, television) or the practice of creative writing, preferably in a collective context.[12] And it is the professors who are responsible for histories of literature, student manuals, textbooks, and anthologies that shape our attitude toward poetry and determine the canon of masterpieces, those works we consider to *be* poetry.

As proof that other options are possible, one need cite only the socialist experience, specifically that of the U.S.S.R. Admittedly, the control the State and Party bring to bear on cultural matters inhibits free artistic creation; admittedly, in the Soviet Union the Academy shapes people's understanding of the past and present at least as much as do lycée or university professors in the West. Nonetheless, for what it is worth, living poets are both published and honored, and thousands of people regularly, enthusiastically attend readings. As for the past, the classics—Pushkin and Lermontov especially—are recognized as symbols of the national culture, and thousands upon thousands of citizens memorize their verse. It is convenient, since the revelation of the gulags, to downgrade everything Soviet. Nonetheless, the prestige enjoyed by poetry in Russia and the passion for poetry in the Russian people are facts that cannot be explained away by the czarist heritage or by "primitiveness" deemed endemic to the Slavic soul.

In the West the *maisons de la culture* experience proves that a potential public awaits and will respond to the right people under the right conditions. This also is a lesson to be drawn from Jean-Paul Gourévitch's survey.[13] Gourévitch recounts the enthusiastic response in the schools to the National Poetry Contest, how young people love poetry, read it with joy, and are eager to compose it on their own. An educated public exists, which buys and reads books, journals, and newspapers, is ready to buy and read poetry. Finally, as suggested in chapter 4, one specific historical event of our time did launch an up-surge of poetry: the Occupation of France and the Resistance move-ment that responded to it. There can be no doubt that from the ap-pearance of Aragon's *Le Crève-Coeur* in 1941 until well after victory poetry had attained an unprecedented stature not only with intellectu-als but with masses of the French people. Significantly, more than one observer of the literary scene, including Benjamin Péret, consider the war years and the school of Resistance poetry to be an aberration, an interlude of no importance in the development of twentieth-century letters. It will not come as a surprise to the readers of this book that I do not share Péret's views. Neither the holocaust of the 1940s nor the verse it called forth is a historical accident. Surely *Brocéliande, Jour de colère,* and *Kyrie* are as representative of our century's life and letters as is *Un Coup de dés* or *Le Cimetière marin.* A sufficient number of master-pieces were created by Aragon, Eluard, Emmanuel, Char, Frénaud, Jouve, Masson, Supervielle, Desnos, and so many others to compare favorably with any other half-decade in the history of world literature.

During the Resistance, for the first time since the age of Hugo (*Châtiments,* 1853; *l'Année terrible,* 1871), the primary function of poetry was to express a public, political voice, to be directed outwardly, toward the community. The war years brought to poets themes and ideas—of patriotism, rebellion, and freedom, of heroism and self-sacrifice, of policy and history—that had ceased to share the limelight for some time. French verse again became epic, satirical, philosophical, and di-dactic as well as lyric; in the hands of the greatest masters, once again it acquired archetypal power and a sense of the sublime.

We find a comparable enlarging of horizons and striving for the sublime in the so-called Catholic school (Jouve, Emmanuel, La Tour du Pin, Grosjean, Renard, Estang) and in the leading poets from Black Africa; for example, Senghor and Tchicaya U Tam'si. Critics often say that our age lacks myths as it lacks a collective consciousness. Yet the alleged lack of myth and disintegration of the collective con-sciousness is itself a powerful modernist myth. The War, the Resis-tance, and class struggle; Communism, Christianity, and negritude; the national tradition and its history—these have in the past and can again in the future provide the poet with themes, doctrines, and a voice that will enable him to recover a true literary public for verse. With such themes the poet inevitably seeks his public, is desperate to involve the reader in his quest for freedom or salvation, to include him in the poem—as a participant, a character, an *actant* as committed as the implied author himself.

In order to involve the reader, one has to reach him. This is surely a major reason why Aragon and Eluard, except when eluding Vichy censorship, renounced *trobar clus* in favor of a more accessible style, rhetorical and adorned with imagery yet bound by the precepts of rhyme and meter, even couched in regular stanzas and imitating popular ballads or the *chanson*. Similarly, in the poetry contests reported by Gourévitch young school versifiers are surprisingly conventional in taste: sixty-three percent of the submissions were in rhyme, and thirty-seven percent in fixed meter; and the themes were on the whole traditional, indeed archetypal, in nature. Rather than bemoan such attitudes, as does Gourévitch, ought we not to profit from them, indeed to learn a lesson? A lesson that also can be derived from the fact that the only major contemporary French poet to achieve paperback status is Prévert, and the most successful poets, in terms of audience appeal, are Brassens and Brel or, for a younger, more militant public, Stivell and Marti! If poetry is to live, it must be renewed. One such renewal entails a return to spoken idiom, for the spoken idiom, meter, and rhyme partake of a thousand-year tradition in France, are inherent in the tongue. *Pace* Derrida, to the extent that the twentieth century, with its phonograph, tape recorder, radio, television, and cinema, evidences a return to the oral, to a medieval, pre-Gutenberg culture, poetry can benefit by exploring its oral potentiality, including, as have Aragon and Prévert, as have poets in Breton and Occitan, its relationship to song.

The relationship between high culture and popular culture over the centuries has been complex. Popular legends contributed to the flowering of high art in the twelfth century. By the time of Louis XIV, the old medieval culture—epics, romances, saints' lives—survived largely in chapbooks (the Bibliothèque Bleue) hawked about the countryside; the masses knew prose versions of *Renaud de Montauban* and *Huon du Bordeaux,* not *Polyeucte* and *Andromaque.* Belles-lettres were reinvigorated by folksong and ballad, by legend and folktale, during the heyday of Romanticism. Today may well be the time for a similarly fruitful interchange.

It should not be forgotten that during the Occupation Aragon employed rhyme and meter in order to enlarge the reading public and also because they were creations of the French Middle Ages, contributions that French poets, the earliest and greatest of the Middle Ages, gave to the rest of Europe. Similarly, song contributed to the dissemination of contraband verse, and song was at the heart of French troubadour art. For political but also for esthetic reasons Aragon was aware of France's past, aware of her culture and proud of it. Unfortunately, in terms of literary culture, an Aragon in verse, a Gracq in prose, are largely exceptions. In terms of influence, of seminal force, the majority of contemporary poets sway back and forth between Baudelaire, Rimbaud, Mallarmé, Lautréamont, the Surrealists, and foreign luminaries who shine for a season on the Parisian stage: Rilke followed by Lorca followed by Pound followed by Mayakovsky followed by a version of haiku. Modernism, French and foreign, for all its virtues, ought not to reign alone over all of culture. And one legacy of Modernism is overvaluation of the modern. However, it is from the past that our contemporaries can receive other legacies: the concept of an organic relationship between poet and public, a realization of the possibilities inherent in rhetoric, the speaking persona, modulation of diction and level of style, an insight into the genres and modes available to be cultivated, and, most of all, that pride in Western culture, that sense of roots, origins, and continuity, without which the composition and dissemination of poetry may well remain peripheral to the main concerns of our society. Fortified by some of these legacies, poets will perhaps find their public—a reasonable, rational, respectable contemporary public, an educated public, the functioning healthy public that is possible in our time—made up of the bourgeois, professional, educated classes and those other people who hunger for culture and can be reached by it.

To be sure, integrating a consciousness of the past into the present, modifying our conception of French literature and making this new conception a reality for poet and public alike—these are Herculean tasks. Creative writers and the public are modern-oriented. Most contemporary critics are willing to accept the contemporary canon as a *fait accompli,* indeed to proclaim as their own the notion "Vox populi, vox dei." Thus Jean Cohen bases his choice of writers and his decision to begin with the seventeenth century on the general consensus. For Robert Goffin the public of today determines what deserves to live from the past, hence his acceptance of Villon and a few lines from Ronsard, hence his statement that d'Aubigné is unreadable.[14] Hans Hinterhäuser includes in his anthology articles on nineteen texts before 1840 and forty texts since that time, a decision, as we saw in chapter 1, he claims to be based not on personal taste but determined by the verdict of history.[15]

It is hardly necessary to insist upon the fact that the average reader historically has made mistakes about his contemporaries, preferring Chastelain to Charles d'Orléans, Desportes to Ronsard, Malherbe to d'Aubigné, and Sully Prudhomme to Verlaine, Rimbaud, and Mallarmé. The average reader sometimes fails to recognize geniuses, who receive their due years perhaps centuries later. A number of great medieval texts have survived in only one manuscript; more than one metaphysical or Baroque poet are appreciated for the first time in our generation.

The general public's taste, in France at any rate, is formed almost exclusively by the schools. People will know the names of authors and be familiar with specific texts uniquely because they were exposed to them in the form of a *dictée* or *lecture commentée*.[16] Thus for members of the lower classes, the word *author* or *writer* will be associated with La Fontaine and Hugo, not Proust and Robbe-Grillet. This means that the people are, or at any rate were, aware of the existence of poetry and of the "classics." On the other hand, it takes at least a generation for the discoveries of university professors to filter down to the C.E.S. and the *école primaire*, for the professors' students to become professors in turn. With a highly centralized, conservative academic establishment such as exists in France, where the impulse to rehabilitate the Middle Ages and the Baroque has come largely from abroad, there is no telling how much time the process will require. What minor reforms that have occurred in the schools concern critical approach or pedagogy, not the canon; reformers are eager to introduce Aimé Césaire or Mayakovsky, not poets six or seven centuries old.

In France literature is an institution, taught in the schools and organized into a canon. In a curious example of tautology, the school manual can be defined as that which selects and contains the national patrimony of masterpieces, the latter defined as those texts chosen to appear in the manual. Critics on the left have demonstrated the extent to which school texts contribute to and are a form of censorship—political, religious, esthetic, and sexual.[17] Literary history, stripped of politics and sex, is envisaged as a uniquely psychological realm in which writers painfully strive for eternal values, they alone embodying the human condition in its essence. Furthermore, the evolution of literature is conceived in what Barthes calls "classico-centrist" terms: a slow rise to, then falling away from, the summit, a high point that purportedly corresponds to the genius of the nation and its language.[18] For all too many teachers of French in the motherland and abroad, Louis XIV classicism is presumed to be quintessentially French, with the additional proviso that what is good is French and what is French is good. That teachers of German and Spanish are plagued by a comparable *deutsche Geist* and *hispanidad* renders the "national tautology" no less unacceptable. In the case of poetry, the old neoclassical summit (Corneille, Molière, Racine, La Fontaine, Boileau) has fortunately been displaced but replaced by a "symbolico-classical" summit (Baudelaire, Verlaine, Rimbaud, Mallarmé, Valéry) as pervasive in its influence on our way of thinking as the old one was on Voltaire's.

A series of factors—political, technical, and ideological—shapes the way that the history of literature is envisaged in French cultural life. If the French Middle Ages, the oldest and richest of the European vernaculars, is neglected in its homeland, this is because of neoclassical prejudice, maintained by a corps of teachers raised on Greek and Latin and conscious of their elite classical status, but also because the teachers of the Third Republic, committed to the Republic and to secularism, scorned the Middle Ages for its allegedly naïve Christianity. Furthermore, since pedagogic and pedantic logic calls for studying the corpus in chronological order, medieval texts were and are inflicted onto the youngest pupils, ill-prepared to cope with what is to them a foreign tongue.

Similarly, the Baroque is downgraded in part because of neoclassical prejudice, in part because of the language, for if La Fontaine and Racine compose in a limpid French more or less communicable to all Francophones today, such is not the case for d'Aubigné and Saint-Amant, famous for the richness, variety, and scope of their lexicon. In addition, religion and sectarian controversy are fundamental aspects of the Baroque: subjects sedulously avoided by Third, Fourth, and Fifth Republic secularists and also by teachers in the Catholic system, who either, as modernists, consider the controversies to be anachronistic or who, as traditionalists, do not care to admit that France was once also a Protestant country. Even in the case of recognized masters, Ronsard will be known primarily for his Cassandre-Marie-Hélène rose sonnets and Hugo as the father of Léopoldine and the grandfather of Adèle, not for their philosophical, satirical, and visionary efforts. This is the case, once again, because teachers are expected to avoid political or religious controversy, and because short poems can be readily included in the manuals, whereas long ones cannot. The situation in France is perhaps unique, given the extent to which foreign scholars—Swiss, German, English, American—have rehabilitated the French Middle Ages and Baroque and have appreciated Surrealism and the *nouveau roman,* in opposition to the classico-centrist bias of the Parisian establishment.

Whether or not people are wrong when judging their contemporaries, people of every age are sometimes wrong in their normative judgments of the past. Ought we not blush with shame at the thought of Horace Walpole proclaiming Dante to be "extravagant, absurd, disgusting, in short a Methodist parson in Bedlam," or Voltaire dismissing Shakespeare as a "village clown," a "drunken savage" with, nonetheless, "some pearls in his enormous dunghill"?[19] It is surely wrong for us to presume that our poetry is superior to that of the past, that our taste is superior, and that we are true poets, whereas our ancestors were not. Fashions in verse, for that matter modes of artistic creation—classicism, mannerism, the Baroque, Romanticism—come in cycles. Each great poet does the best he can, adhering to the esthetic and the sensibility of his age. We have the right to prefer one culture to another on moral or ethical grounds (*et encore!*), but not on esthetic ones. To condemn a century or mode from the past is to fall into the prescriptive heresy, to establish à la Boileau a prescriptive, normative, universal dogmatism: absurd when Boileau claimed the values of his age to be superior to Villon's or Ronsard's, no less absurd if we merely substitute *purifier les mots de la tribu* to an earlier period's *Longtemps plaire sans jamais lasser.*

Here it must be said that some sort of pedagogical duty is incumbent upon specialists of older literature, to make it accessible to the general reader and to those students who will become teachers of general readers a generation hence. An earlier stage in the language, the inaccessibility of cultural contexts, and unfamiliarity with literary conventions from another age—these questions must be faced honestly and without either cynicism or despair by those who believe in the value of what they do and who wish criticism and the history of literature to play a dynamic, living role in the making of our world.

One of the great adventures in modern culture, in England, America, Germany, and Spain, has been the quest for tradition in order to renew our contact with history. Many writers of today are not stifled by the past, as they would like us to believe, but, on the contrary, ignorant of it. A versifier who knows only the present or the present plus the immediate past is to some extent frivolous. The future contains the past as well as the present. To integrate the tradition of French verse, however, we must first envisage it anew, accept it in its totality, and rethink the structures by which we understand it and relate it to ourselves. Only then will it become a vital, living organic force and not the object of antiquarianism.

7

THE HISTORY

French literature of the Middle Ages is the oldest and richest in Europe, one of the most dynamic, creative periods in literature. These centuries gave rise to the refined, stylized, jewel-like courtly lyric examined in chapter 2 and, in *fin' amor*, the most important literary doctrine of the Middle Ages and the source of the romantic love tradition so important in the West ever since. Still more significant, at least for the early centuries, is narrative poetry. The trouvères have left us a good one hundred *chansons de geste* (of which a dozen or so are masterpieces), one hundred courtly romances (including at least a dozen masterpieces), and many, many fine erotic allegories or dream visions. This is a flood, an outpouring of storytelling in verse, unprecedented in the West, comparable only to the Sanskrit epic in India. For a century and more the three genres coexisted, enjoyed by different audiences or competing for attention within the one feudal-aristocratic public.

As noted in chapter 6, early epic reflects the ethos of the ruling class, the feudal aristocracy, in all its splendor, emphasizing prowess, loyalty, and heroism in the face of death, the virtues of a *miles Christi* concretized in poems of national history. Certain texts, especially the epics of the Cycle of Rebel Barons, deal concretely with socioeconomic problems that divide France. The crisis within the feudal system, the conflict between feudal and family loyalties, the reaction against a corrupt or aggressive central monarch, the danger of civil war, the role of money and land as a motivating force in the community— these are scrutinized in a problematic, introspective, "realistic" fictional world. Courtly romance is on the whole less oriented toward contemporary reality. Chrétien and his followers generally resolve sociopolitical tensions in a wish-fulfillment world of fantasy. However, by so doing, the romance develops a theme no less crucial for the subsequent evolution of literature: the rise of the individual. Fiction by Chrétien de Troyes and his most gifted disciples explores inner psychology, self-awareness, and a personal *crise de conscience*, the protagonist's growth over a period of years, and his relationship to society. For Chrétien attempts a synthesis of *fin' amor* and marriage, the quest for adventures and service to the community, King Arthur's court and the *gaste forest* of supernatural adventure. The protagonist—Erec, Lancelot, Yvain, Perceval—undergoes a symbolic and moral *itinéraire*, as in a sense does the society in which he lives, shifting from a shame to a guilt culture. Thus the aristocratic class, and specifically the *juvenis* of the petty nobility, is integrated into society, achieves being and fulfillment in an ideal *ordo*.

At the same time romances and late epics depict a world of folklore, fantasy, and the marvelous, exploiting the theme of the quest where the hero undergoes ordeals and rites of passage in a supernatural ambiance. Such texts revel in an atmosphere of refinement and luxury, in court festivities dominated by beautiful clothes, banquets, castles, color, light, and sheen, where the protagonist, a warrior, is also an aristocrat, an elegant, charming, handsome youth given to eloquence. In Chrétien, the most complex single poet of the age, we find a combination of mystery, psychological analysis, and sophisticated elegance, given form in a *genus temperatum* containing wit and the poetry of the heart, tension and the relaxation of tension, romance and antiromance. Chrétien is the greatest, but he does not stand alone. The romances of Chrétien, Beroul, Thomas, and Jean Renart, and epics such as *Girart de Roussillon, Renaud de Montauban,* and *Huon de Bordeaux* are works of high art, of complex esthetic synthesis. This period, the early French Middle Ages, and these narratives manifest a bursting forth of creativity that gave the world some of its most famous heroes of myth: Roland, Oliver, and Charlemagne; the Four Sons of Aymon and the great horse Bayard; Ogier the Dane; Tristan, Isolt, and King Mark; Lancelot, Guinevere, and King Arthur; Sir Gawain; Sir Perceval and the Holy Grail—and, in the comic, parodic register, Reynard the Fox and his merry friends and adversaries.

Although in the later Middle Ages myth tends to disappear, in its place the sense of complexity, of psychological and artistic self-consciousness, increases. Allegories of love portray an inner quest where the hero struggles with personified abstractions that are often aspects of his own psyche. The plot recounts his initiation to Eros. However, in a masterpiece such as Jean de Meun's *Roman de la Rose,* in continuation of Guillaume de Lorris, courtliness is transformed. Jean abandons Guillaume's delicate allegorical equilibrium, poetry, and exemplary *fin' amor,* in favor of a strident, sarcastic demystification of romance. Although Jean proposes an ideal of universal copulation for the purposes of reproducing the species, he is no less interested in unmasking the hypocrisy of *fin' amor* and in teaching us the truth of the human condition. He exposes the human comedy in all its richness, governed by duplicity and manipulation, the exploitation of man by woman and of woman by man, and the place in our lives occupied by material concerns. His is the preeminent antiromance of the Middle Ages, a secular "anatomy" in which the entire world is held up to scrutiny.

In the following century Guillaume de Machaut and Jean Froissart bring the *dit amoureux* to its culmination, refining the work of their predecessors. Sometimes Machaut renews the dream-vision topos of poetry and beauty in a garden of delight; sometimes he ridicules *fin' amor,* undermining conventions of erotic allegory. The canon of Reims relishes a new literary type: the inept, blundering narrator, who is also an inept, blundering lover. This pseudoautobiographical character is prone to cowardice, sloth, snobbery, misogyny, and pedantry. By mocking his own persona as narrator and lover-hero, by playing with point of view and illusion-reality, Machaut exploits the possibilities inherent in the first-person narrative; he anticipates some of the most exciting subsequent developments in the history of fiction. He also follows Jean de Meun in manifesting extraordinary self-consciousness and pride in his function as a poet. He does so by introducing a version of himself as the protagonist; by claiming mastery in his craft and elaborating the myth of the artist; by composing "poetic pseudoautobiographies" that presume to explain how certain of his own lyrics came to be written; thus by making the craft of writing, indeed the writing of the book, the subject of the book. Not until du Bellay and Ronsard, not until Vigny and Hugo, will the dignity and importance of the poetic vocation again be so exalted.

The central tradition, then, is narrative, didactic, and satirical as well as lyric; the relationship of poet to public is organic; the literary style is flexible and colloquial. For perhaps the only time in history the spoken idiom of court and castle proves to be a free creative medium for literature. The elegant middle style serves as a norm for the masterpieces of Chrétien de Troyes and Guillaume de Lorris; yet it is also possible for Jean de Meun to soar on flights of eloquence, to attain the utmost in force and vigor, and for the authors of fabliaux and *Le Roman de Renart* to integrate low speech, including obscenity, into works of high art. At its best, all medieval verse maintains a colloquial freshness and vitality, also a tough reasonableness, and the ripeness and urbanity that are hallmarks of the provincial courts. For this is the creative period par excellence, the age when myths are elaborated, when poetry exudes archetypal power as it never has since.

There is, then, nothing primitive or childlike about the French Middle Ages, a time that exalted the image of the book and its creator (*auctor*) as author and authority, that exalted the role of education and rhetoric as no subsequent period has been able to do. This is a time of convention, of reverence for examplars of the genre and for the Latin classics, when almost all works of art are intertexts, an age embodying realism and stylization, dynamism and artistic self-consciousness. In the early centuries we find the power of *Raoul de Cambrai* and the refined court elegance of *Cligès* and *Yvain;* in the late ones the even more refined elegance of Charles d'Orléans and the cutting, corrosive, eternally poignant mockery of François Villon. The Middle Ages is neither primitive, oral, childlike, and dark, nor a universal, univocal age of faith. Rather, it is a period of creativity and culture, of art and artistic awareness, giving rise to the discovery of the individual, delving into the mysteries of the human condition, exalting "joie de vivre" and literature.

As pointed out in chapter 5, French literary historians have traditionally emphasized the barriers separating the Middle Ages from the Renaissance. But the differences between the two periods have been exaggerated. Traits presumed to be hallmarks of the new times—a passion for classical letters; the desire to embellish contemporary writing with Greco-Roman myth; a rich, lusty enjoyment of love, life, and nature; the exaltation of man in his secular destiny—are amply manifest in the works of Chrétien de Troyes, Guillaume de Lorris, Jean de Meun, and Guillaume de Machaut. Thus the twelfth century has been rightly called an *aetas ovidiana,* and no one in all of French literature was so familiar with classical *auctores,* was so capable of revering them and mocking them at the same time, as was Jean de Meun.

Similarly, quite a few so-called medieval practices—alchemy, astrology, allegory, typology, even witchcraft—extended well into the seventeenth century. Petrarchan love, so important an inspiration to du Bellay, Ronsard, Desportes, and d'Aubigné, is medieval, the Italian version of *fin' amor* come back to the land that gave it birth. And much that in Marot and Scève scholars have called Petrarchan is in fact a direct manifestation of the earlier native court tradition, uncontaminated by Italian influence. Allegorical theology or the figurative method of interpretation applied to Holy Writ and to the classics of Antiquity—this medieval cultural phenomenon thrives in the Renaissance, when, for the first time, it inspires sublime poetry in the vernacular: Ronsard's *Hymnes,* d'Aubigné's *Tragiques,* and, later, Christian epics by Saint-Amant and Le Moyne. The Renaissance continues a medieval tradition of didacticism, acting on the assumption that poets have a duty to teach virtue and celebrate glory. The pagan gods are retained, for writers seek to reconcile classical and Christian culture by recuperating, by Christianizing, the myths, which in turn provide vernacular authors with numen, enthusiasm, lyricism, and fervor. We find a syncretic bond not only between the Christian and the classical but also between sacred *caritas* and profane Eros: in Scève and du Bellay the two loves are juxtaposed, bound, and fused on several levels.

Finally, with the mode of "scientific poetry" (Scève, Peletier du Mans, Ronsard, Belleau, du Bartas, Lefèvre de la Boderie) anticipating the stance of the Romantics, the poet assumes traits of a magus, a seer as well as an encyclopedist. He practices and teaches *musica instrumentalis, musica humana,* and *musica mundana;* he is subject to melancholia and frenzy; he is the beloved of the Muses, a teacher as well as an entertainer of men. As teacher, and as one dependent upon his patron, the author constructs his work following the precepts of classical and medieval rhetoric, cultivating the techniques of judicial, deliberative, and panegyric oratory, his texts meant to serve as an encomium of the prince and the prince's people. Last of all, the great Renaissance writers, like their medieval forebears, were consciously reactionary in politics. Ronsard and d'Aubigné, no less than Turold, Chrétien, and the trouvères of *Raoul de Cambrai* and *Garin le Lorrain,* castigate contemporary failings by pointing to a bygone Golden Age, exalting the past over the present and stasis over change.

However, we must not exaggerate continuity between the Middle Ages and the Renaissance. It is in people's attitudes toward time and history that evolution can most clearly be discerned. In the sixteenth century men sensed differences between themselves and preceding ages, whether the medieval or the Greco-Roman. It has been said that this epoch marks the beginnings of French literary history, with Renaissance humanists, dating back, it is true, to the end of the fourteenth century, for the first time distinguishing between literary periods, thus becoming aware of period divisions.[1] Suffering from an inferiority complex in the face of Antiquity, envisaging the Ancients in a new light, Ronsard and his successors sought to imitate classical genres, not just to incorporate myths, themes, or rhetorical figures; to revitalize form as well as content. This inferiority complex vis-à-vis the Ancients was compensated for by a strident superiority complex vis-à-vis the immediate past, the tradition of the French Middle Ages. The Christian, typological view of time and history was supplemented by a new cyclical vision: positing a Golden Age in the distant past, assimilated to Eden before the Fall, to the glory of Greece and Rome, or to pastoral Arcadia, followed by a period of barbarism and/or decadence (the Dark Ages) extending up to the recent past, followed by the return of Astraea, the Renaissance or Rebirth, a New Golden Age under the aegis of a gifted, semidivine prince, assimilated to the present or the immediate future, conceived in terms of Utopia or the millenium.

It is for these reasons that, in the *Deffence et Illustration de la Langue Françoyse,* du Bellay calls for a break with the past, condemns the French Middle Ages, and urges linguistic and literary innovation based upon the imitation of Antiquity. His ideas are typical of an intellectual climate in mid-sixteenth-century France, therefore accurately reflect sixteenth-century mentalities. They also helped provide inspiration for an entire generation of poets. However, we moderns must not assume that du Bellay and Ronsard were historically or esthetically right in their value judgments or that the path they chose to take was the only one open to them. The examples of England and Spain prove the contrary. According to the science of linguistics, one language is as good as another; therefore Renaissance French cannot be considered superior or inferior to medieval French or, for that matter, superior or inferior to the French of Louis XIV. A period of enriching the lexicon with terms from Latin did indeed occur, but it was largely a fourteenth- and fifteenth-century phenomenon, all but over by 1549; and there was never a serious danger of French being replaced by Latin in those same 1540s. In fact, du Bellay and Ronsard came at the end of a great period of civilization, not at the beginning of one. Unbeknownst to themselves, they had four centuries of outstanding poetry behind them. Therefore, the modern reader is wrong to accept their all too subjective, all too emotionally involved condemnation of their predecessors. The reality of those centuries was one of slow evolution and broad continuity, the continuity of a syncretic classical-Christian civilization in synthesis: containing love and war, the individual and the community, religion and satire, classical Antiquity and Christian faith, the rules of rhetoric and the glory of the individual artist.

In the sixteenth century French is a rich, exciting tongue, organically alive, concrete, dense, pithy, in no way inferior to the language of the *chansons de geste* and *romans courtois.* The invasion of Greco-Roman culture heralded a flood of new myths, themes, motifs, and even literary genres to be exploited. At its best the Renaissance maintains tough reasonableness, vitality, force, strength, and high culture. Indeed, Ronsard and d'Aubigné attain a sublime style rare in the earlier age. And Renaissance poets do not permit the divorce of form and matter, of idea and expression: They have ideas and fight for them. In the Baroque period especially, Sponde, d'Aubigné, Chassignet, and La Ceppède combine seriousness and wit, density and elegance, force and urbanity. They are metaphysical poets in every sense of the term.

Marot, Scève, du Bellay, and Ronsard ought to be known not for a few pieces in anthologies but for the sweep and range of their genius, their capacity to master a number of artistic genres and modes. Clément Marot's solid six volumes in the modern edition contain epistles, satires, complaints, songs, elegies, canticles, epithalamia, eclogues, *rondeaux, ballades,* epitaphs, *étrennes,* translations of the psalms, and a mass of epigrams.[2] Always the court poet, adopting the appropriate voice and mask, a master of urbane wit, Marot is the most varied of writers. The same can be said for the six volumes by du Bellay, creator of love sonnets, sonnets of satire and nostalgia, mythological poems, poems of praise and of blame, official texts such as the epithalamium and *tombeau,* religious texts, and the *jeu rustique;* and for the twenty volumes by Ronsard.[3] As we saw in chapter 2, Ronsard sings of high love, low love, nature, war, satire, the cosmos, and God. He writes Pindaric odes, Horatian odes, Petrarchan sonnets, encomiastic hymns, philosophical hymns, satirical-religious discourses, pastoral eclogues, epistles, elegies, epithalamia, funeral dirges, epitaphs, epigrams, *folastries, blasons, voeux,* songs, inscriptions, *mascarades* and *cartels,* poems on God and death, and an epic. Like Goethe or Pushkin, he is a universal poet, having practiced all genres, all registers, all styles, having mastered the entire past European tradition and having brought it to a new acme of perfection.

The outpouring of French verse does not cease with the Pléiade; on the contrary, succeeding generations prove to be even richer in scope and achievement. However, the post-Pléiade writers have never been fully integrated into the modern academic canon. These poets, now called Baroque, were relegated by Lanson to a shelf for "attardés et égarés."[4] Even today, the Baroque is appreciated more in Germany, Italy, and Spain than in France. Scholars have delved into the Baroque mentality. They claim with good reason to find a series of themes or mental traits, a phenomenology, that distinguishes this period from the High Renaissance that precedes it and the classicism that follows it. These traits include mutability and metamorphosis, ostentation and spectacle, a sense of paradox, the play of illusion and reality, a myopic, disconnected vision, multiple-sense imagery, the macabre and the morbid, emotionalism, monumentality, and an opening-out toward nature.

The great Baroque poets are at the same time magnificent and

militant. They revel in pomp, spectacle, and declamation; they strive
for new horizons and the richness of the universe; and they are profoundly Christian, children of the Reformation or the Counter-Reformation, passionate in their missionary zeal, seeking union with God
for themselves and their readers. Thus they indulge in meditative,
private lyrics in the devotional style and in public, biblical epics; yet
their heroism is one of sacrifice, and their epic protagonists are vir-
gins and martyrs. The Baroque is a "modern" style, nonconformist
and eccentric, that reacts against the classically oriented perfection
and genre decorum of du Bellay, Ronsard, and Belleau. In reaction to
the Pléiade, the Baroque masters seek irregularity and *désinvolture;*
they disdain hard work and pedantry; they are eager to please a
broad-based contemporary public; and they experiment with varied
registers of style, including the idiom of the court and that of the
marketplace. In the Baroque we find Moses, David, and the Holy
Ghost as models in addition to, even supplanting, Virgil and Horace.
Truth, the *veritas* of Scripture, supplements the formal perfection and
secular wisdom of the earlier generation.

Ronsard in the *Discours* and *Derniers Vers* and Jodelle throughout
his career are forebears of the Baroque style. Around 1570, Huguenots—du Bartas, d'Aubigné, Constans, Goulart, La Roche-Chandieu—
launched the new antipagan, antiformalist, antielitist mode, which was
then adopted by Catholic poets in the 1590s: Chassignet, La Ceppède,
and Favre, among others. Another current is "Black Neopetrarchism"
in the line of Desportes and the lyricists who came after him, including
La Roque, Bernier de la Brousse, and again d'Aubigné, who revel in a
world of madness, erotic transgression, and demonic, masochistic punishment. With the end of the Wars of Religion a flood of verse poured
from the presses, the decade from 1600 to 1610 proving to be especially rich. Decline set in only with the advent of neoclassicism. The
immense Baroque production can be divided chronologically into two
currents or modes. The first one, which has been assimilated to Mannerism or the English metaphysical school, includes, as we have seen,
du Bartas, d'Aubigné, Sponde, Chassignet, and La Ceppède. They reveal a curious blend or juxtaposition of passion and thought, concern
with ontological problems, concrete, functional imagery, and living
speech. Theirs is an unusually compact, dense style with both a metaphysical core and Mannerist embellishment. The second group contains Théophile de Viau, Saint-Amant, Tristan l'Hermite, and, in the
1640s, Le Moyne, Bussières, Martial de Brives, and du Bois-Hus.
Theirs is an ornate style based upon rhetoric and descriptive amplification, richly decorative, joying in artifice, revealing disunity of structure,

apocalyptic vision, and an obsession with the "modern"—with Tassian *meraviglia* and the latest trends south of the Alps and Pyrénées.

Today's reader is most astonished by the variety of stance in the Baroque: the dense, questioning, private, Christian devotional register; the passionate, tortured Neopetrarchan erotic register; the flamboyant, rhetorical, religious, epic register; the soft, gentle, mellifluous pastoral register; the witty, ironic, caustic demotic register of the caprice or the burlesque. A number of poets assume more than one voice. D'Aubigné is a masochistic, suffering, dying love slave in the *Hécatombe à Diane* as well as the militant Christian hero-poet prophet of *Les Tragiques*. Saint-Amant indulges in *genus grande* for epic and the sacred; *genus medium* for descriptive, philosophical, and meditative poems on love and nature; and *genus humile* or a mixture of styles for mock-encomia of food and drink, satire on Rome and England, and experiments in the grotesque. The leading poets in Occitan—Pey de Garros, Bellaud de la Bellaudière, Pierre Paul, Godolin—manifest an unusually rich, sensuous style and juxtaposition of styles. They combine sumptuous rhetoric and the popular voice, composing poetry of passion, of pastoral, of contemporary reality, and of the Faith. The Baroque is one of the most fascinating periods in the history of world literature, and in its sense of fragmentation and frustration, of multiplicity, intellectuality, and the concrete, its obsession with ideas and with the "modern," it is peculiarly like our own age.

Quite unlike our own is the succeeding period, that of neoclassicism followed by Rococo and the Enlightenment. From the vantage point of Romanticism or Symbolism the century and a half extending from 1660 to 1820 can be viewed as a desert, but from its own perspective and in the totality of world literature, it is an exciting age indeed. Five of the greatest figures in literature composed in verse: Corneille, Molière, Racine, La Fontaine, and Boileau. It is not fair to deny them their place in the pantheon. True, three of the five are dramatists but masters of poetic theater, of the same type and importance as Marlowe and Shakespeare, Lope and Calderón, Goethe, Schiller, Kleist, and Grillparzer. In addition, La Fontaine and Boileau are poets in the very first rank, who dominate their age and the entire European neoclassical tradition. La Fontaine introduced two genres central to the canon for over a century: the *fable* and the *conte*. (He also composed superb narrative, elegiac, and lyrical verse.) Boileau did the same for the satire, the familiar epistle, the *ars poetica,* and the mock-epic. These six genres reached their acme, their summum of perfection, in the late seventeenth century. They were often to be imitated but seldom equaled and never surpassed.

While perhaps less rich in genius, the eighteenth century provides excitement of creativity in the hands of Voltaire and Chénier, the greatest masters of the century, and a good twenty other figures. Although with less range than in the Baroque, these men practiced a variety of modes and genres: the heroic epic; the philosophical, theological, didactic, or descriptive long poem; the sublime secular ode; the sacred ode, cantata, or psalm; the pastoral, eclogue, idyll, elegy, and heroid; the mock-epic; the satire; the *conte en vers;* the familiar epistle; and all sorts of fugitive verse. Some will specialize in the sacred (Louis Racine and Lefranc de Pompignan), some in the sublime ode and witty epigram (Jean-Baptiste Rousseau and Lebrun), some in the *conte* and *poésie de circonstance* (Gresset, Grécourt, Piron), some in the erotic elegy and pastoral (Bertin, Léonard, Parny), some in descriptive verse on nature (Saint-Lambert, Roucher, Delille). Voltaire, Dorat, and Rousseau cultivate many genres, perform surprisingly well in most or all of them, and have to be considered universal poets in the same sense as Ronsard, Saint-Amant, La Fontaine, Hugo, and Aragon.

The first century of classicism is a time of vitality through freshness and wit, through the use of a comic speaker-persona, a Horatian voice who follows the rhetorical precepts of *captatio benevolentiae,* shaping and molding the reader's beliefs and norms, appealing to his instincts, emotions, and culture, seeking his approbation at every turn. Malherbe, Boileau, and Voltaire maintain a close organic bond with the community; they also insist that poetry exists in order to teach, therefore that the *dulce* and *utile* are indissolubly fused. Theirs is still a public muse. The Horatian persona's principal mode is satirical: The Speaker manipulates his reader through laughter and mockery. He attacks, thrusts, and parries, duels with imaginary adversaries, creates dialogues of dispute and wit. This is a poetry of worldliness, verse that is based upon, reflects, and contributes to an ordered social existence, a system of public gestures and values, man's functioning in the community. It is an urban, urbane style, where the subject of verse is social pleasure and the cultivation of manners, the visual and the transient. In so worldly and refined an ambiance, it is only appropriate that mock-epic (*Le Lutrin, Ver-vert, La Pucelle, La Guerre des Dieux*) predominates, that parody and pastiche evoke, rely upon, seek complicity with, and play off against the cultural past, that texts comment upon and fulfill the texts of others, that verse as intertext subsumes pre-texts and allows for *mise en abyme.* The work of art is truly an artifice. Recognized as such by writer and reader alike, it becomes, in the best sense of the term, a *jeu d'esprit,* an increment of the spirit *sub specie ludi.*

Furthermore, this Horatian tradition appears in a variety of subcurrents during the Rococo-Enlightenment age. The official academic high style, inherited from Malherbe and Boileau, perpetuated by Voltaire, is one such current. More interesting perhaps is what has been called "individualist poetry," represented especially by Chaulieu, La Fare, Jean-Baptiste Rousseau, Gresset, Lefranc, Bernis, and Louis Racine, a current of modernism, striving for freedom from rules, oriented toward pleasure rather than the didactic, relishing variety, sentiment, and the esthetics of negligence in an aura (illusion?) of artless simplicity, lightness, and charm. No doubt emanating from this school we also find the poetics of nostalgia and wish-fulfillment sentiment in the pastoral, the poetics of desire and exotic fantasy in the *conte*, and a new sort of heroism, the spiritual prowess of the religious leader or the Christian poet creating sacred verse.

Finally, allied with the Rococo style is a mode that will come to the forefront during the half-century following upon the publication of *La Nouvelle Héloïse:* one that reveals erotic and sentimental intimacy, high-flown moral and sentimental rhetoric, a new classicism under the banner of Horace, Tibullus, Ovid, and Virgil, obsession with nature (gardens, woods, the four seasons, and the Alps), and a mood of *tragédie larmoyante,* romantic sensibility, and an appeal to the heart. This is a literature either of sensibility and sensual or tragic passion or of didacticism and description, mastering the world by describing it and praising God through his creation.

With Gilbert and Chénier, with Roucher and Parny, we approach Romanticism. And with Romanticism we arrive at the modern era, with poetry that has found its place in today's academic canon. The shift from the classical-Christian tradition to the modern is more significant than, say, the progression from the Middle Ages to the Renaissance or from the Baroque to neoclassicism. If not the subject of this book, it is the cause and the fundamental presupposition behind it.

One manifestation of the Romantic age is the problematic hero—centered in the novel but appearing also as a speaker or protagonist in verse (Lamartine, Vigny, Hugo)—one who, struggling against his fate, seeks authenticity in a degraded, reified world. Another is the Biedermeier structure of *ora et labora, Sammeln und Hegen:* the exaltation of the petty bourgeois or rustic home, with emphasis on the hearth, the family, and domestic intimacy, presented in a mood of idyllic realism and melancholy. This type of writing is concerned with humble people in the provinces and the valorization of their daily concerns, little people taken seriously and endowed with tragic or at least melodra-

matic dignity, a mode of existence deemed to possess universal significance and in which a new kind of heroism is considered possible (Lamartine, Hugo, Brizeux, Laprade; in Occitan, Mistral and Aubanel).

The classical-Christian synthesis, based upon a vision of cosmic harmony, a functioning social order, the triumph of reason, and Christian
revelation, assuming the acceptance of hierarchy, order, stasis, and the
community, is turned around. This is, in the world of letters, literally a
revolution. From Romanticism on, the poet exalts external nature, far
from the cities of men and angels, and the individual, in a man-created
universe, the protagonist of which is an alienated poet-lover-rebel,
whose essence is sentiment, who lives and suffers on his own, without
direction from sacred theology or the literary classics. Goodness and
innocence no longer derive from authority, human or divine; they are to
be found through self-awareness, not social integration. The poet seeks
the dark inside of man, not the light of heaven. In Northrop Frye's
terminology, the old male-oriented, god-centered, rational, conservative, and heroic myth, exalting man as warrior and thinker, inherent in
Virgil, *chansons de geste,* and the sublime verse of the Renaissance, gives
way to a second myth: female-oriented, centered on the mother goddess,
radical, sentimental, and erotic, exalting man as lover and victim.[5]

It is not surprising that, convergent with Romanticism, melodrama
arose as a specific theatrical genre and as a mode of the imagination.
What has been called the Byronic hero, to be found in Lamartine,
Vigny, Hugo, and Musset, is a rebel, an individualist, perhaps a bandit
or political revolutionary, perhaps a noble savage close to nature, most
certainly a man of sensibility, passion, and enthusiasm, a tragic figure
who has suffered *le mal du siècle.* He is a seeker, wanderer, mystic,
solitary prophet and visionary, a magic figure because of his soul, his
inner self. The archetypal hero of the age is Satan or a comparable
embodiment of the fallen angel (Lamartine, Vigny, Hugo, Soumet,
Baudelaire), and the wish-fulfillment fantasy of poets is that Satan be
redeemed. With Satanism comes a profusion of demonic imagery—
prison, tower, tomb, bat, owl, night, autumn, decay, the *femme fatale*
and the *beau ténébreux,* a pattern of imagery and a mentality that dominated early literature only during the Baroque. Poets also hold for the
first time a vision of history as totality, and they seek to incorporate a
total structure, both cosmology and world history, in their own creative
works. This leads to social concerns, indeed an obsession with Napoleon and the Revolution of 1789, and the creation of new, syncretic
religions. It also leads to a renewed obsession with epic, with the desire
to construct a *Gesamptkunstwerk* that would include and transcend all
previous models and genres.

After 1850 in France, after 1890 in the rest of Europe, the reaction against bourgeois values and bourgeois idealism predominates. Leading writers repudiate the present either to dream of the future or to exalt the past. The tragic, individualized hero of Romanticism is transformed into a pathetic or ironically alienated antihero. Dislocation of form expresses inner dislocation, an antirational sentiment, and the negation of the very idea of society. The Rimbaud or Mallarmé speaker exists apart from time and space, ahistorical and ageographical, uniquely in the pages of a book. According to Lukács, the modern condition is defined by man's alienation from concrete objective reality.[6]

Thus in the course of the nineteenth century, alongside the enthusiasm of Hugo, his sense of an active involvement with history, and the private erotic vision of Lamartine, alongside and in reaction to public or intimate optimism, grow the flowers of evil and a private *noia*. In reaction to propaganda, to bourgeois or mass vulgarity, the poet proclaims his alienation; he denounces the myth of progress, he appeals to the antisocial or the arcane. Symptomatic of this worldview is the demystification of Paris, embodied in the theme of the demonic city, become perhaps the dominant motif of Modernism. Although Hugo and Aragon relish the metropolis, the demonic vision is present in Baudelaire, Lautréamont, Verhaeren, Bely, Döblin, Dos Passos, Eliot, Lorca, and Pierre Emmanuel, to name the most eminent. A second nexus centers around the *femme fatale* or *belle dame sans merci*, woman conceived as the Medusa, macabre and devouring, a castrating Kali figure in the line of Salome, Lilith, and Ishtar. True, the Surrealists rehabilitate romantic love (*l'amour fou*) and the ideal of the woman and, in their reaction to what they consider to be capitalist oppression, hope to change life as well as verse, to synthesize Freud and Marx for the benefit of mankind. However, since World War II, poets are convinced not only that the old culture is gone but that no new culture can replace it. The fall of Western civilization has left a void that cannot be filled by haiku and Zen or the proletarian myths elaborated by Mayakovsky and Brecht.

From Hugo and Vigny to Roubaud and Pleynet, poets nevertheless agree on one point: their own crucial, unique importance as poets. The repudiation of rules, genres, models, and the esthetic hierarchy led the Romantics and their successors not to greater humility but to pride in themselves. No longer a craftsman, no longer a moralist useful to society and working in harmony with it, the poet is imagined to be the hero of his own quest, a rebel and victim, the most recent incarnation of Lucifer the light-bearer. And the writer is deemed to be a priest, a seer, a visionary, a new Orpheus. The Orpheus theme becomes one of the great seminal ideas in modern literature, from Ballanche to Pierre Emmanuel and Marie-Jeanne Durry, for the Greek harrower of Hades, at one time assimilated to Christ, now is proclaimed to figure the artist, unique in his passion and glory.

It has been said that there are two dominant currents in Modernist verse: the seer-prophetic, but also the scholar-hermetic.[7] Many of the great twentieth-century texts reveal complex patterns of imagery but no mimesis, no argument as such. With them the principal, indeed unique, subject of poetry becomes the writing or criticism of poems. In this sense they are pure art and pure language, autotelic and metapoetic in the extreme. Yet often they also contain revelation and prophecy, if only revelation and prophecy about themselves as poems.

Be this as it may, it would still be a mistake to exaggerate the uniqueness of the modern and its divergence from all previous poetic endeavor. That the modern functions within a continuum, forming one stage in the evolution of poetry, is after all the theme of this book. Artistic self-awareness and the theme of art and the artist were scarcely invented by Hugo and Vigny. The poem itself as an image, the notion that the subject of a poem is poetry or the writing of poems by a poet, goes back to the earliest masterpieces in Occitan, and it is a constant throughout the nine-century history of French verse. The *trobar ric* and *trobar clus* of the troubadours, the high hermetic style of the Rhétoriqueurs, testify to "medieval modernism." We find the figure of the poet as lover and creator, as a self-reflexive consciousness mocking, analyzing, and elaborating itself, in Machaut, Froissart and Charles d'Orléans. With Scève, du Bellay, Ronsard, Baïf, and Jodelle are exhibited the conscious elaboration of *stylus duris,* an artificial, difficult, allusive register produced by a *poeta vates,* an inspired genius possessed by the muses, subject to *furor poeticus* and conscious of his glory.

Closest to the modern is the period of the Baroque, an age of ornate or mixed style, rich metaphor, concrete imagery, violence, and the quest for new horizons. Sponde, Chassignet, d'Aubigné, Tristan, Théophile, Saint-Amant, and Le Moyne elaborate such themes as solitude, melancholia, passionate Eros, the four seasons, external nature, the horrors of the night, and typically Baroque traits that are also typical of verse since Baudelaire: death, the macabre, cruelty, deception, inconstancy, and change. Furthermore, the old poetry—medieval, Renaissance, and Baroque—gave voice to the collective unconscious and to myth, either to reworking old Greco-Roman myths or, especially in the Middle Ages, to creating new, contemporary ones. The great period of mythmaking is the century of Roland, Tristan, Lancelot, the four sons of Aymon, and Reynard the Fox, not the century of *le peuple* and *Paris aux barricades*.

We must recognize that poetic production since Lamartine or since Baudelaire is more varied than most people realize and that it contains and amplifies much of the past tradition. Whatever critics say, great modern poets persist in cultivating a kind of epic or long poem (Lamartine, Hugo, Saint-John Perse, Aragon, Emmanuel), drama in verse (Hugo, Soumet, Rostand, Claudel, Milosz), even a form of Pindaric ode (Claudel, Perse, Jouve). Hugo, Baudelaire, and their successors are masters of symbolism but also of allegory; the new allegory, scarcely the same as the one illustrated by Guillaume de Lorris and Pierre Le Moyne, nonetheless exists and is pervasive in our time. Much has been written on the classicism of the Romantics. Suffice it to say that not only was the generation of Hugo nurtured on the French tradition extending from Malherbe to Delille but that the Romantics continued the classification and separation both of genres and of stylistic registers. A case can be made that, like their forebears of the Pléiade, French Romantics consciously specialized: Lamartine in the *élégie*, Vigny in the *poème*, Hugo in the *ode* (high style), while Musset reserved for himself genres appropriate to the Horatian voice. The old literary kinds were renewed and regenerated, never discarded. According to Hugo Friedrich, all modern verse derives from the Baudelaire-Mallarmé current.[8] It is true that the most dominant presence in recent French verse springs from the "Hermetic school" of Nerval, Mallarmé, and Valéry: It includes the work of Char, Bonnefoy, Dupin, du Bouchet, and Jaccottet, to name but a few. However, other traditions in our century prove to be no less productive. Among them are post-Symbolism, with Régnier and Verhaeren the most respected voices from 1900 to 1920; the Ecole romane; the *fantaisistes*, derived from Laforgue, including Apollinaire, who gave expression to *Esprit nouveau*, and his many disciples or those influenced by him; Cubism, Dada, and Surrealism in its full range of influence; and the Catholic revival. More recently appears another form of classicism, poets who employ rhyme and meter and respect the traditional modes: among others can be cited Supervielle, Aragon, Audiberti, Cassou, the late Eluard, Jammes, Lanza del Vasto, and Emmanuel.

Since World War II we find a profusion of trends that derive from the currents mentioned above or cut across the same literary terrain. These are concrete and spatialist verse, *lettrisme* and *spatialisme* (Isou, Garnier); a phenomenological school, sometimes called *chosisme*, obsessed with material things (Ponge, Guillevic); the *tranche d'écriture* antipoetry of the *Tel Quel* and *Change* groups (Deguy, Pleynet, Roche,

Roubaud); "cosmic counter-humanism" (Jouve, Perse, Char); a pseudo-popular tradition (Prévert, Brassens, Vian); poetry of commitment (Aragon, Eluard); and "realists" who return to concrete simplicity, including the Ecole de Rochefort (Cadou, Manoll, Follain). In other words, in the supposedly Mallarmé-dominated twentieth century we find poetry of humor, wit, and elegant sociability (Apollinaire, Jacob, Jammes, Supervielle, Michaux, Queneau, Prévert, Desnos); love poets with the passion and lyrical commitment that extends back to the troubadours (Claudel, Breton, Eluard, Aragon, Jouve, Perse); writers who revel in and evoke the life of the provinces (Péguy, La Tour du Pin, Char, the Ecole de Rochefort); the great Catholic school (Péguy, Claudel, Jammes, Jacob, Milosz, La Tour du Pin, Jouve, Emmanuel, Cayrol, Jaccottet, Grosjean, Renard); and above all the poets of the Resistance, who combine political commitment with the desire to appeal to a vaster public through simple, traditional artistic forms. The most recent trends reveal a denial of lyric inspiration in favor of metapoetics and the patient, rational elaboration of *écriture* by a *scripteur*.

Modernists and post-Modernists share a knowledge of and desire to perpetuate a tradition, even though it is not the same obviously as those known to Machaut, Ronsard, and Boileau. When in the history of verse certain means, techniques, or effects are no longer needed and disappear from practice, they are replaced by new means, techniques, and effects. Thus the rhyme and rhetoric of the Romantics give way to density of metaphor and an exotic lexicon with the Symbolists; thus the rich lexicon and generally traditional word order of the Symbolists are replaced by broken syntax and traditional vocabulary with the Surrealists.

The nature of artistic creation ensures a continuity of archetype, of deep structures and inner form, from the Middle Ages to the present, even when, in a bourgeois age, the old heroism and romance are displaced to a register of low mimesis or irony. *Fin' amor* persists in the guise of an adoring Speaker-lover in Lamartine, Hugo, and Aubanel, as *amour fou* with Breton, Eluard, and Aragon. Woman as temptress or virgin, muse or bride, Ishtar or Mary, remains the obsession of French writers. *Ennui* and *spleen*, those peculiarly Baudelairean states of the soul, the hallmark of modern letters, are but the last embodiment of the old melancholia and *acedia*, endured by poets born under the sign of Saturn, from the troubadours to Machaut, Charles d'Orléans, du Bellay, and Théophile de Viau. The Biedermeier and post-Biedermeier current in Lamartine, Brizeux, and Mistral, in Cadou and Follain, is after all but the last reincarnation of the pastoral convention central to our culture since the Renaissance. Although, except for the poetry of Resistance, martial heroism has gone, in its place we find a new unheroic or antiheroic hero, who turns inward, suffers from transgression, traverses his own dark night of the soul, and aims at transcendence and the attainment of metaphysical absolutes. Christian imagery, typology, and mental structures not only pervade the work of the Catholic school but also suffuse all the great writers of our time, Marxist atheists as well as believers. They form part of our culture now as a thousand years ago, one pattern of myth in a century of mythmaking, a century obsessed with reinterpreting the great classical heroes (Orpheus, Oedipus, Prometheus, Narcissus) and the Christian ones (Satan, Cain, Jacob, Job, Christ) and with creating new figures in their stead: Joan of Arc, Marianne, Paris, le peuple. Modern mythmakers—Hugo, Leconte de Lisle, Mallarmé, Valéry, Claudel, Apollinaire, Saint-John Perse, Jouve, Char, Emmanuel, Bonnefoy—perpetuate the tradition of their forebears, from Chrétien de Troyes and Guillaume de Lorris to Racine and Chénier.

Over the nine centuries of French verse, what patterns can we discover? what trends and forces for growth? One crucial element of evolution from the Middle Ages to the twentieth century is the steady decline of poetry, not in quantity or quality but in what we can call its centrality within the tradition. In the twelfth century all literature in French was in verse; in the twentieth century all but the rarified lyric is in prose. As we saw in chapter 6, one after another the major genres or modes—history, narrative fiction, philosophy, satire, comedy, tragedy—all have left the domain of the muses. The center of gravity has shifted from epic to lyric and from poetry to prose. Along with the loss of centrality, universality, and gravity, eventually had to follow loss of prestige. For centuries the highest seats in the pantheon were occupied as a matter of course by poets—epic, tragic, and lyric. Although today we rightly assume the greatness of, say, Rabelais, Montaigne, Pascal, and La Bruyère, the public in the past considered them to be inferior to their contemporaries who composed in verse. This state of affairs persisted until the middle of the nineteenth century, when, still, Lamartine and Hugo enjoyed more glory than Balzac, Stendhal, and George Sand. When a writer composed in both prose and verse—Molière, Voltaire, Hugo—verse was chosen for compositions in the sublime and prose for works in a lower register, and the writer expected immortality from his poetry but not his prose.

It is also true that as a result of the process we now call the esthetics of reception, poetic evolution, corresponding to the evolution of fiction and the theater, assumes a steadily increasing fund of sources and influences, of models subject to imitation. Such is inevitably the case as a tradition builds up over the centuries and writers have more and more predecessors to choose from. Such is also the case vis-à-vis foreign authors, when an old, relatively homogeneous culture such as the French discovers the developing cultures of its neighbors. French was the oldest, the richest, and the most autonomous literature in the Middle Ages. Aside from Celtic myth, the trouvères were familiar only with Latin and Occitan texts in addition to French ones. The twelfth century has rightly been called an *aetas ovidiana,* and Ovid, Virgil, and the Latin Bible were the formative influences of the age. With the Renaissance, Homer, Hesiod, Pindar, the tragedians, Anacreon, the Anthology, and Theocritus were added to the list, as were Petrarch, Boccaccio, Ariosto, and Bembo, then Tasso, Marino, and the Burlesque school. In time the English muse came to inspire verse in France: Shakespeare, Milton, Pope, Young, Thomson, then the Romantics, with Byron in the lead. Germany followed, with Klopstock, Goethe, Schiller, and those German Romantics who were readily translated. The French poet of today, like his German or American counterpart, ranges over all of world literature, from the *griot* songs of the Caribbean or black Africa to Japanese tanka and haiku by way of Lorca, Hölderlin, and Mayakovsky. With regard to models, foreign and native, French verse has evolved in the direction of variety and diversity, a sort of freedom, an "opening out" as it were, as has, for that matter, the literary tradition in its entirety.

Granting this, it is also true that poets, whether of the past or present, are not scholars, that their knowledge of literature is necessarily fluctuating and limited. Some of the greatest are well-read, open to a culture of worldwide proportions (Jean de Meun, Ronsard, d'Aubigné, Saint-Amant, La Fontaine, Hugo, Apollinaire, Aragon, Emmanuel), others noticeably less so (the singers of *geste,* Charles d'Orléans, Malherbe, Boileau, Rimbaud, Saint-John Perse, Prévert). Furthermore, as the centuries flow past, although new works enter the current, old ones are lost to all but a few antiquaries or professors of literature. Even within the Middle Ages, for example, although Guillaume de Lorris was familiar with Virgil, Ovid, Boethius, Chrétien de Troyes, and the troubadours, it is quite likely that *chansons de geste* no longer formed part of his background. Those few Renaissance poets who did appreciate the Middle Ages (Marot, even Ronsard) cite Jean de Meun, Chartier, certain Rhétoriqueurs, and Jean Lemaire de Belges; however, literature prior to 1250 and, for the subsequent period, Machaut, Froissart, Charles d'Orléans, even Villon are forgotten. A later generation, while relishing the great Italians (or condemning them), will no longer be influenced by the native tradition, be it medieval or Renaissance. Marot survives largely as a model of style for the *conte;* du Bellay and Ronsard are scarcely better loved than

Jean de Meun and Villon. Finally, in our time poets have at their
fingertips resources of staggering richness, but, in the process, almost
all of the national tradition prior to Baudelaire and Hugo plus the
earliest of the great foreign models have ceased to function. With the
exception of Dante, Italian poetry has lost its seminal force, and authors once so powerful, giants of influence—Petrarch, Boccaccio, Ariosto, Tasso, Marino—have become more "obscure" than French Arthurian romance and the *discours* of the Wars of Religion.

One explanation for this process of exclusion, or one result that has
come of it, is a steadily recurring pattern of repudiation in the course
of French literature, a pattern whereby young poets appear to deny
their immediate predecessors while seeking inspiration or critical support from the practice of an earlier age, to repudiate their "fathers"
while relying upon their safely dead "grandfathers." In the thirteenth
century we find the old epics copied in England and created anew in
Italy while, inside France, the texts were modernized or abandoned
utterly, literary taste having shifted to romance. Similarly, in the fourteenth century, whereas the French and Occitan courtly lyric was still a
source of inspiration in Italy, Spain, and Portugal, Machaut succeeded
in supplanting the old genres with the *ballade, rondeau,* and *virelai.* Du
Bellay and Ronsard effectuated a more violent break with the medieval
heritage than was to be the case elsewhere in Europe. They condemned
their great medieval predecessors for alleged ignorance, for failing to
imitate the Greco-Roman classics with enthusiasm and erudition. Then,
in an act of unconscious poetic justice, the generation of Boileau repudiated the Renaissance—for too much enthusiasm and pedantry, for
failing to approximate the spoken idiom of the court—with as much
finality and as much injustice as the Pléiade had rejected the Middle
Ages. They were then to be repudiated in turn by the Romantics for
purported lack of sentiment, for an excess of intellect and stylization.
The pattern of rejection continues from generation to generation,
from *cénacle* to *cénacle,* from manifesto to manifesto: a succession of
romantics, Parnasse, symbolists, the Ecole romane, Dada, surrealists,
existentialists, structuralists, up to our own day.

This structure of rejection corresponds to and helps explain the phenomenon of canon formation that will be discussed later, the fact that
most poetic generations posit a Golden Age sometime in the past, condemn their immediate predecessors, and praise themselves for the condemnation and for their desire to rejoin the golden ancestors. I have
come to believe that in all cases the *cénacles* are wrong as critics (though
not as poets), wrong historically, for in each case the repudiated fathers
are as great as the sons and the grandfathers, and the rejection of, say,

Jean de Meun and Villon by Ronsard and du Bellay, of du Bellay and Ronsard by Malherbe and Boileau, of Malherbe and Boileau by Lamartine and Hugo, tells us a great deal about the repudiators but nothing whatsoever about the repudiated. Of course, du Bellay's, Boileau's, and Hugo's being "wrong" as critics in no way diminishes their greatness as poets, nor the fact that as poets they were perhaps "right" to carve out a place for themselves in order to build upon it.

Such being the case, Harold Bloom's challenging, brilliantly controversial thesis of "anxiety of influence" and "creative misreading" for English poetry since the Enlightenment[9] is also valid for the history of verse in France and from the early Middle Ages on. Bloom is surely correct to underscore that the claim to originality on the part of modern poets, the fierceness with which they deny influence from the past, seeks to mask but in fact reveals their debt to the past. Furthermore, each school, each *cénacle*, each new generation does indeed commit distortion, perverse, willful revisionism, and self-serving caricature— misreading of their predecessors—simply in order to exist. Greater creative health on the Gallic side of the Channel can perhaps be explained by the fact that the pattern of repudiation is more dominant, pervasive, and universal in France than in England. French poets either assimilate (by devouring) their predecessors with alacrity or repudiate them with no less alacrity. They never, except perhaps for sections of the eighteenth century, allow themselves to be weighed down, stifled, and stultified by the mighty dead. In the face of the myth of a Golden Age in the past and an Age of Iron or Clay in the present, they either presume confidently to restore the Golden Age (Ronsard), revere it with mockery (Boileau), or deny it and all it entails with gusto (Breton).

One cause for the pattern of repudiation, and one outcome of it, is a cyclical shift, movement, or recurrence in style over the centuries. Not only are *trobar ric* or *trobar clus* and *trobar plan* manifest throughout the literary history of France, but one style predominates in various periods only to yield place to the other. As suggested in chapter 3, heightened diction, complex metaphor, conscious patterns of imagery, striving for a personal voice, and archetypal power are typical of some troubadours, Villon, Scève, d'Aubigné and the great Baroque lyricists, Hugo and the Romantics, Baudelaire, Rimbaud, and the Symbolists, and such major twentieth-century figures as Saint-John Perse, Breton, Char, Aragon, Jouve, and Bonnefoy. For different reasons *chansons de geste* also adhere to the category of stylized, archetypal verse, far from the register of colloquial speech. On the other hand, plain imagery, diction corresponding to the spoken idiom, and a conventional persona fall in the province of Chrétien de Troyes, Guillaume de Lorris, Machaut, Charles d'Orléans, Marot, du Bellay, La Fontaine, the eighteenth-century tradition, Corbière, Laforgue, and, more recently, Supervielle and Prévert. A case can be made for the cyclical recurrence of the two styles: one, "Baroque" or "Romantic," prevalent during certain historical periods (1100–1150; the 1400s; 1570–1660; 1820–); the other, "Classical" or "Mannerist," predominating at different times (1150-1400; 1500–1570; 1660–1820). This recurrence of styles, a shift back and forth from Classical-Mannerist to Baroque-Romantic and from Baroque-Romantic to Classical-Mannerist, proves to be central to the evolution of literary history, a diachronic structural pattern of the first importance. And the fact that we have been now in a Baroque-Romantic phase, under Baroque-Romantic ideals, for almost two centuries may explain our unwillingness to accept the Classical-Mannerist tradition and even Baroque-Romantic texts from the past, which, because they are from the past, we assimilate to the Classical-Mannerist mentality: as if there were only one Father, and he has to be slain for the Son to live.

Accounting for the ebb and flow of styles, the alternance of a Classical and a Romantic temperament over the ages, it may then be possible to elaborate broader, more inclusive patterns that make sense of *longue durée*. For example, concerning the long poem, I have postulated a recurrent pattern of evolution: Epic bursts on the scene with an archaic or experimental work of power, idealism, and almost classical perfection. The mode then develops in two directions: (1) toward realism, concreteness, political commitment, and formal diffuseness; and (2) toward concern with Eros and the theme of the quest, the wish-fulfillment world of romance. The romance element remains dominant for a time but eventually yields to a spirit that can be qualified as anti-Romantic, characterized by encyclopedic or didactic pretensions and social satire, which undermine the notion of epic as most people conceive it. With this extreme form of sophistication the genre peters out; the cycle is complete and free to begin again.

Whether a comparable deep structure can be determined for other genres or modes (satire, pastoral, the erotic lyric) or for poetry as a totality, I cannot say. The possibility exists. For the evolution of epic and of French poetry in general adheres reasonably well to the cyclical theory proposed by art historians to explain the evolution of architecture, sculpture, and painting in the sixteenth and seventeenth centuries. We find, in literature as in the arts, an experimental phase (Lemaire de Belges, Marot, Scève) followed by High Renaissance, a moment of classical perfection (du Bellay, Ronsard, Belleau), followed by a period of Mannerism (Jodelle, the late Ronsard, Desportes, Sponde, Chassignet), followed by a Baroque synthesis (d'Aubigné, La Ceppède, Théophile, Saint-Amant, Le Moyne). It can be said that this curve was preceded by a comparable, analogous medieval sequence: the Romanesque (experimental) achievement of the early trouvères and singers of *geste,* leading to the Gothic (classical) perfection of Chrétien de Troyes, Guillaume de Lorris, and the *Prose Lancelot,* leading to the Rayonnant Mannerism of Jean de Meun, Machaut, and Froissart, leading to a Flamboyant, Baroque-like synthesis in the century of Villon and the great mystery plays. And the Renaissance-Baroque may have been succeeded by a third sequence, still another curve of experiment (the *burlesque,* the *précieux,* Corneille, Rotrou), of Classicism (La Fontaine, Racine, Boileau), of Rococo Mannerism (the century of Voltaire, Gresset, Dorat, and Chénier), and of a new Baroque, the Romantic synthesis of Lamartine, Musset, and Hugo, the Hugo of *Notre Dame-de-Paris, Les Burgraves, La Légende des Siècles,* and *La Fin de Satan.* If I am correct, the modern period, represented by Baudelaire, Rimbaud, and Mallarmé in letters, Cézanne and Picasso in painting, and Debussy and Ravel in music, is in the process of launching a new experimental phase, the fourth in the history of French letters, and our twentieth-century art forms represent the beginning of a style that will take centuries to evolve before it can be assimilated in the annals of history. All the more reason why it is so difficult for us to relate to the tradition that, as Curtius puts it, begins with Homer and ends with Goethe, to relate to it and assimilate it into our consciousness.

A case can also be made that the culture of the twentieth century represents, in more than one respect, a return to the Middle Ages and that medieval poetry can be more readily appreciated by people today than at any other time since the Renaissance. Certainly the current vogue of medieval doings—in film à la Bresson and Rohmer, in fantasy literature à la Tolkien and Lewis, in the phenomenon of "medievalism" now recognized in academic circles—brings weight to my argument. To some extent our age embodies a repudiation of the notions of progress, technology, materialism, and secularism, the collective *idées reçues* derived from Voltaire and Michelet; it represents a return to symbolic thinking, religious anguish, and mythmaking; it even manifests a partially oral culture based on film, radio, and television. Both medieval and contemporary writers operate in an esthetic that does not value the realism prevalent from Molière to Malraux. They share this trait with the novelists of imperial China and Japan and with the oral narrative of black Africa and the Native American. Similarly, the epic theater of Brecht rejoins the epic theater of the mystery plays, and twentieth-century art proclaims an opening-out and a renewal of forms under the influence of Japanese prints, Chinese bronzes, African masks, and our own Romanesque and Gothic. Last but not least, contemporary critical approaches—Freudian, Jungian, phenomenological, and structuralist— also prove to be closer to medieval *mentalités,* to the spirit of the Middle Ages, than positivistic philology or literary history ever were.

It is obvious that my view of the history of French verse runs counter to that held by the average educated Frenchman, the average lycée professor, the average university professor (except for specialists in the Middle Ages or the Baroque), the average newspaper critic, and, last but not least, the average poet. For a certain generation and social class French poetry really means Lamartine, Vigny, and Hugo. For another generation and somewhat different class, "bad poetry" begins with Lamartine and "good poetry" with Baudelaire. Both groups recognize, behind Lamartine, a vague stretch of "history," containing, at most, a few brief texts by Villon, du Bellay, and Ronsard, and of course the classics: lyrical, satirical, and dramatic poets of the Age of Louis XIV envisaged not as poets but as classics. In essence, both groups are largely unaware of literature prior to French classicism, to some extent unaware of all poetry prior to the nineteenth century.

It is this view, this canon, that I cannot accept. And it is no less obvious that, explicitly and implicitly, I wish to revise the canon of French verse. The theoretical considerations elaborated in the first six chapters of this book demand such change in the canon; or my desire to revise the canon implies a preliminary, preceding, preexistent revision of the theory of what is poetry.

To restate a position taken in chapter 1, the contribution of the Anglo-American New Criticism and the more recent myth-criticism of Northrop Frye lies in the fact that these movements not only gave us insights into the nature of the critical or interpretive process, that they taught us how to read and to teach, but they also made us rethink English literary history; they shook up the canon. Thus the New Critics rehabilitated Donne, Crashaw, Dryden, and Pope; they brought them back into the "Temple du goût" and, in the process, displaced Milton, Shelley, and Tennyson. In reaction to Eliot, Leavis, and Brooks, Northrop Frye then reintroduced Spenser and Milton and helped install Blake. Meanwhile, literary historians in the States have fought all along as to whether the genuine American tradition is embodied in Hawthorne, James, Eliot, and Tate, or in Whitman, Twain, Hemingway, and Sandburg. Alas, nothing comparable has occurred in France. The only creative writer from the past to have been elevated by the structuralists, poststructuralists, and deconstructionists is the Marquis de Sade. With the exception of

Jean Rousset,[10] has any major Francophone critic in our century, for the literature of the past (pre-Hugo), made a significant effort to alter the pattern of French literary history elaborated by Lanson, a pattern that he himself had borrowed in large measure from Brunetière and Faguet, who inherited it from Sainte-Beuve? Lanson's shortcomings as a critic lie not in his methodology, the most progressive of its day, but in his vision of French literature, oriented toward neoclassicism and prose. We have been suffering under its weight now for almost a century.

Are other structures possible? Indeed, they should be. It ought to be possible to revise the canon of French verse, to recast our notions of value and our conception of how the tradition evolved. Such revaluations would be extremely healthy for the profession because they could set poems and poets in a new order, then bring about that rethinking of the literary tradition that ought to occur every other generation or so if the history of literature is to survive as an exciting, vital discipline. One such revaluation, à la F. R. Leavis, based upon the example of New Criticism in England, would be to exalt the Middle Ages and the Renaissance, the period of verse extending from 1100 to 1600 or 1650, for its flexible and colloquial style, freshness, vitality, tough reasonableness, and strength, then to denigrate (but for isolated exceptions, such as La Fontaine or Apollinaire) much of the poetry that has appeared since that age for its purported subjectivism, pretentiousness, sentimentality, and narcissism.

I shall not, however, propose this or any other structure, even one seemingly congenial to the principles enunciated in the preceding chapters. This is because I do not subscribe to a universal reductionist view of poetry based upon inclusion and exclusion, upon the alleged rise and fall or birth and death of genres, and upon categorical judgment of value. Since the Renaissance at least, western Europe in general and France in particular have been plagued by classico-centrist canon formation and distortions of the national heritage to conform to it. Through the centuries the classico-centrist curves adhere to the same fundamental pattern. For the men of the Renaissance, say, Ronsard's generation, the pattern is conceived as a *tempus aureum* in Greco-Roman Antiquity, falling off to the nadir of the Middle Ages but then curving back to form a new summit in the present, the return of Astraea and the rebirth of classical learning and beauty. The age of Louis XIV in essence adopts the same curve, simply legating the Pléiade, and the Baroque also for that matter, to the medieval nadir and, of course, reserving for itself and its Jupiter-figure, King Louis, the upward swing to a new Golden Age. The Romantics evolved a more complex structure, in line with their discovery of world literature. They imagined a first summit with the Greeks, also including the Old Testament and India; they did not, however, allow a place for Rome, now relegated to the decline. A second high point of inspiration is ascribed to the Middle Ages (formerly in the nadir) and/or early Renaissance, a second nadir to all of neoclassicism and, as always, a revival of true poetry in the present.

A somewhat more academic and more humble variation on the curve occurs when the present generation considers itself not to be the creators of a New Golden Age but the inheritors of one established in the recent past. Hence Voltaire and his fellows accepted the Louis XIV pattern, placing themselves in a position slightly below the acme achieved by Molière, Racine, La Fontaine, and Boileau. Similarly, for many people today the Golden Age is evoked by a succession of writers extending from Baudelaire to Claudel and Valéry, and poetic production in the twentieth century is deemed to be on the right track but nonetheless inferior to the giants of Modernism. For our generation the rise and fall of Modernism or Symbolism forms a relatively narrow curve, given that the Moderns, at least in their overall esthetic judgments and sense of canon formation, no longer have the same dynamic relationship to Greece, Rome, and the early national tradition that was taken for granted in the past. Last of all, we discover a structure endemic to the Middle Ages. Although medieval poets were less inhibited by canon formation and a normative poetics, they certainly did consider their work inferior to the classics of ancient Rome. *Chevalerie* and *clergie* may well have shifted from Greece and Rome to France; nonetheless, Frenchmen, even with the gift of Faith, could only esteem themselves dwarfs seated on the shoulders of giants. Variations on this relatively simple, linear pattern (not limited to poetry) are proposed in the twentieth century by conservatives, joying in nostalgia for the past, who posit steady decadence from the Middle Ages to the present; or by Marxists and/or proponents of avant-garde, joying in the myth of progress, who posit steady rise from "feudalism" to the highly self-conscious, self-reflexive metatexts of today that they themselves compose.

Each age, then, establishes its own canon and its canon curve, based upon a subjective evaluation of the nature of poetry, deriving above all from the needs of creators in the present who react against the immediate or distant past. The present-day view is no worse and no better than any of the canon formations in the past. Each epoch, including our own, expresses in its vision of poetry its own sensibility; the poets and practicing critics of each age are equally subjective in terms of value judgments; and, finally, each age is probably correct in judging its own poetic production. The poetry of a specific period never goes wrong, is always appropriate to that period, because there is no such thing as "right poetry" as opposed to "wrong poetry," no normative esthetics valid for all generations.

There is no progress in literature and no decadence either. Baudelaire is greater than Ponsard, just as Chrétien is greater than Gautier d'Arras, Villon greater than Chastelain, Ronsard greater than Pontus de Tyard, and Racine greater than Quinault. However, Chrétien, Villon, Ronsard, and Racine are equals, supreme each in his own domain, and each is the equal of Baudelaire or Mallarmé. If we base value judgments on a few quite specific, limited criteria, such as tension, irony, ambiguity, density, originality in diction, and a narcissistic esthetic self-consciousness, supremacy can be claimed for certain modern poets: Baudelaire, Rimbaud, Lautréamont, Mallarmé, and Valéry, among others. On the other hand, by positing other criteria—elegance, charm, wit, grace, and variety in the manipulation of stylistic register; or, on the contrary, archetypal power, political commitment, passion, élan, and the creation of myths—we can accord preeminence equally well to Chrétien de Troyes, Machaut, Marot, La Fontaine, and Musset; or to singers of *geste*, d'Aubigné, Le Moyne, and Hugo. Would it not be better to make our criteria more flexible and more varied, thus to admit a greater variety of poets and kinds of poetry in the canon?

The supreme ages of poetry manifest such variety in style, mode, tone, and register. This is true for the twelfth and thirteenth centuries, which contain the passion, commitment, and élan of the epics of revolt and epics of the Guillaume cycle; the elegance, charm, psychological penetration, and evanescent poetic aura of Thomas, Chrétien, Jean Renart, and Guillaume de Lorris; the abstract, gemlike purity of the courtly lyric; and the magnificently bawdy, festive, satirical, life-hungry juxtaposition and undermining of styles typical of Jean de Meun, the *fabliaux* and *Le Roman de Renart*. This is true for the Baroque, which contains religious commitment and dense, metaphysical analysis in Sponde, Chassignet, and La Ceppède; satirical, archetypal power and élan in d'Aubigné; formal rigor and pastoral elegance in Théophile, Racan, and Maynard; and the rich, festive outpouring of language and fantasy, mock-encomium, and the concreteness of realia in Régnier, Motin, and Saint-Amant. The mid-fifteenth century gives birth to Charles d'Orléans *and* Villon, the mid-sixteenth to Scève *and* du Bellay, the mid-nineteenth to Hugo *and* Baudelaire.

Furthermore, poets speak out to each other, consciously or unconsciously, by imitation or by archetype, over the centuries. Guillaume de Lorris, Guillaume de Machaut, Charles d'Orléans, Marot, La Fontaine, Gresset, and Musset form a continuity of elegant, witty *préciosité*,

l'art de causer en vers. For the tragic, engaged poets of government, war, and apocalypse, the wielders of *saeva indignatio*, the chain extends from the authors of *Raoul de Cambrai, Garin le Lorrain,* and *Renaud de Montauban* through Jean de Meun, the Ronsard of the *Discours,* d'Aubigné, the Voltaire of the *Poëme sur le désastre de Lisbonne,* Hugo, and Aragon. For florid, lyrical, passionate élan, the outpouring of erotic emotion, and the illusion of personal authenticity, a continuum of *trobar leu* extends from the early trouvères to Villon, much of Ronsard, the young d'Aubigné, Théophile de Viau, Lamartine, Hugo, Verlaine, Eluard, and Aragon. And, for a dense, convoluted, intellectual register and commitment to language and the art of poetry, one need only consider *trobar clus* in Guiraut de Bornelh and Arnaut Daniel, the Rhétoriqueurs, Scève, and the modern tradition from Rimbaud to Yves Bonnefoy.

The notion of progress in literature is a heresy. The notion of universal *Zeitgeist* is no less a heresy. The medieval Age of Belief, the sixteenth-century Renaissance of Letters and Joy in Life, the Splendid Century of neoclassical restraint and order, or the era dominated by Enlightenment ideas—these are gross oversimplifications that distort, diminish, restrict, and corrupt the richness and variety of poetry that came into being in those days. Each century of the past is rich and beautiful, each has something that corresponds to present concerns, each contains contradictions, conflicts, discoveries, obsessions, and anxieties comparable to the ones that we pride ourselves on being ours. In all periods, including of course the Middle Ages, we find people asking the same questions and often offering the same answers. In all periods the concerns and obsessions are love, war, justice, politics, satire, God, and the exaltation of the poet, his craft, his art. The human condition remains essentially the same. And the tradition of French literature, the oldest and richest in Europe, manifests a surge of masterpieces over the centuries from the *Saint-Alexis* and *Roland* to the present. There are no weak centuries; there are not even weak generations. The vitality and totality of the tradition, its uninterrupted nine-hundred-year continuity, is comparable to the great literatures of the East: those of India, China, and Japan.

It can be said that ours is an age without history, an age where provincialism in time has replaced provincialism in space. For many people, history means nostalgic, *rétro* films evoking the 1940s or the 1950s. Seldom has there been a time so parochial, so cut off from its own past, one where the vast majority of people read uniquely contemporary books. The nature of literature is not to be provincial and parochial. And literature abandons nothing en route. Each period con-

tributes to the whole, is part of the whole, therefore contributes to the modern and is part of it. To know the present, we must know the past; to know the past is to know the present. For, according to Eliot, one is "to write not merely with his own generation in his bones but with a feeling that the whole of literature of Europe from Homer and within it the whole literature of his own country has a simultaneous existence and comprises a simultaneous order."[11] Living poets bear the burden of the mighty dead, struggle against them, also learn from them, assume their glory and contribute to it and to their own. The mighty dead weigh on our shoulders, but we shape them in turn, assimilate, integrate, and devour them, re-creating them for us and our posterity in our image. Our sense of belatedness can be a virtue in disguise and inspire us to create; we must not shake it off through barbarism and ignorance.

The opportunity for our century is to accept, to integrate, indeed to welcome the tradition, to "recuperate" the past as we create in the present, to make it as vital for us as the work of our contemporaries is. Thus we can hope not to replace the old restrictive, prescriptive canon with a new one, but to enlarge the canon in order to include all masterpieces from all periods, on a level of equality, each as an ontological whole. One goal surely of our century is to expand horizons, to inaugurate a *bibliothèque imaginaire* alongside Malraux's *musée imaginaire*, a truly Goethean notion of world literature that will perpetuate the cultural masterpieces of the past for their own sake and in order that they inspire the cultural masterpieces of the present and the future. Poetry perhaps will then be envisaged as a diachronic as well as a synchronic entity, and texts will exist not only as ontological wholes but also as part of a tradition and a continuity, intertextual and intercultural, forming part of a universal civilization available for the instruction and the pleasure of all men. In his course at the Collège de France (spring 1980), Georges Duby stated that the history of love in the West has yet to be written. I should add that, despite the extraordinary triumphs of modern criticism, an authentic, total history of Western literature also is waiting to be written.

APPENDIX

THE MODERN VIEW OF POETRY IN FRANCE

Passages from twenty-five books on poetry (general studies) published in France, Belgium, and Switzerland over a twenty-year period (1959 to 1977).

François Germain, *L'Art de commenter un poème lyrique: De l'inspiration et du style lyriques avec applications à la composition française* (Paris: Foucher, 1959).

La raison d'être du lyrisme est bien de créer un domaine où la sensibilité de l'auteur, si étrange qu'elle soit, puisse librement s'épanouir, une sorte de paradis intérieur, où l'on vive à sa mesure. (9)

Disons simplement que la poésie est incompatible avec l'indifférence du coeur ou même avec la tiédeur sentimentale; il n'y a de lyrisme que par la *ferveur* . . . (14)

Si le poète est l'écho sonore de la nature, c'est que la nature d'abord est l'écho du poète. *Etre lyrique, c'est donc projeter sa sensibilité sur toute chose* et recueillir, dans une récolte miraculeuse, la sensibilité de l'univers. . . . Si les idées font la dignité du lyrisme, c'est bien dans la chaleur des sentiments qu'il puise la force, proprement lyrique, de transformer l'univers. (15)

. . . *il y a poème lyrique quand l'auteur nous présente son émotion directement, sans recourir à un récit, à des personnages, à une action dramatique, quand il parle lui-même, saisi par l'émotion.* (30–31)

. . . le poème est un genre bref. (33)

René Ménard, *La Condition poétique* (Paris: Gallimard, 1959).

La Poésie est un bien capable de tous les autres biens. (23)

Elle [une telle poésie] témoigne sur l'homme qui la produit, avec une sincérité quelquefois effrayante. Conscience elle-même, elle n'a nul besoin de se réclamer d'autres vérités que de la sienne. (36)

... ce que nous appelons Poésie ressortit à la connaissance du sacré; à telle enseigne que l'histoire de l'une et de l'autre sont intimement liées, soit qu'elles se confondent, soit qu'elles se complètent. De même que le sacré se résout lentement dans l'humain, la Poésie, dans ses intentions et ses formes successives, se dissout dans le discours. (39)

Mais je ne crois pas que quiconque puisse méditer de bonne foi sur la Poésie sans se réclamer d'une liberté totale. (48)

... la Poésie qui inspire l'image, n'est pas dépendante de l'esprit humain, n'est pas une superstructure subjective, mais une réverbération du sens essentiel du monde sur notre esprit. Elle n'est pas créée par lui, mais découverte, dévoilée. Le monde est une pensée incarnée, indépendante des hommes, pourtant accessible, traduisible par la Poésie. (97)

Alain Bosquet, *Verbe et vertige: Situations de la poésie* (Paris: Hachette, 1961).

Pendant des siècles, la poésie française abdiquera ses pouvoirs les plus absolus. Elle ne pourra rencontrer l'universel que dans l'absolu—tout relatif—de sa perfection formelle; elle oubliera jusqu'au milieu du XIXe siècle l'universel inquiétant: celui qui encourage la redéfinition de la nature humaine. (20–21)

Une poésie [celle de Racine] qui, obligatoirement, se plie aux exigences d'une psychologie d'où tout écart est exclu—d'où, aussi, tout recours au merveilleux est éliminé—et qui doit tenir compte d'une succession de faits déterminée, pour rester à chaque vers conforme à l'état d'esprit de qui la récite sur scène, est, par définition condamnée, en tant que poésie. (30–31)

Pour rien au monde, il [le poète moderne] ne retournerait à l'espèce de bonne santé superficielle de ses ancêtres, les poètes capables de dire d'avance ce que seront leurs poèmes; pire encore: capables d'affirmer qu'ils demeureront, eux, poètes, les mêmes citoyens, après leurs poèmes, qu'avant. (90)

Que le poète le veuille ou non, la poésie est alors une perpétuelle remise en cause de lois fondamentales et de *valeurs en déséquilibre parfait*. . . . *Elle est une sainte subversion:* qui n'écoute pas ses décrets injustifiables commet un crime et une impiété. (108)

Jacques-G. Krafft, *Poésie corps et âme: Etude sur l'esthétique de la poésie suivie de quelques généralisations* (Paris: Vrin, 1961).

Le vers français est d'abord une unité, comme le disait Luc Durtain. Ainsi, de la prose à la poésie, la langue a été passée à l'estompe de la désignification et à un syncrétisme, une conglomération unitaire. Elle en arrive à l'illogicité foncière du discours, une absence de toute cursivité raisonnable ou déductivité; ce pendant qu'une rhythmisation s'opère. (21)

On peut prononcer des choses fort intéressantes, aujourd'hui encore, sur la genèse du poème, sa conception, sa maturation, sa venue au jour; —dire qu'il est communication instantanée et éternelle, *ex cathedra humili,* du tréfonds de l'âme au tréfonds d'une autre âme. . . . La poésie aussi est un tout en soi, à soi, pour soi. Elle est son propre but. Elle est devenue, par le feu . . . sacré, expression totale, globale, combiné définitif de la chose dite et de la façon adoptée pour la dire: corps et âme. (25)

Par jeu, par l'ébat en ouverture ou fermeture de notre diaphragme optique mental, nous voyons tout à coup plus grand, plus général, plus total, plus universel, plus beau, en tout cas différemment des autres et de ce que nous voyions nous-même hier et verrons peut-être demain. Inspiration! (248)

Georges Mounin, *Poésie et société* (Paris: Presses Universitaires de France, 1962).

D'abord, il faut constater que l'histoire de la poésie tout entière est l'histoire d'une succession de langages—à des degrés divers—absolument neufs. Et de langages qu'il a fallu chaque fois que le public apprenne, assez lentement. (46)

C'est très lentement, même après le XVIe siècle, que les hommes ont appris à rechercher "la poésie" pour y trouver de plus en plus consciemment la vitamine poétique qui s'y trouve contenue. Et tout l'art poétique, depuis Racine jusqu'au Surréalisme, paraît avoir été de rechercher des concentrations toujours plus élevées de cet élément spécifique de toute poésie, trop dilué pour un goût de la poésie qui devenait de plus en plus conscient de sa recherche. Par élimination de toute finalité didactique, de toute finalité narrative, de toute finalité moraliste, de toute finalité rhétorique, et de toute finalité mnémotechnique, *la poésie est devenue de plus en plus la poésie.* La poésie à haute dose, la poésie à l'état pur, a été une invention continue. (87)

Robert Champigny, *Le Genre poétique: Essai* (Monte-Carlo: Regain, 1963).

Un poème doit être bref, plus bref sans doute que ne le demandait Poe à une époque où la technique poétique s'embarrassait encore d'éloquence, de narration, de description et de commentaires. (18)

Le langage poétique trouve sa justification propre et suffisante dans l'acte de prononcer, dans l'appréciation du poème. . . . la poésie ne nomme pas les choses; la poésie chose les noms. (94)

Comment la situation de la poésie (de langue française) peut-elle être caractérisée, alors que s'est close la première moitié du XXe siècle? . . . seuls, quelques poèmes de quelques poètes me paraissent constituer, dans l'ensemble comme dans le détail, une réalisation, aussi pure et juste qu'on puisse raisonnablement l'espérer, de l'idée de la poésie comme telle. Il semblerait donc que, du point du vue sémantique, la poésie n'en soit qu'aux prémices de la maturité. (232)

Si donc l'on se borne à un examen de la situation intérieure, la poésie telle que nous l'avons définie ne se présente pas comme un genre épuisé: il semble bien plutôt qu'elle vienne de reconnaître son domaine propre. (233)

Robert Goffin, *Fil d'Ariane pour la poésie* (Paris: Nizet, 1964).

Comment discerner la fissure certaine entre la poésie pure et celle qui ne l'est pas! Comment faire sentir toute l'irrémédiable différence entre la prose rimée qui raconte, qui narre, qui peut se résumer, et la véritable poésie qui met si longtemps à se trouver un chemin à travers les adhésions? (12)

Il est évident que la sensibilité et l'intelligence sont deux domaines qui ont des fins propres; l'une est la matière de la poésie ou de l'art, et la seconde est celle de la prose. . . . Et si nous poussons plus avant nos prospections, nous pouvons affirmer que la poésie venant de la sensibilité s'adresse à la sensibilité, par la voie de la suggestion; lorsqu'elle rejoint la perception de l'intelligence, elle retourne souvent à la prose! (16)

Au début, la poésie française semble être purement et simplement un récit d'exploits héroïques ou amoureux dont le jeu plaît à une aristocratie de seigneurs. La poésie est à ce moment une prose pure et simple avec quelques particularités techniques qui doivent aider la mémoire et apporter à la jouissance auditive une collaboration mnémotechnique. (35)

Jusqu'au romantisme, dans tout le fatras poétique publié qui est souvent illisible, il y a eu un ou deux grands poètes par siècle.

Mais voici le XIXe siècle, la royauté de Victor Hugo est proche et, en cent ans, la poésie française trouvera plus de génies qu'elle n'en a jamais eu. (45)

N'est-il pas essentiel de connaître les maîtresses à qui s'adressent les poèmes de Ronsard ou d'Apollinaire? n'est-il pas intéressant de pénétrer dans les arcanes de Rimbaud et de Verlaine et même jusqu'à l'attitude amoureuse de Mallarmé, si ces notions apportent des éclaircissements? (61)

Jean Cohen, *Structure du langage poétique* (Paris: Flammarion, 1966).

Le fait poétique devient alors un fait mesurable. Il s'exprime comme fréquence moyenne des écarts par rapport à la prose présentés par le langage poétique. . . . Le style poétique sera l'écart moyen de l'ensemble des poèmes, à partir duquel il serait, théoriquement, possible de mesurer le "taux de poésie" d'un poème donné. (15)

Dans de telles conditions, on peut aller jusqu'à dire que l'esthétique classique est une esthétique antipoétique et que si le génie du créateur, d'un Racine ou d'un La Fontaine, réussit à percer l'obstacle, l'art de la poésie ne pourra vraiment s'épanouir que dans le climat de liberté que le romantisme a le mérite d'avoir introduit dans l'art. . . . Le romantisme n'a pas inventé la poésie, mais on peut dire qu'il l'a découverte. (20)

La poésie s'est faite de plus en plus "poétique" au fur et à mesure qu'elle avançait dans son histoire. Phénomène qui est peut-être généralisable, et qui permettrait de définir la modernité esthétique, chaque art *involuant* en quelque sorte, par une approche toujours plus grande de sa propre forme pure, la poésie du poétique pur comme la peinture, à travers l'art abstrait, du pictural pure. (21)

Jacques Garelli, *La Gravitation poétique* (Paris: Mercure de France, 1966).

On voit donc que la création poétique ne se mesure pas à la mise en circulation d'idées abstraites. N'importe quelle proclamation en prose en est capable. Le poème ne se situe pas à ce niveau de désignation du langage. Plus simplement, l'écriture poétique va présenter des objets sonores qui en se faisant écouter révèlent par leur structure matérielle comme par leur sens ou leur détournement de sens logique la présence sourde et opaque d'un monde. (132)

Rien de tel pour le poème qui ne renvoie à aucune réalité extérieure à lui-même et qui ne fait voir qu'en se faisant voir. Non-sens ouvrant sur la chose et sens à la fois, il est à lui-même son propre monde, parce qu'il est issu de son propre vide; et cela parce que la réceptivité de l'imagination créatrice ne se réduit pas à la soumission de la sensibilité du sujet à l'empreinte réaliste du monde extérieur, mais qu'elle procède de la mise en forme créatrice de l'imagination transcendantale qui est l'oeuvre temporelle du néant. (157)

Jean-Paul Gourévitch, *La Poésie en France* (Paris: Editions Ouvrières, 1966).

La poésie a très longtemps été faite pour la déclamation et la récitation publique. Le passage à la lecture silencieuse marque un enrichissement. (47)

Ecrire et plus particulièrement poétiser, c'est faire passer le maximum d'univers possible entre la plume et le papier; c'est faire le dénombrement des terres où substituer sa propre création à celle qui nous est offerte. . . . Faire un poème relève d'une dimension ontologique et engage, qu'il en soit conscient ou non, le poète dans l'Universel. (88)

Bien comprendre que la poésie a de plus en plus cherché une concentration élevée de la "vitamine poétique" en abandonnant progressivement toute finalité narrative ou didactique ou dramatique ou moraliste ou rhétorique ou mnémotechnique et qu'on est peut-être, comme sembleraient le prouver les mouvements d'avant-garde, à l'époque de l'abandon de toute finalité émotionnelle, voire même de toute finalité linguistique. (110)

Il n'y a pas de problème plus important pour la poésie que le langage. Tout art est une réflexion sur les moyens de l'art. Parallèlement, toute poésie est une élucidation du langage. (144)

Georges Jean, *La Poésie* (Paris: Seuil, 1966).

La poésie ne peut en *aucune manière* aider à expliquer la science, ou à enseigner la philosophie, la morale, les structures du monde. (38)

Ce que le langage versifié lui révèle, ce sont ses propres sentiments; il [le poète] découvre dans les mots savoureux dont il use un moyen unique de parvenir à saisir ce qui lui échappe de lui-même; la qualité de *son* plaisir, la brûlure de *son* chagrin, la douceur terrible ou apaisée de *son* amour, pour un être ou pour le monde extérieur. . . . Et ceci depuis toujours. (40–41)

Dans ce cas particulier de l'homme en situation de poésie, le sentiment vibre avec une intensité aiguë, brûle et épuise, l'émotion renverse tous les équilibres intérieurs, mais, dans tous les cas, de cette cendre qui reste dans le coeur du poète peut renaître le Phénix. (62–63)

. . . nous sommes perpétuellement coincés entre le réel et l'imaginaire au point de ne pas toujours bien les distinguer l'un de l'autre. Le poète proclame, lui, leur identité, ou plutôt il pense que seule l'imagination contient le réel. . . . Au fond de la nuit la plus obscure, l'imagination poétique est une déesse aux yeux ouverts. (70–71)

Mais ne peut-on penser aussi que chaque grand poète crée en même temps que son propre univers son propre langage; que chaque univers poétique implique de ce fait une "vision du monde" originale. (90–91)

La poésie c'est l'anticonformisme sur tous les fronts. (149)

Guy Belleflamme, *Approche du phénomène poétique: Notions de théorie littéraire, Initiation à la lecture des poèmes lyriques* (Liège: Dessain, 1967).

La poésie lyrique est l'art du langage le plus personnel, le plus subjectif qui soit. Ou le poète nous livre ses émotions (ses enthousiasmes, ses déceptions . . .), en un mot ses sentiments personnels, ou il nous livre sa propre vision du monde. (17)

C'est de cette faculté d'invention que procède la création poétique. Ainsi, le lyrisme apparaît comme le terrain d'élection où s'exerce l'imagination. . . .

Une image ne peut procéder que d'une sensation réelle ou d'une imagination authentique. (63)

Il est donc important que l'image poétique donne du monde une vision nouvelle, *inédite.* Son pouvoir tient en partie dans son caractère de nouveauté, de suprise; et c'est en cela qu'elle est création. (64)

Car, enfin, tous les gens d'esprit ne sont pas nécessairement des gens de coeur. Le lyrisme est étranger au concettisme, tout comme il ne s'accommode guère de la satire, du genre didactique ou du dithyrambe exalté. . . . S'il s'y manifeste, c'est accidentellement et malgré les exigences du genre. (89–90)

On a donc accoutumé d'appeler *inspiration* toute impulsion spontanée et enthousiaste qui échappe au contrôle de la raison et que seul celui qui l'a reçue en don peut transformer en poème s'il est artiste. Le poète sera cet élu. (104)

Marcel Thiry, *Le Poème et la langue* (Brussels: La Renaissance du Livre, 1967).

Le poète modifie, c'est sa fonction. Nous savons, et cette étymologie n'est que trop souvent rappelée, que le poète est celui qui fait. Mais le prosateur aussi invente et fabrique; le don du poète est de changer la nature de ce qu'il touche. La vue des choses ni les lois de la société ne sont plus les mêmes après que l'aventure poétique les a rencontrées et traversées.

Les choses existaient avant que le poète les eût dites, mais un sens d'elles ne s'était pas révélé à tous, et c'est donc une nouvelle modalité d'existence qui leur est venue, si exister, c'est être connu. (13)

Le poème est revêtu d'une autorité sacerdotale . . . (42)

L'écrivain se distingue du poète, on en trouve ici la confirmation. C'est donc que d'écrire n'est pas une activité essentielle du poète, et même que le métier ou l'effort d'écrire n'est pas très compatible avec sa nature . . . (47–48)

Jean-Charles Payen and Jean-Pierre Chauveau, *La Poésie, des origines à 1715* (Paris: Colin, 1968).

La poésie, dans cette perspective, n'est plus seulement discours, "littérature", au sens objectif, et quelque peu suspect, du terme. Elle est manière d'être présent au monde, à la fois état d'âme, mode de connaissance et aventure spirituelle. . . . Aventure spirituelle, la poésie exige du poète qu'il renonce à tout ce qui n'est pas elle, au bonheur individuel, au confort, à la paix, qu'il s'engage corps et âme dans une entreprise qui le dépasse et dont il ignore l'issue, sinon les risques. Le vrai poète ne peut en effet se satisfaire d'aucun conformisme, encore moins se contenter d'appliquer des recettes . . . (8)

Ornement ou rhétorique, savant discours, "perle de la pensée", la poésie antérieure au symbolisme n'a fait trop souvent que pressentir sa véritable nature, art de dire, parmi d'autres, plutôt que moyen de conquête spirituelle. (10)

Il faudra sans doute attendre—en France du moins—Nerval, Baudelaire, Rimbaud et Mallarmé pour qu'enfin les poètes aient une claire conscience d'être autre chose que des artisans du vers et aspirent à cultiver la poésie pour la poésie. . . . Cette lente découverte de la poésie par elle-même s'achemine vers une conscience plus aiguë du mystère poétique dans sa grandeur et dans sa folie. (10–11)

Marcel Clémeur, *Alchimie et chimie poétiques: Essai* (Paris-Brussels: Sodi, 1969).

D'autre part, le poème prend volontiers pour thème son mystère prénatal, la merveille de ses aubes en voie de dépliement, ce qui n'intéresse, en principe, que les auteurs. La poésie, au lieu de chanter le monde et l'homme, s'analyse. (16)

Le plus haut potentiel chimique et alchimique caractériserait le verbe poétiquement élaboré, la métaphore supérieure, la formule magique. . . .

On attend la phrase, le mot, la syllabe, la lettre ou le signe qui résume et dévoile les secrets de l'univers. (18)

Le vers peut prétendre à un certain hiératisme, s'il atteint au sublime. Le poème engendre la synthèse des réalités symplectiques, l'une à l'autre irréductibles, et d'autant plus qu'une âme d'apparence étrangère les modifie, transpose, corrompt et régénère.

En principe, le poème n'est pas là pour expliquer. Il impose un chant, un charme, une fascination, un cauchemar, une folie. (33–34)

Venue d'ailleurs, la poésie réside en moi avant d'habiter le poème. . . . Là se reflètent mes certitudes, mes incertitudes, mes solutions, mes problèmes, ma valeur et ses ombres. (56)

On n'apprend pas à créer.

On naît créateur comme on naît poète. (372)

Robert Montal, *Introduction à la poésie française* (Paris-Brussels: Sodi, 1970).

C'est qu'aujourd'hui la poésie nous paraît manquer son but lorsqu'elle n'exprime pas les sentiments personnels de son auteur; le caractère essentiellement lyrique de sa vocation ne fait plus de doute pour personne. Elle a cessé d'être une mémoire collective pour devenir un langage individuel; son destin n'est plus d'être déclamée en public, mais déchiffrée sur la page blanche d'un livre; elle n'a plus partie liée ni avec l'histoire, ni avec la foi, ni avec la morale, ni avec la science; elle est un cri du coeur, un appel, un chant de joie, une prière, un balbutiement; elle est "de l'âme, pour l'âme", comme disait Rimbaud; elle ne concerne plus que le poète lui-même et les quelques personnes qui ont encore le temps de l'écouter. (106)

Jean-Claude Renard, *Notes sur la poésie* (Paris: Seuil, 1970).

Le poète, en écrivant, devient d'une certaine manière le poème qu'il écrit—et le poème, en s'écrivant, devient d'une certaine manière le poète qui l'écrit: l'un et l'autre s'identifiant en se modifiant l'un et l'autre et l'un par l'autre. (39)

Car il [le poème] entre en rapport avec ce qui ne se représente pas, ne se mesure pas et ne se juge pas. Il fait apparaître l'énigme, puis le mystère. (43)

C'est ainsi, par exemple, que le langage poétique, à force de chercher à se purifier de ce qui ne serait pas sa nature véritable, n'apparaît plus seulement comme un producteur de mythes, mais comme un mythe lui-même, ayant sa propre autonomie . . . (58)

Il n'existe peut-être pas de définition de la poésie parce que la poésie n'est mesurée par rien d'autre qu'elle-même . . . (75)

Nos propres poèmes (quels qu'ils soient) nous révèlent par suite tôt ou tard, clairement ou obscurément, nos propres secrets comme nos propres obsessions (et il advient même qu'ils prédisent), sans que nous puissions fausser leur parole. (105)

Camille Souyris, *L'Aventure poétique: Essai d'introduction générale à une Poétique moderne* (Cannes: La Diaspora Française, 1972).

Original, il [le poète] l'est dans son langage: c'est un homme qui ne parle pas comme tout le monde. . . . C'est peut-être en raison de cette modulation, de cette carmination, de ce chant sacré de la poésie qu'il doit d'être sincère avec lui-même, de croire, à la différence des autres hommes, en ce qu'il dit, au moment où il le dit: c'est qu'il se prend au sérieux et veut qu'on le prenne au sérieux. (19–20)

Le Poète est celui qui sait, celui qui a cheminé tout au long d'une voie mystérieuse pour arriver au Temple et en franchir le seuil sacré, avant de contempler la Réalité face à face, de saisir *"les splendeurs situées derrière le tombeau."* (23)

Le caractère spontané du jaillissement verbal nous est apparu la marque fondamentale de toute création poétique. (60)

Mais il va de soi que son *"message"* s'inscrit surtout dans l'Eternel et que, de toute façon, il se révélera efficace pour l'avenir. Car il dépasse son temps et présage de grands bouleversements: le poète n'est-il pas un *"prophète"*, un *"mage"*, un *"Voyant"*? (120–21)

Georges-Emmanuel Clancier, *La Poésie et ses environs* (Paris: Gallimard, 1973).

Le poète est cet enfant, cet homme qui plonge dans sa nuit intérieure, y redevient pareil à l'enfant qu'il a été, naïf, émerveillé, à peine encore séparé du monde et de ses mystères, et il tente cette aventure spirituelle pour dérober, au coeur de la nuit (là où la raison avoue son impuissance, là où règnent les secrets des rêves), sinon le feu total de la connaissance, du moins des fragments, des étincelles de ce foyer, de ce coeur ardent de la vie. (27)

Employant le langage de tous, *le poète doit pourtant créer, dans et par ses poèmes, un langage personnel et nouveau.* (31)

De même que "Il était" pourrait être la clef—au sens musical—du roman, "Je suis" est la racine du chant. Cette affirmation ne relève pas de l'égoïsme, elle fonde plutôt le centre nécessaire où l'univers et l'être qu'il investit ne sont plus qu'une seule et même flamme.

Le poème en son essence—autrement dit, épuré de tout ce qui n'est pas lui-même: récit, anecdote, discours, leçon, décor—se compose des harmoniques qu'éveille cette évidence. (70)

Pierre Dufayet and Yvette Jenger, *Le Comment de la poésie* (Paris: Les Editions E S F, 1973).

Vivre ce que nous appelons l'expérience immédiate de poésie, c'est, en plus de tous les aspects que nous avons essayés de dégager, dépasser les limites que le langage de prose impose à la pensée. (40)

Cette tentative d'écrire de la poésie comme une création *ex nihilo* est une pure vue de l'esprit, et c'est, sans doute, pourquoi aucune oeuvre notable n'a pu naître de cette intention.

En effet, ce que le dire fait exister porte la marque de l'essence qui lui a donné naissance, et vouloir faire quelque chose de rien revient, en fait, à exprimer sa personne la plus profonde et la plus authentiquement personnelle. (53)

L'être de la poésie est transcendant; à ce titre, il se dérobe à mon dire, même si je peux en avoir une certaine conscience, qui est déjà une forme de connaissance; cette connaissance est du domaine de l'ineffable, je ne peux en prendre possession. (62–63)

Marc Eigeldinger, *Poésie et métamorphoses* (Neuchâtel: La Baconnière, 1973).

Selon une vision schématique, on peut affirmer que l'histoire de l'affranchissement de l'imagination s'étend, dans la littérature française, de Rousseau au surréalisme, en passant par Victor Hugo, Baudelaire et Rimbaud. (8)

La pensée poétique est de type analogique parce qu'elle traduit des alliances imprévues entre des objets occupant des points ou des niveaux différents de l'espace grâce à ces multiples métamorphoses dont la puissance créatrice de l'imagination détient l'aptitude souveraine. L'image, flèche de lumière, célèbre la présence de l'homme dans l'univers, elle chante leur union substantielle à la faveur de sa mobilité. Semblable à l'opération alchimique, elle métamorphose la *boue* en *or* et transfigure tout objet sensible en un corps surréel qui acquiert les propriétés solaires par les effets de la transmutation verbale. (16)

Si le poète est disposé à lui témoigner sa confiance, le langage devient le miroir de l'univers, le lieu de rencontre entre l'homme et le monde, le centre où le verbe humain peut communiquer avec le Verbe divin . . .

Soumise à l'incarnation du Verbe, la poésie est un langage sacré qui exprime la dimension spirituelle du monde, l'altitude intérieure des êtres et des choses. (36–37)

Roger Laufer and Bernard Lecherbonnier, *Littérature et langages: Les genres et les thèmes,* vol. 2: *le conte, la poésie* (Paris: Nathan, 1974).

Devenu célèbre en France avec Rimbaud, ce terme [voyant] définit fréquemment cette faculté ultra-lucide qui aboutit à la *connaissance* poétique du monde. . . . Après Gérard de Nerval, authentique "voyant", le premier à être passé de l'autre côté des choses . . . , c'est Baudelaire qui, avant Rimbaud, nous persuadera "que tout est hiéroglyphique". (114–115).

La force du désir consiste à orienter l'imagination dans le sens d'une réalisation de ses rêves. Ce pourrait être la définition même de la poésie: dépassement de la raison, des apparences du réel, enchantement du quotidien, tension vers le rêve et l'idéal. Extase acquise dans le vertige du désir. (138)

La plupart des grands artistes n'étaient-ils pas atteints eux-mêmes de troubles de la personnalité, ou mal adaptés à la vie sociale, comme pourraient d'ailleurs le laisser supposer les cas bien connus de Blake, Musset, Nerval, Poe, Van Gogh . . . ? Une oeuvre d'art ne tiendrait-elle pas sa "valeur" plutôt de son authenticité que de son élaboration, toujours mensongère parce qu'artificielle? (217)

La prose communique quelque chose d'extérieur à elle-même. Elle est outil. La poésie ne fait que se communiquer en tant qu'acte de langage. (254)

R.-J. Charpentier, *Survol critique de la poésie française, des origines à nos jours (Vers une poésie totale): Essai* (Paris: Editions de l'Athanor, 1975).

Le seul but de la Poésie ... est de se manifester. ...

La Poésie ne peut avoir d'autre but qu'elle-même, car en principe elle constitue dès lors, de par son essence même, le summum de la connaissance par l'ampleur sans égale de ses moyens d'investigation. (13)

... *originalité* dans le déroulement de la pensée, dans les images, et même dans les mots qui en sont le substratum ... *sincérité et fidélité du texte transcrit aux idées et aux images résultant de la "prise de conscience".* (17)

Tant il est vrai que *la véritable Poésie se rit des "arts poétiques" et autres guide-ânes, et ne connaît de règles que celles dictées au poète par son propre génie* ... (34–35)

En cent ans d'histoire la poésie française parcourera plus de chemin qu'au cours des dix siècles précédents, et cela aussi bien du point de vue fond que du point de vue forme. (104)

Marceline Desbordes-Valmore ... a réussi, avec les humbles mots de chaque jour, avec de simples mots de femme, d'amante, de mère ou d'épouse, à atteindre aux plus hauts sommets de l'art, parce qu'*elle n'a jamais rien écrit qu'elle n'ait profondément senti.* (106)

Jean-Louis Joubert, *La Poésie* (Paris: Colin and Gallimard, 1977).

Les poètes nous apprennent à découvrir (ou inventer) le monde et nousmêmes ... (24)

Le projet des poètes les plus conscients est de tendre au maximum cette distance ou cette opposition entre poésie et *"langage ordinaire".* ...

Comme la danse, la poésie ne va nulle part; elle trouve sa fin en ellemême. ... La poésie est d'abord une aventure de langage. (53)

La poésie est un acte de rébellion et d'invention. Rébellion: le refus de l'arbitraire du signe, le refus de l'échec du langage; ce que dit le mimétisme poétique, c'est d'abord cette révolte. Invention: les mots du poème suscitent des mondes nouveaux; ils libèrent tous les possibles; ils laissent affleurer un désir qu'ils tendent à réaliser. (68–69)

La poésie est la forme du langage par laquelle l'homme (se) donne à voir. Elle est révélation, dévoilement, et par là même ouverture sur l'être. (70)

Michel Patillon, *Précis d'analyse littéraire,* vol. 2: *Décrire la poésie* (Paris: Nathan, 1977).

Avec la poésie, l'homme joue son langage et il y enferme des mondes. (8)

La fonction poétique détermine chez le destinataire une attitude particulière à l'égard du message: au lieu de le lui faire traverser, comme la fonction référentielle, elle l'y arrête. On dit que le message poétique est *intransitif*. (15)

La notion de motivation poétique découle du caractère *intransitif* du message poétique. Elle se définit comme l'existence de relations non arbitraires entre le contenu et l'expression d'un texte poétique, telles que la signification totale est inséparable de la forme du message. (22)

NOTES

CHAPTER 1

1. Novalis, *Schriften: Die Werke Friedrich von Hardenbergs,* ed. Paul Kluckhohn and Richard Samuel; vol. 2, ed. Richard Samuel et al. (Stuttgart: Kohlhammer, 1965), 592.

2. Jean-Paul Sartre, *Situations, II* (Paris: Gallimard, 1948), 55–330, esp. 63–70.

3. D. J. Mossop, *Pure Poetry: Studies in French Poetic Theory and Practice, 1746 to 1945* (Oxford: Clarendon Press, 1971).

4. For the relevant texts, see *L'Art poétique,* ed. Jacques Charpier and Pierre Seghers (Paris: Seghers, 1956); Alain Bosquet, *Verbe et vertige: Situations de la poésie* (Paris: Hachette, 1961); *Modern French Poets on Poetry: An Anthology,* ed. Robert Gibson (Cambridge: Cambridge University Press, 1961); Henri Lemaître, *La Poésie depuis Baudelaire* (Paris: Colin, 1965), 77–161; and, for an excellent brief selection, Peter Broome and Graham Chesters, *The Appreciation of Modern French Poetry (1850–1950)* (Cambridge: Cambridge University Press, 1976), 56–59.

5. See note 4.

6. Jean Cohen, *Structure du langage poétique* (Paris: Flammarion, 1966), also *Le Haut Langage: Théorie de la poéticité* (Paris: Flammarion, 1979).

7. Roland Barthes, *Le Degré zéro de l'écriture* (Paris: Seuil, 1953), especially the essays "Y a-t-il une écriture poétique?" and "Triomphe et rupture de l'écriture bourgeoise."

8. Robert Champigny, *Le Genre poétique: Essai* (Monte-Carlo: Regain, 1963).

9. See *Revue d'Histoire Littéraire de la France* 35 (1928): 152.

10. André Gide, "Préface" to his *Anthologie de la poésie française,* Bibliothèque de la Pléiade (Paris: Gallimard, 1949), viii.

11. Arthur Rimbaud, *Œuvres complètes,* ed. Antoine Adam, Bibliothèque de la Pléiade (Paris: Gallimard, 1972), 250.

12. *Le Conte, la poésie: Textes et travaux,* ed. Roger Laufer and Bernard Lecherbonnier, vol. 2 of *Littérature et langages: Les genres et les thèmes* (Paris: Nathan, 1974).

13. François Germain, *L'Art de commenter un poème lyrique: De l'inspiration et du style lyriques, avec applications à la composition française* (Paris: Foucher, 1959).

14. *Interpretationen französischer Gedichte,* ed. Kurt Wais (Darmstadt: Wissenschaftliche Buchgesellschaft, 1970).

15. *Die französische Lyrik: Von Villon bis zur Gegenwart,* ed. Hans Hinterhäuser, 2 vols. (Düsseldorf: Bagel, 1975).

16. The bibliography is immense. In the course of this book I have profited especially from the following recent studies on periods, currents, and genres of poetry: André Baïche, *La Naissance du baroque français: Poésie et image de la Pléiade à Jean de La Ceppède* (Toulouse: Université de Toulouse–le Mirail, 1976); Karl-Heinz Bender, *König und Vasall: Untersuchungen zur Chansons de geste des XII. Jahrhunderts* (Heidelberg: Winter, 1967); Terence C. Cave, *Devotional Poetry in France, c. 1570–1613* (Cambridge: Cambridge University Press, 1969); Dorothy Gabe Coleman, *The Gallo-Roman Muse: Aspects of Roman Literary Tradition in Sixteenth-Century France* (Cambridge: Cambridge University Press, 1979); Guy Demerson, *La Mythologie classique dans l'oeuvre lyrique de la "Pléiade"* (Geneva: Droz, 1972); Anny Detalle, *Mythes, merveilleux et légendes dans la poésie française de 1840 à 1860* (Paris: Klincksieck, 1976); Roger Dragonetti, *La Technique poétique des trouvères dans la chanson courtoise: Contribution à l'étude de la rhétorique médiévale* (Bruges: De Tempel, 1960); Robert Finch, *The Sixth Sense: Individualism in French Poetry, 1686–1760* (Toronto: University of Toronto Press, 1966); Hugo Friedrich, *Die Struktur der modernen Lyrik von Baudelaire bis zur Gegenwart* (Hamburg: Rowohlt, 1956); Robert W. Greene, *Six French Poets of Our Time: A Critical and Historical Study* (Princeton: Princeton University Press, 1979); Robert W. Hanning, *The Individual in Twelfth-Century Romance* (New Haven: Yale University Press, 1977); John Porter Houston, *The Demonic Imagination: Style and Theme in French Romantic Poetry* (Baton Rouge: Louisiana State University Press, 1969); idem, *French Symbolism and the Modernist Movement: A Study of Poetic Structures* (Baton Rouge: Louisiana State University Press, 1980); idem, *The Rhetoric of Poetry in the Renaissance and Seventeenth Century* (Baton Rouge: Louisiana State University Press, 1983); Erich Köhler, *Ideal und Wirklichkeit in der höfischen Epik: Studien zur Form der frühen Artus- und Graldichtung* (Tübingen: Niemeyer, 1956); Henri Lafay, *La Poésie française du premier XVIIe siècle (1598–1630): Esquisse pour un tableau* (Paris: Nizet, 1975); Sylvain Menant, *La Chute d'Icare: La crise de la poésie française, 1700–1750* (Geneva: Droz, 1981); Daniel Poirion, *Le Poète et le prince: L'évolution du lyrisme courtois de Guillaume de Machaut à Charles d'Orléans* (Paris: Presses Universitaires de France, 1965); Laurence M. Porter, *The Renaissance of the Lyric in French Romanticism: Elegy, "Poëme" and Ode* (Lexington: French Forum, 1978); Jean-Pierre Richard, *Onze études sur la poésie moderne* (Paris: Seuil, 1964); Bernard Weinberg, *The Limits of Symbolism: Studies of Five Modern French Poets* (Chicago: University of Chicago Press, 1966).

17. Roman Jakobson and Claude Lévi-Strauss, " 'Les chats' de Charles Baudelaire," *L'Homme* 2:1 (1962): 5–21, reprinted in Jakobson, *Questions de poétique* (Paris: Seuil, 1973), 401–19; and *"Les Chats" de Baudelaire: Une confrontation de méthodes,* ed. Maurice Delcroix and Walter Geerts (Namur: Presses Universitaires de Namur, 1980), 19–35.

18. Julia Kristeva, *La Révolution du langage poétique: L'avant-garde à la fin du XIXe siècle, Lautréamont et Mallarmé* (Paris: Seuil, 1974); Cohen, *Structure du langage poétique* and *Le Haut Langage;* Michael Riffaterre, *Essais de stylistique structurale* (Paris: Flammarion, 1971), *La Production du texte* (Paris: Seuil, 1978), and *Semiotics of Poetry* (Bloomington: Indiana University Press, 1978).

19. A. J. Greimas et al., *Essais de sémiotique poétique* (Paris: Larousse, 1972); Tzvetan Todorov et al., *Sémantique de la poésie* (Paris: Seuil, 1979); "Le Groupe μ," *Rhétorique de la poésie: Lecture linéaire, lecture tabulaire* (Paris: Presses Universitaires de France, 1977). In addition, see Nicolas Ruwet, *Langage, musique, poésie* (Paris: Seuil, 1972); and, oriented toward the schools, M. Patillon, *Précis d'analyse littéraire,* vol. 2: *Décrire la poésie* (Paris:

Nathan, 1977), and Jean Molino and Joëlle Tamine, *Introduction à l'analyse linguistique de la poésie* (Paris: Presses Universitaires de France, 1982).

20. Henri Meschonnic, *Pour la poétique, I: Essai* (Paris: Gallimard, 1970) and the subsequent volumes; and Greimas, "Pour une théorie du discours poétique," in *Essais de sémiotique poétique*, 5–24.

21. Paul Eluard, ed., *Première Anthologie vivante de la poésie du passé*, 2 vols. (Paris: Seghers, 1951); Thierry Maulnier, ed., *Introduction à la poésie française* (Paris: Gallimard, 1939); Roger Caillois, *Les Impostures de la poésie* (Paris: Gallimard, 1945), and *Art poétique* (Paris: Gallimard, 1958); and Francis Ponge, *Pour un Malherbe* (Paris: Gallimard, 1965). See also A. Kibédi Varga, *Les Constantes du poème: A la recherche d'une poétique dialectique* (The Hague: Van Goor Zonen, 1963), repr. *Les Constantes du poème: Analyse du langage poétique* (Paris: Picard, 1977); and René-Albert Gutmann, *Introduction à la lecture des poètes français* (Paris: Nizet, 1967). In English, see Frederic O. Musser, *Strange Clamor: A Guide to the Critical Reading of French Poetry* (Detroit: Wayne State University Press, 1965).

22. Ernst Robert Curtius, *Kritische Essays zur europäischen Literatur* (Berne: Francke, 1950), especially the essays on Virgil and Goethe.

CHAPTER 2

1. Perhaps the most cogent theoretical discussion on the subject remains E. M. W. Tillyard and C. S. Lewis, *The Personal Heresy: A Controversy* (London: Oxford University Press, 1939).

2. T. S. Eliot, "Tradition and the Individual Talent," in his *Selected Essays*, new ed. (New York: Harcourt, Brace and World, 1950), 3–11, esp. 7–8, 10.

3. Barbara Herrnstein Smith, *On the Margins of Discourse: The Relation of Literature to Language* (Chicago: University of Chicago Press, 1978), chap. 2; and Robert C. Elliott, *The Literary Persona* (Chicago: University of Chicago Press, 1982), chap. 4.

4. See John C. Lapp, *The Esthetics of Negligence: La Fontaine's "Contes"* (Cambridge: Cambridge University Press, 1971).

5. Boileau, *Œuvres complètes*, ed. Antoine Adam and Françoise Escal, Bibliothèque de la Pléiade (Paris: Gallimard, 1966), 187–222 and 1004–20, esp. 221–22.

6. Curtius, *Europäische Literatur und lateinisches Mittelalter* (Berne: Francke, 1948), chap. 8.

7. *Œuvres complètes de Voltaire*, ed. Louis Moland (Paris: Garnier, 1877), 10: 83–88.

8. Caillois, *Art poétique*, 70.

9. *Gace Brulé, trouvère champenois: Edition des chansons et étude historique*, ed. Holger Peterson Dyggve (Helsinki: Société Néophilologique, 1951), 332–35.

10. *Chansons attribuées au Chastelain de Couci (fin du XIIe–début du XIIIe siècle)*, ed. Alain Lerond (Paris: Presses Universitaires de France, 1964), 68–71.

11. *Les Chansons de Thibaut de Champagne, roi de Navarre*, ed. A. Wallensköld, Société des Anciens Textes Français (Paris: Champion, 1925), 26–30.

12. Pierre de Ronsard, *Œuvres complètes*, vol. 5, ed. Paul Laumonier, Société des Textes Français Modernes (Paris: Hachette, 1928), 196–97.

13. Ronsard, *Œuvres complètes*, vol. 17, pt. 2, ed. Paul Laumonier, revised and completed by Isidore Silver and Raymond Lebègue, Société des Textes Français Modernes (Paris: Didier, 1959), 125.

14. Ronsard, *Œuvres complètes*, ed. Gustave Cohen, Bibliothèque de la Pléiade (Paris: Gallimard, 1950), 1: 10–11.

CHAPTER 3

1. An excellent recent study on this topic is David Hillery, *Music and Poetry in France from Baudelaire to Mallarmé: An Essay on Poetic Theory and Practice* (Berne: Lang, 1980). For more general information, see Marie Naudin, *Evolution parallèle de la poésie et de la musique en France: Rôle unificateur de la chanson* (Paris: Nizet, 1968); and James Anderson Winn, *Unsuspected Eloquence: A History of the Relations Between Poetry and Music* (New Haven: Yale University Press, 1981). For the contemporary period, see Lucienne Cantaloube-Ferrieu, *Chanson et poésie des années 30 aux années 60: Trenet, Brassens, Ferré . . . ou les "enfants naturels" du surréalisme* (Paris: Nizet, 1981).

2. Northrop Frye, *Anatomy of Criticism: Four Essays* (Princeton: Princeton University Press, 1957), 23–24.

3. Champigny, "Le Français comme langue poétique," *French Review* 30 (1956–57): 207–10. On this problem, see also Efim Etkind, *Un Art en crise: Essai de poétique de la traduction poétique* (Lausanne: L'Age d'Homme, 1982).

4. Walther von Wartburg, *Französisches Etymologisches Wörterbuch: Eine Darstellung des galloromanischen Sprachschatzes,* 14 vols. (Bonn: Klopp; Leipzig and Berlin: Teubner; Basel: Helbing and Lichtenhahn; Zbinden, 1928–67); Paul Imbs, *Trésor de la langue française: Dictionnaire de la langue du XIXe et du XXe siècle, 1789–1960,* vol. 1–(Paris: Klincksieck, 1971–).

5. I have benefited enormously from Leonard Forster, *The Poet's Tongues: Multilingualism in Literature* (London: Cambridge University Press, 1970). See also H. J. Chaytor, *From Script to Print: An Introduction to Medieval Vernacular Literature* (Cambridge: Heffer, 1945), chap. 3.

6. F. R. Leavis, *Revaluation: Tradition and Development in English Poetry* (London: Chatto and Windus, 1936), 53.

7. Houston, *The Rhetoric of Poetry.*

8. On the general topic of medieval obscenity, see Hans Robert Jauss, "Die klassische und die christliche Rechtfertigung des Hässlichen in mittelalterlicher Literatur," 143–68; and Wolf-Dieter Stempel, "Mittelalterliche Obzönität als literarästhetisches Problem," 187–205, in *Die nicht mehr schönen Künste: Grenzphänomene des Ästhetischen,* ed. H. R. Jauss (Munich: Fink, 1968).

9. *Raoul de Cambrai, chanson de geste,* ed. Paul Meyer and Auguste Longnon, Société des Anciens Textes Français (Paris: Didot, 1882).

10. Mikhail Bakhtin, *Rabelais and His World* (Cambridge, Mass.: MIT Press, 1968).

11. *Le Roman de Renart: Première Branche,* ed. Mario Roques, Classiques Français du Moyen Age (Paris: Champion, 1957).

12. Guillaume de Lorris and Jean de Meun, *Le Roman de la Rose,* ed. Félix Lecoy, 3 vols., Classiques Français du Moyen Age (Paris: Champion, 1965–70). Texts cited from vol. 1.

13. *Le Testament Villon,* ed. Jean Rychner and Albert Henry, Textes Littéraires Français (Geneva: Droz, 1974), vol. 1, vv. 1591–627.

CHAPTER 4

1. Barbara Hardy, *The Advantage of Lyric: Essays on Feeling in Poetry* (London: Athlone Press, 1977), 1. Quoted in Christopher Clausen's valuable and insightful study, *The Place of Poetry: Two Centuries of an Art in Crisis* (Lexington: University Press of Kentucky, 1981), 5.

NOTES 195

2. On this topic, see Predrag Matvejevitch, *La Poésie de circonstance: Etude des formes de l'engagement poétique* (Paris: Nizet, 1971). For the relationship of the poet to the community in general, see F. W. Bateson, *English Poetry: A Critical Introduction*, rev. ed. (New York: Barnes and Noble, 1966).

3. *Œuvres complètes de Voltaire*, ed. Louis Moland (Paris: Garnier, 1877), 10: 526.

4. *Œuvres complètes de Voltaire*, 10: 269–71.

5. Pierre de Ronsard, *Œuvres complètes*, vol. 8, ed. Paul Laumonier, Société des Textes Français Modernes (Paris: Droz, 1935), 47–72.

6. See chapter 2, note 5.

7. Edwin Honig, *Dark Conceit: The Making of Allegory* (Evanston: Northwestern University Press, 1959), 11; see also Angus Fletcher, *Allegory: The Theory of a Symbolic Mode* (Ithaca: Cornell University Press, 1964). On medieval and Renaissance allegory, see Rosemond Tuve, *Allegorical Imagery: Some Medieval Books and Their Posterity* (Princeton: Princeton University Press, 1966); and Maureen Quilligan, *The Language of Allegory: Defining the Genre* (Ithaca: Cornell University Press, 1979).

8. Charles d'Orléans, *Poésies*, ed. Pierre Champion, 2 vols., Classiques Français du Moyen Age (Paris: Champion, 1923–27), 1: 88–89.

9. *Poésies*, 1: 130–31.

10. *Poésies*, 2: 477–78. On this text, see Jean Starobinski, "L'encre de la mélancolie," *Nouvelle Revue Française* 11 (1963): 410–23.

11. See William Calin, *A Muse for Heroes: Nine Centuries of the Epic in France* (Toronto: University of Toronto Press, 1983).

CHAPTER 5

1. See Paul Bénichou, *Le Sacre de l'écrivain, 1750–1830: Essai sur l'avènement d'un pouvoir spirituel laïque dans la France moderne* (Paris: Corti, 1973).

2. Lewis, *The Personal Heresy*, 103.

3. George Steiner, *In Bluebeard's Castle: Some Notes towards the Redefinition of Culture* (New Haven: Yale University Press, 1971).

4. In French studies there are no analogues to Hoxie Neale Fairchild, *Religious Trends in English Poetry*, 6 vols. (New York: Columbia University Press, 1939–68), not even the equivalents of Vincent Buckley, *Poetry and the Sacred* (London: Chatto and Windus, 1968), or Helen Gardner, *Religion and Literature* (New York: Oxford University Press, 1971). Henri Bremond's famous *Histoire littéraire du sentiment religieux en France depuis la fin des guerres de religion jusqu'à nos jours*, 11 vols. (Paris: Bloud and Gay, 1916–33), treats seventeenth-century devotional writing in the broadest sense of the term, with little direct attention to verse.

5. Eliot, "Religion and Literature," in *Selected Essays*, 343–54, esp. 345–46.

6. *Les Miracles de Nostre Dame par Gautier de Coinci*, ed. V. Frederic Koenig, Textes Littéraires Français, vol. 1 (Geneva: Droz; and Lille: Giard, 1955), 44–46.

7. On *contrafactum*, see Bruce W. Wardropper, *Historia de la poesía lírica a lo divino en la cristiandad occidental* (Madrid: Revista de Occidente, 1958); on "le registre pieux," see Pierre Bec, *La Lyrique française au Moyen Age (XIIe–XIIIe siècles): Contribution à une typologie des genres poétiques médiévaux, Etudes et textes*, 2 vols. (Paris: Picard, 1977–78), 1: 142–50; 2: 65–85.

8. Sponde, *Poésies*, ed. Alan Boase and François Ruchon, Les Trésors de la Littérature française (Geneva: Cailler, 1949), 241.

9. Jean de La Ceppède, *Les Théorèmes sur le sacré Mystère de notre rédemption: Reproduction de l'édition de Toulouse de 1613–1622*, ed. Jean Rousset, Travaux d'Humanisme et Renaissance (Geneva: Droz, 1966), 297.

10. On the devotional revival and its influence on the culture and poetry of the times, see Louis L. Martz, *The Poetry of Meditation: A Study in English Religious Literature of the Seventeenth Century* (New Haven: Yale University Press, 1954); and, for France, the excellent volume by Cave, *Devotional Poetry in France*.

11. Eliot, "Dante," in *Selected Essays*, 199–237, esp. 218–19.

CHAPTER 6

1. "La Poésie en France," ed. Jérôme Garcin, *Les Nouvelles Littéraires*, no. 2583 (5–12 May 1977), 15–26. This issue made national headlines. See also Georges Mounin, *Poésie et société* (Paris: Presses Universitaires de France, 1962); Jean-Paul Gourévitch, *La Poésie en France* (Paris: Editions Ouvrières, 1966); Georges Jean, *La Poésie* (Paris: Seuil, 1966); Robert Montal, *Introduction à la poésie française* (Paris and Brussels: Sodi, 1970).

2. David Perkins, *A History of Modern Poetry: From the 1890s to the High Modernist Mode* (Cambridge, Mass.: Harvard University, Belknap Press, 1976), chap. 1.

3. These ideas are proposed by Mounin, *Poésie et société;* Gourévitch, *La Poésie en France;* Jean, *La Poésie;* and Montal, *Introduction à la poésie française*. See also Henri Peyre, *Writers and Their Critics: A Study of Misunderstanding* (Ithaca: Cornell University Press, 1944), emended as *The Failure of Criticism* (Ithaca: Cornell University Press, 1967).

4. Pierre Kuentz, "Diffuser la culture: mais quelle culture?" in *L'Enseignement de la littérature: Crise et perspectives*, ed. Michel Mansuy (Paris: Nathan, 1977), 195–205, and his comment, 213–14.

5. György Lukács, *Studies in European Realism: A Sociological Survey of the Writings of Balzac, Stendhal, Zola, Tolstoy, Gorki, and Others*, trans. Edith Bone (London: Merlin Press, 1972), 208.

6. Curtius, "Über die altfranzösische Epik," in his *Gesammelte Aufsätze zur romanischen Philologie* (Berne: Francke, 1960), 106–304, especially his essays on *Aspremont* and *La Chevalerie Ogier*, 204–13 and 214–27.

7. I apologize for inflicting on the reader the equivalent of a mustering of the troops in the *Iliad* or the *Aeneid*. It is the only way I know to convince skeptics to accept the predominantly aristocratic, provincial character of early French poetry, a fact that a number of writers on literary subjects, including Sartre and Barthes, tend to ignore.

8. Jauss, "*La douceur du foyer:* Lyrik des Jahres 1857 als Muster der Vermittlung sozialer Normen," in his *Ästhetische Erfahrung und literarische Hermeneutik*, vol. 1 (Munich: Fink, 1977), 343–76.

9. For data in this historical section I have profited from Reto R. Bezzola, *Les Origines et la formation de la littérature courtoise en Occident (500–1200)*, pt. 2, vol. 2, and pt. 3, vols. 1 and 2 (Paris: Champion, 1960–63); and John Lough, *Writer and Public in France: From the Middle Ages to the Present Day* (Oxford: Clarendon Press, 1978).

10. *La Pucelle d'Orléans*, ed. Jeroom Vercruysse, vol. 7 of *Les Œuvres complètes de Voltaire* (Geneva: Institut et Musée Voltaire, 1970).

11. Leavis, "Retrospect 1950," in the 1950 edition of his *New Bearings in English Poetry: A Study of the Contemporary Situation* (London: Chatto and Windus, 1932 and 1950).

12. See, for example, Jean Ricardou, "Travailler autrement," in *L'Enseignement de la littérature*, 13–22, plus his comments and those of his friends during the discussion.

13. Gourévitch, *La Poésie en France*, 155–248.

14. Robert Goffin, *Fil d'Ariane pour la poésie* (Paris: Nizet, 1964).

15. Hinterhäuser, "Anthologien französischer Lyrik und literarischer Geschmackswandel," in *Die französische Lyrik*, 1: 9–20.

16. Robert Escarpit et al., *Le Littéraire et le social: Eléments pour une sociologie de la littérature* (Paris: Flammarion, 1970).

17. See the articles in the issue of *Littérature* entitled "Le discours de l'école sur les textes," no. 7 (October 1972); and Bernard Mouralis, *Les Contre-littératures* (Paris: Presses Universitaires de France, 1975).

18. Barthes, "Réflexions sur un manuel," in *L'Enseignement de la littérature: Centre culturel de Cerisy-la-Salle, 22 au 29 juillet 1969*, ed. Serge Doubrovsky and Tzvetan Todorov (Paris: Plon, 1971), 170–77.

19. René Wellek, "Criticism as Evaluation," in his *"The Attack on Literature" and Other Essays* (Chapel Hill: University of North Carolina Press, 1982), 48–63, esp. 49.

CHAPTER 7

1. Franco Simone, *Il Rinascimento francese: Studi e ricerche* (Turin: Società Editrice Internazionale, 1961), and *Storia della storiografia letteraria francese: Due capitoli introduttivi* (Turin: Bottega d'Erasmo, 1969).

2. Clément Marot, *Les Epîtres, Œuvres satiriques, Œuvres lyriques, Œuvres diverses, Les Epigrammes, Les Traductions*, ed. C. A. Mayer, 6 vols. (London: Athlone Press, 1958–70; Geneva: Slatkine, 1980).

3. Joachim du Bellay, *Œuvres poétiques*, ed. Henri Chamard, 6 vols., Société des Textes Français Modernes (Paris: Cornély; Droz; Hachette, 1908–31); Pierre de Ronsard, *Œuvres complètes*, ed. Paul Laumonier, Isidore Silver, and Raymond Lebègue, 20 vols., Société des Textes Français Modernes (Paris: Hachette; Droz; Didier, 1914–75).

4. Gustave Lanson, *Histoire de la littérature française* (Paris: Hachette, 1985), pt. 4, bk. 1, chap. 2.

5. Frye, *The Stubborn Structure: Essays on Criticism and Society* (Ithaca: Cornell University Press, 1970), chap. 9, esp. 158; also *The Secular Scripture: A Study of the Structure of Romance* (Cambridge, Mass.: Harvard University Press, 1976).

6. Lukács, *Wider den missverstandenen Realismus* (Hamburg: Claassen, 1958).

7. Marcel Raymond, *De Baudelaire au surréalisme: Essai sur le mouvement poétique contemporain* (Paris: Corrêa, 1933); and, more recently, Greene, *Six French Poets of Our Time*.

8. Friedrich, *Die Struktur der modernen Lyrik*.

9. Harold Bloom, *The Anxiety of Influence: A Theory of Poetry* (New York: Oxford University Press, 1973); see also other volumes, of practical criticism, by Bloom, and W. Jackson Bate, *The Burden of the Past and the English Poet* (Cambridge, Mass.: Harvard University, Belknap Press, 1970).

10. Jean Rousset, *La Littérature de l'âge baroque en France: Circé et le paon* (Paris: Corti, 1954), and *L'Intérieur et l'extérieur: Essais sur la poésie et sur le théâtre au XVIIe siècle* (Paris: Corti, 1968).

11. Eliot, "Tradition and the Individual Talent," 3–11, esp. 4.

INDEX

Adam de la Halle, 44–45, 53
allegory, 63–66, 78–80, 86–94, 107–8, 121, 151, 152–54, 165
Amyot, Jacques, Bishop of Auxerre, 135
Anacreon, 168
Anouilh, Jean, 100, 141
anticourtly texts, 37, 63–70
antifeminism, 59–70, 163
Apollinaire, Guillaume, 3, 10, 35, 42, 45, 53, 165–68, 174, 182
Aragon, Louis, 14–15, 23, 35, 42, 45, 55, 73, 85, 86, 96, 97, 106, 107, 122, 125, 139, 145, 146, 160, 163, 165, 166, 168, 170, 177
Argile, 100
Ariosto, Lodovico, 9, 24, 25, 139, 140, 141, 168, 169
aristocratic literature, 134–36
Arnaut Daniel of Ribérac, 17, 177
Arnold, Matthew, 99
Arp, Hans, 51
Aubanel, Théodore, 162, 166
Aubigné, Théodore Agrippa d', 4, 10, 25, 35, 48, 56, 57, 73, 79, 83–84, 87, 88, 95, 96, 101, 104, 105, 107, 109, 122, 132, 134–136, 147, 149, 154–59, 164, 168, 170, 172, 176, 177
Auden, W. H., 9, 143
Audiberti, Jacques, 42, 165
Augustine, Saint, 86, 106

Bachelard, Gaston, 84
Baïf, Jean-Antoine de, 15, 45, 94, 104, 135, 164
Bakhtin, Mikhail, 62
ballade, 45, 66–69, 88–92, 120, 169
Ballanche, Pierre-Simon, 100, 126, 164
Balzac, Honoré de, 95, 126, 137, 167
Banville, Théodore Faullain de, 135
Baroque period, 8, 20–21, 24, 57–59, 83–84, 87–88, 102, 105–6, 115–21, 132, 135–36, 149, 157–59, 164, 170–72, 176–77
Barthes, Roland, 2, 5, 10, 51–53, 148
Bataille, Georges, 10
Baudelaire, Charles, 3, 4, 5, 8, 9, 10, 20, 23, 43, 46, 47, 55, 99, 107, 126, 147, 148, 162–66, 170, 172, 173, 175, 176, 185, 188
Beatriz, Countess of Die, 135
Beaumanoir, Philippe de Remi, sire de, 135
Beaumarchais, Pierre Augustin Caron de, 126
Beckett, Samuel, 51
Beckford, William, 50
Bécquer, Gustavo Adolfo, 9
Bellaud de la Bellaudière, Louis, 159
Belleau, Remy, 95, 104, 135, 155, 158, 171
Bely, Andrey, 163

Bembo, Pietro, Cardinal, 25, 168
Bérimont, Luc, 45
Bernart de Ventadorn, 17, 82, 139
Bernier de la Brousse, Joachim, 158
Bernis, François Joachim de, 106, 135, 161
Béroul, 130, 152; *Tristan et Iseut*, 139
Bertaut, Jean, Bishop of Sées, 135, 136
Bertin, Antoine, 95, 160
Bertran de Born, 82
Bertrand, Louis Jacques Napoléon (Aloysius), 126
Bèze, Théodore de, 45–46, 83, 104
Bibliothèque Bleue, 146
Biedermeier, 161, 166
biographical criticism, 13–17
Blake, William, 173, 188
Bloom, Harold, 25, 170, 197
Boccaccio, Giovanni, 24, 88, 168, 169
Bodel, Jean, 39
Boethius, 26, 90, 168
Boileau-Despréaux, Nicolas, 4, 6, 21–22, 42, 53, 54, 56, 58, 80–82, 83, 96, 102, 106, 122, 135, 136, 139–41, 142, 148, 150, 159, 160, 161, 166, 168, 169, 170, 172, 175
Boisrobert, François Le Metil de, 135, 136
Bonnefoy, Yves, 42, 54, 100, 125, 165, 167, 170, 177
Bosquet, Alain, 5, 6, 10, 180
Bossuet, Jacques-Bénigne, 88
Boufflers, Stanislas-Jean, chevalier de, 135
Brassens, Georges, 45, 146, 166
Brébeuf, Georges de, 135, 136
Brecht, Bertolt, 86, 163, 172
Brel, Jacques, 45, 46, 146
Bremond, Henri, 2
Breton, André, 23, 166, 170
Brizeux, Julien Auguste Pélage, 106, 161, 166
Broch, Hermann, 139
Brooks, Cleanth, 9, 173
Browning, Robert, 6, 9, 101
burlesque, 57–59, 139–41
Bussières, Jean de, 158
Byron, Lord (George Gordon), 125, 168

Cadou, René-Guy, 166
Calderón de la Barca, Pedro, 122, 159

Campistron, Jean Galbert de, 139
Camus, Albert, 86
canon, literary, 8–9, 11, 169, 173–76
cantiques, 46
carpe diem, 35–36, 76–77
Cassou, Jean, 42, 165
Cats, Jacob, 50
Cayrol, Jean, 166
cénacles, 169, 170
Cendrars, Blaise, 73
Césaire, Aimé, 86, 122, 148
Chandieu, Antoine de Laroche de, 158
Change, 86, 165–66
chanson, 45–46, 146
chanson de geste, 59–61, 82, 103, 127, 128–31, 151–152, 170
Chanson de Roland (Song of Roland), 9, 11, 60–62, 82, 103, 108, 126, 128, 129, 139, 177. *See also* Turold
Chanson de Saint-Alexis, La, 4, 101, 103, 177
Chapelain, Jean, 135, 140, 141
Char, René, 42, 43, 45, 54, 85, 86, 100, 125, 143, 145, 165, 166, 167, 170
Charles d'Orléans, 4, 15, 18, 43, 45, 53, 54, 55, 73, 87, 88–94, 135, 147, 154, 164, 166, 168, 171, 176
Chartier, Alain, 128, 168
Chassignet, Jean-Baptiste, 105, 122, 136, 157, 158, 164, 172, 176
Chastelain, Georges, 147, 176
Chateaubriand, François René, vicomte de, 8
Chaucer, Geoffrey, 6, 9, 107
Chaulieu, Guillaume Amfrye de, 74, 135, 161
Chénier, André, 4, 6, 7, 8, 11, 25, 43, 56, 73, 94, 95, 160, 161, 167, 172
Chevalerie Ogier, La, 129
Chin P'ing Mei, 35
Chrétien de Troyes, 16, 26, 43, 53–56, 84, 96, 103, 104, 109, 127, 128, 130–32, 139, 142, 143, 151–55, 167, 168, 171, 172, 176
circonstance, poésie de. See verse, occasional
classicism, 21–22, 24–25, 52, 53, 54, 56, 57, 80–82, 83, 106, 139–41, 148, 159–61, 170–72, 174–75
Claudel, Paul, 4, 42, 45, 73, 102, 106, 122, 165, 166, 167, 175

Cocteau, Jean, 45, 100
Cohen, Jean, 5, 6, 10, 51–53, 147, 182–83
Coignard, Gabrielle de, 118
comedy, 52, 56, 61–66, 74–77, 126, 138, 167
conjat, 32–33
Conon de Béthune, 135
Constans, Jacques de, 158
contrafactum, 110–15
convention, poetry of, 26–39
Corbière, Tristan, 3, 55, 171
Corneille, Pierre, 5, 43, 48, 52, 56, 59, 73, 84, 106, 107, 122, 132, 136, 140, 146, 148, 159, 172
court and courtly life, 78, 115–16, 128–33, 153–54
courtly love. See *fin' amor*
courtly lyric, 26–33, 42–45, 49, 88–94, 134–35, 151; and *contrafactum*, 110–15
Crashaw, Richard, 173
creed, 99–123
criticism, 12, 13–17, 41–57, 71–73, 100, 122, 127, 143–50, 169–70, 173–74, 179–90
Cubism, 165
Curtius, Ernst Robert, 12, 21, 79, 131, 140, 172
Cyrano de Bergerac, Savinien, 126, 136

Dada, 47, 165, 169
Damas, Léon-Gontran, 86
D'Annunzio, Gabriele, 50
Dante Alighieri, 6, 9, 49, 59, 86, 87, 122, 134, 147, 169
Darío, Rubén, 9
Dassoucy, Charles Coypeau, 57, 58, 139, 140
Day Lewis, Cecil, 143
death and rebirth, 35–39, 113, 164
deconstructionism, 11, 143, 173
Deguy, Michel, 165
Delille, Abbé Jacques, 135, 160, 165
Derrida, Jacques, 100, 146
Desbordes-Valmore, Marceline Félicité Josèphe, 189
Deschamps, Eustache, 45
Desmarets de Saint-Sorlin, Jean, 88
Desnos, Robert, 85, 145, 166

Desportes, Phillippe, 35, 43, 109, 136, 138, 139, 147, 154, 158, 172
Dickens, Charles, 126
Diderot, Denis, 106, 126
Diop, David, 86
discourse, natural and fictive, 16–17
dits amoureux, 13–14, 17–18, 153
Döblin, Alfred, 163
Donne, John, 9, 54, 172
Dorat, Claude-Joseph, 56, 95, 160, 172
Dorat, Jean, 88
Dos Passos, John, 163
dreams, 2, 151, 153
Dryden, John, 9, 48, 54, 173
Du Bartas, Guillaume de Salluste, sieur, 26, 73, 105, 135, 136, 155, 158
Du Bellay, Joachim, 4, 10, 15, 20, 25, 26, 37, 43, 50, 52, 87, 104, 115, 134–36, 142, 153–58, 164, 166, 168–71, 173, 176
Du Bois-Hus, Gabriel, 105, 135, 158
Du Bouchet, André, 100, 165
Dumas, Alexandre, 131
Du Perron, Jacques Davy, Cardinal, 135, 136
Dupin, Jacques, 100, 165
Durry, Marie-Jeanne, 164

écart (poetry vs. prose), 2–5, 10, 51–56, 59
education, 1, 7–9, 72–73, 143–44, 147–50, 154
eighteenth century, 4–5, 22–23, 43, 50, 73–77, 84–85, 106, 137, 141–42, 160–61, 168, 170–72, 175–77
Eliot, T. S., 9, 11, 16, 47, 48, 51, 54, 55, 107, 122, 163, 172, 178
Eluard, Paul, 10, 11, 23, 42, 55, 73, 85, 86, 122, 145, 146, 165, 166, 177
Emmanuel, Pierre, 4, 42, 85, 96, 97, 100, 102, 107, 108, 125, 145, 163–68
Empson, William, 9
encomiastic, 77–82, 133–34, 155
L'Ephémère, 100
epic, 49, 56, 57–61, 82, 96–97, 103, 120, 127–31, 139–41, 151–52, 165, 171
epigram, 74–76
Estang, Luc, 145
esthetics: of negligence, 20, 134, 161; of reception, 138–39, 167–69

fantaisistes, 45, 165
Favre, Antoine, 105, 108, 118, 158
Fénelon, François de Salignac de la
    Mothe, 141
Ferré, Léo, 45
feudalism, 128–35, 151–54
fin'amor, 26–33, 88–94, 103–4, 130–33,
    152–54; parodied, 63–70; sacred par-
    ody, 109–15
Flamenca, 103
Flaubert, Gustave, 95
Florian, Jean-Pierre Claris de, 135
Follain, Jean, 166
Fontanes, Louis Jean Pierre, marquis de,
    135
Fontenelle, Bernard le Bovier, sieur de,
    95
Foucault, Michel, 100
France, Anatole, 106
Frederick II, King of Prussia, 50
free verse, 41–43
Frénaud, André, 145
French language, 46–51
Freud, Sigmund, 163
Froissart, Jean, 26, 87, 96, 133, 135, 153,
    164, 168, 172
Frye, Northrop, 11, 47, 83, 162, 173

Gace Brulé, 26–31, 35, 39, 45
García Lorca, Federico, 147, 163, 168
Garcilaso de la Vega, 9
Garin le Lorrain, 129, 155, 177. See also
    Lorrains Cycle
Garnier, Pierre, 165
Gautier d'Arras, 128, 176
Gautier de Coinci, 52, 99, 103, 104, 107,
    108, 109–15, 122
genus (grande, medium, humile), 56–70, 159
Geoffroy, Count of Brittany, 135
George, Stefan Anton, 50, 122
Gerhardt, Paul, 122
Gide, André, 6, 7, 23
Gilbert, Nicolas Joseph Laurent, 161
Girart de Roussillon, 103, 129, 152
Giraudoux, Jean, 141
Glissant, Edouard, 86
Godeau, Antoine, Bishop of Grasse, 88,
    135
Godolin, Peire, 159

Goethe, Johann Wolfgang von, 72, 100,
    126, 157, 159, 168, 172, 178
Goll, Ivan, 51
Góngora y Argote, Luis de, 6, 9, 49, 53;
    (góngoristas), 105
Gorki, Maksim, 196
Goulart, Simon, 158
Gower, John, 50
Gracq, Julien, 146
grand chant courtois (canso). See courtly lyric
Greban, Arnoul, 108
Grécourt, Jean-Baptiste Joseph Willart de,
    74, 135, 160
Greimas, Algirdas Julien, 10, 51
Gresset, Jean-Baptiste Louis, 58, 74, 95,
    139, 160, 161, 172, 176
Grillparzer, Franz, 159
Gringore, Pierre, 136
Grosjean, Jean, 102, 107, 108, 125, 145,
    166
Guérin, Maurice de, 135
Guerne, André Charles Romain, vicomte
    de, 135
Gui, Châtelain de Couci, 14, 26–31, 35,
    39, 43, 135
Guillaume IX, duc d'Aquitaine, 135, 139
Guillaume de Degulleville, 87
Guillaume de Ferrières, vidame de
    Chartres, 135
Guillaume de Lorris, 26, 34, 55, 56, 63,
    87, 93, 96, 104, 128, 132, 142, 152–53,
    154, 165, 167, 170, 172, 176. See also
    Romance of the Rose
Guillaume de Machaut, 4, 8, 14, 17–18,
    26, 42, 43, 45, 46, 54, 55, 73, 78, 87,
    90, 93, 96, 104, 128, 133, 135, 139, 153,
    154, 164, 166, 168, 169, 171, 172, 176
Guillevic, Eugène, 125, 165

Hamilton, Anthony, 50
Hawthorne, Nathaniel, 86, 173
Hemingway, Ernest, 173
Heredia, José María de, 50, 135
Héroët, Antoine, 135
Hesiod, 168
Hölderlin, Friedrich, 100, 168
Hoffmann, Ernst Theodor Amadeus, 100
Homer, 72, 113, 140, 141, 168, 172, 178.
    See also *Iliad*

Horace, 25, 26, 55, 101, 161
Horatian tradition, 20, 54, 76, 160–61, 165
Housman, A. E., 6
Hue de Rotelande, 43
Hugo, Victor, 3, 4, 5, 10, 15, 42, 52, 53, 56, 72, 73, 85, 96, 99, 100, 101, 122, 125, 126, 134, 137, 139, 145, 147, 149, 153, 160–68, 170, 172, 173, 176, 177, 182, 188
Hugues de Berzé, 135
Huon de Bordeaux, 146, 152
Huon d'Oisy, 135

"I" narrator, 17–25, 58, 153
Iliad, 61, 140. *See also* Homer
Imitatio Christi, 106
intertextuality, 25–26, 34–35, 49, 121, 139–43, 154
Ionesco, Eugène, 51
irony, 18, 72, 166
Isherwood, Christopher, 143
Isidore of Seville, 86
Isou, Isidore, 165

Jaccottet, Philippe, 42, 165, 166
Jacob, Max, 106, 166
Jakobson, Roman, 9, 10
James, Henry, 173
Jammes, Francis, 42, 106, 165, 166
Jarry, Alfred, 10
Jaufre Rudel, 17, 135
Jauss, Hans Robert, 137
Jean de Meun, 17, 26, 34, 56, 63–66, 67, 73, 83, 87, 90, 96, 101, 104, 122, 132, 152–53, 154, 168, 169, 170, 172, 176, 177. See also *Romance of the Rose*
Jean Renart, 8, 43, 128, 152, 176
Jodelle, Etienne, 158, 164, 172
Jonson, Ben, 54
Jouve, Pierre Jean, 35, 43, 54, 85, 100, 102, 107, 145, 164, 166, 167, 170
Joyce, James, 48
Juan de la Cruz, 9
justice and injustice, 78–80, 82–86

Kafka, Franz, 86
Kleist, Heinrich von, 159

Klopstock, Friedrich Gottlieb, 168
Kristeva, Julia, 10

Labé, Louise, 136
La Bruyère, Jean de, 126, 167
Lacan, Jacques, 100
La Ceppède, Jean de, 4, 8, 52, 53, 55, 105, 107–9, 118–21, 122, 135, 136, 157, 158, 172, 176
La Fare, Charles Auguste, marquis de, 161
La Fontaine, Jean de, 4, 24–25, 43, 49, 53, 54, 55, 78, 95, 101, 102, 106, 109, 133, 134, 139, 141, 143, 148, 149, 159, 160, 168, 171, 172, 174, 175, 176, 182
Laforgue, Jules, 3, 53, 55, 165, 171
Lamartine, Alphonse de, 3, 4, 5, 15, 43, 45, 52, 55, 56, 95, 96, 100, 101, 106, 125, 134, 135, 137, 139, 161–67, 170, 172, 173, 177
Lancelot-Grail Cycle, 104, 126, 128. See also *La Mort le roi Artu* and *Prose Lancelot*
language, 2–3, 41–70, 71–72, 156
La Noue, Jean-Baptiste Sauvé, 74–76
Lanza del Vasto, 42, 165
Laprade, Pierre-Martin-Victor Richard de, 135, 162
La Rochefoucauld, François, duc de, 126
La Roque, Siméon-Guillaume de, 158
Latini, Brunetto, 50, 126
La Tour du Pin, Patrice de, 107, 145, 166
Lautréamont, comte de (Isidore Ducasse), 23, 100, 147, 163, 176
Leavis, F. R., 9, 11, 54, 143, 173, 174
Lebrun (Ponce Denis Ecouchard-Lebrun), 160
Leconte de Lisle, Charles Marie, 3, 96, 167
Lefèvre de la Boderie, Guy, 136, 155
Lemaire de Belges, Jean, 8, 52, 78, 88, 133, 168, 171
Le Moyne, Pierre, 83, 88, 95, 105, 108, 109, 155, 158, 164, 165, 172, 176
Léonard, Nicolas Germain, 95, 160
Leopardi, Giacomo, 9
Lermontov, Mikhail Yurievich, 144
lettrisme, 165
Lévi-Strauss, Claude, 9
Lewis, C. S., 172

Lorrains cycle, 130. See also *Garin le Lorrain*
Lortigue, Annibal de, 136
Louÿs, Pierre, 6
love, 13–16, 26–39, 52, 58, 62–69, 76–
    77, 88–94, 103–4, 109–15, 120, 151–
    54, 155, 158, 161–64, 170, 171. See also
    fin' amor
Lucretius, 122
Lukács, György, 128–29, 163

MacNeice, Louis, 143
MacOrlan, Pierre, 46
madness, 31, 32, 89, 158
Maeterlinck, Maurice, 50
Mage, André, sieur de Fiefmelin, 135,
    136
Malherbe, François de, 5, 11, 35, 43, 83,
    135, 136, 139, 147, 160, 161, 165, 168,
    170
Mallarmé, Stéphane, 3, 4, 5, 10, 20, 43,
    46, 52–55, 99, 100, 101, 128, 143, 147,
    148, 163, 165, 166, 167, 172, 176, 182,
    185
Malraux, André, 172, 177
Mannerism, 171–72
Manoll, Michel, 166
Manzoni, Alessandro, 9
Marguerite, Queen, consort of Henry II,
    King of Navarre, 95, 104, 135
Marino, Giambattista, 168, 169
Marivaux, Pierre Carlet de Chamblain de,
    16–17, 126
Marlowe, Christopher, 159
Marolles, Michel, abbé de, 88
Marot, Clément, 4, 5, 45–46, 53, 54, 55,
    78, 88, 94, 104, 109, 133, 136, 138, 139,
    154, 157, 168, 171, 176
Martial de Brives, 105, 158
Marx, Karl Heinrich, 101, 163, 166
Masson, Loys, 85, 145
Mayakovsky, Vladimir Vladimirovich, 86,
    122, 147, 148, 163, 168
Maynard, François de, 35, 176
meaning, 71–97
melancholia, 29, 89, 92–94, 155, 161, 164,
    166
melodrama, 161–62
Melville, Herman, 86
Merrill, Stuart, 50

metapoetry, 3, 71–73, 164, 166
meter, 42, 47, 53, 55, 146, 165
Michaux, Henri, 10, 55, 86, 166
Michelet, Jules, 172
Middle Ages, 4–5, 8, 13–14, 17–20, 26–
    33, 49–50, 59–70, 78, 82–83, 87–94,
    102–4, 109–15, 126–36, 138, 149,
    151–54, 164, 166–77
Milosz, Oscar Vladislas de Lubicz, 165, 166
Milton, John, 6, 9, 48, 54, 55, 122, 141,
    168, 172, 173
Mistral, Frédéric, 95, 162, 166
mock-encomium, 176
mock-epic, 62, 80–82, 139–41, 159, 160
Modernism, 1–11, 41–49, 147, 163–67,
    175, 179–90
Mörike, Eduard, 49
Molière (Jean-Baptiste Poquelin), 5, 52,
    106, 126, 136, 148, 159, 167, 172, 175
Molinet, Jean, 135
Monluc, Blaise de Lasseran-Massencome,
    seigneur de, 136
Montaigne, Michel Eyquem de, 126, 134,
    136, 167
Montchrestien, Antoine de, 136
Montesquieu, Charles de Secondat, baron
    de, 106
Moréas, Jean, 50
Mort le roi Artu, La, 131. See also *Lancelot-*
    Grail Cycle and *Prose Lancelot*
Motin, Pierre, 176
multilingualism, 41, 49–51
music, 41, 43–46, 146, 155
Musset, Alfred de, 53, 55, 106, 126, 134,
    135, 162, 165, 172, 176, 188
mystery plays, 102, 103, 107, 172
myth and mythology, 32–39, 78–80, 87,
    99–100, 104–5, 107, 130–31, 137, 145,
    152, 153–54, 162–65, 167, 172

narrative technique, 5, 13–25, 115–18,
    118–21, 153
Neruda, Pablo, 122
Nerval, Gérard de, 5, 10, 45, 99, 100,
    165, 185, 188
Nietzsche, Friedrich, 101
nineteenth century, 3–4, 42–44, 50, 85,
    99, 101, 106, 125–26, 137–38, 161–63,
    166–68, 170–76

Noot, Jan van der, 50
nouveau roman, 142, 143, 149
Novalis (Baron Friedrich von Harden-
    berg), 2, 100

obscenity, 59–70
ode (*odelette*), 33–37, 45, 106, 160
Orphic stance, 4, 99–100, 163–64
Orwell, George, 86
Ovid, 25, 26, 87, 94, 107, 139, 161, 168

panegyric, 73, 77–82
Parny, Evariste-Désiré de Forges, vicomte
    de, 95, 135, 139, 159, 161
Pascal, Blaise, 84, 88, 167
pastoral, 37, 94–96, 108, 116, 132
patronage system, 131–33
Paul, Pierre, 159
Péguy, Charles, 102, 106, 166
Peire Vidal, 17
Peletier du Mans, Jacques, 155
Péret, Benjamin, 85, 145
persona, 13–39, 67, 121, 132–34, 155–53,
    160
personification, 34–37, 89–94
Petrarch, 6, 9, 15, 24–26, 37, 56, 88, 94,
    154, 157, 168, 169; "Black Neope-
    trarchism," 158
Pey de Garros, 159
phonology, 43–44
Pindar, 168
Piron, Alexis, 74, 95, 160
Pizan, Christine de, 45, 87
Plato, 99
Pléiade, La, 25, 53, 104, 134, 157, 158,
    164, 169, 174
Pleynet, Marcelin, 163, 165
Poe, Edgar Allan, 3, 99, 188
poet, nature of the, 1–4, 13–15, 73, 101–
    23, 134–36, 162–64
poetry: concrete, 165; crisis of, 1, 125–27,
    142–50; decline of, 167–78; history of,
    1–12, 17–23, 49, 57, 72, 82–86, 102–
    7, 126–39, 151–78; modes of, 73–97;
    narrative, 96–97, 151–54; occasional,
    73–77; opposed to prose, 2–3, 5–6, 10,
    41–42, 51–56, 72, 125–26, 167; philo-
    sophical, 73; *poésie engagée,* 86, 145,
166; *poésie pure,* 3, 74, 85, 164; political-
    satirical, 82–86; sacred, 99–121; scien-
    tific, 73, 155; spatialist, 165
Polo, Marco, 50, 125
Pompignan, Jean-Jacques Lefranc, mar-
    quis de, 106, 135, 159, 161
Ponge, Francis, 10–11, 43, 165
Ponsard, François, 176
Pope, Alexander, 6, 9, 48, 168, 172
Porchères, Honorat de Laugier, sieur de,
    136
postmodernism, 166
poststructuralism, 173
Pound, Ezra, 9, 48, 51, 100, 122, 139, 147
Pradon, Nicolas, 139
préciosité, 58, 172, 176
pre-romanticism, 94
Prévert, Jacques, 45, 54, 55, 146, 166,
    168, 171
Prose Lancelot, 131, 172. See also *Lancelot-
    Grail Cycle* and *La Mort le roi Artu*
Prose Tristan, 125
prosody, 41–43, 47–48, 51
Proust, Marcel, 17, 148
public, 55–56, 74, 77, 125–50; aristo-
    cratic, 128–36, 138; bourgeois, 136–38;
    modern, 142–50
Pushkin, Aleksandr Sergeyevich, 49, 101,
    144, 157

Queneau, Raymond, 166
quest theme, 67, 90, 152, 163, 171
Quinault, Philippe, 176
Quinet, Edgar, 126

Rabelais, François, 48, 134, 136, 167
Racan, Honorat de Bueil, marquis de, 35,
    135, 176
Racine, Jean, 4, 5, 10, 43, 48, 49, 52, 56,
    73, 78, 84, 100, 106, 107, 122, 140, 146,
    148, 149, 172, 175, 180–82
Racine, Louis, 106, 108, 160, 161, 167
Raimon Jordan, 135
Raimon Vidal de Besalù, 49
Rambaut, Lord of Orange, 135
Raoul de Cambrai, 59–61, 66, 67, 129, 130,
    131, 154, 155, 177
Rapin, Nicolas, 136

realism, 60, 166, 171, 172, 176
reality, 68–69, 71–73
Régnier, Henri François Joseph de, 165
reification, 68, 69, 77, 91, 116, 161
rejection, structure of, 169–70
religion, 2, 26, 29, 57, 68–69, 78–80, 82–84, 87–88, 92, 95–96, 99–123, 128, 154–55, 159, 161, 166, 167, 172
Renaissance, 4–5, 10, 24–26, 33–39, 43, 45–46, 50, 52–54, 56–57, 73, 78–80, 83, 87–88, 94–96, 104–5, 115–18, 126, 127, 133–36, 154–57, 164, 176–77
Renard, Jean-Claude, 107, 145, 166, 186
Renaud de Montauban, 103, 129, 146, 152, 177
René I, d'Anjou, King of Naples and Jerusalem, 135
rhetoric, 25, 34–35, 53–57, 59, 68, 78, 108, 128, 155, 160
Rhétoriqueurs, 52, 99, 127, 134, 164, 168, 177
rhyme, 42, 43, 47, 53, 146, 165, 166
Richard I, King of England, 135
Riffaterre, Michael, 10, 192
Rilke, Rainer Maria, 50, 100, 147
Rimbaud, Arthur, 2, 3, 5, 6, 10, 47, 52, 100, 126, 143, 147, 148, 163, 168, 170, 172, 182, 185, 186, 188
Robbe-Grillet, Alain, 148
Roche, Denis, 165
Rococo, 159, 161
Rodenbach, Georges, 50
Roman de Renart, Le, 60, 61–63, 66, 127, 142, 153, 176
Roman du Castelain de Couci, Le, 14
romance, 90, 103–4, 130–32, 151–53; roman courtois, 4
Romance of the Rose (Roman de la Rose), 9, 26, 35, 63–66, 67, 73, 83, 86, 91, 104, 139, 152–53; See also Guillaume de Lorris and Jean de Meun
Romanesque, 172
romanticism, 1–9, 15, 49, 50, 52–54, 71, 99–101, 106, 125, 137–38, 161–67, 169–71, 174–75
rondeau, 45, 92–94, 120, 169
Ronsard, Pierre de, 4–6, 8, 10, 14–15, 20, 24–26, 33–37, 37–39, 42–46, 52, 53, 56, 57, 73, 73–80, 83, 87, 88, 94–96,

99, 101, 104–5, 109, 113, 122, 133–37, 139, 142, 147, 149, 150, 153–58, 160, 164, 166, 168–74, 176, 177, 182
Rostand, Edmond, 165
Rotrou, Jean de, 136, 172
Roubaud, Jacques, 10, 163, 165
Roucher, Jean-Antoine, 160, 161
Rousseau, Jean-Baptiste, 95, 106, 160, 161
Rousseau, Jean-Jacques, 8, 160, 161, 188
Rousset, Jean, 174
Ruiz, Juan, Archpriest of Hita, 9
Rulhière, Claude Carloman de, 135
Rutebeuf, 52, 103, 107, 109, 122

Sade, Donatien Alphonse François, marquis de, 173
Saint-Amant, Antoine Gérard, sieur de, 8, 20–21, 24, 25, 52, 57, 88, 95, 96, 105, 133, 134, 136, 149, 155, 158, 159, 160, 164, 168, 172, 176
Sainte-Beuve, Charles-Augustin, 174
Saint-John Perse (Alexis Saint-Leger Leger), 47, 48, 54, 85, 96, 97, 165–68, 170
Saint-Lambert, Jean-François, marquis de, 95, 135, 160
salon, 137
Sand, George, 167
Sandburg, Carl, 173
Sannazaro, Iacopo, 94
Sarasin, Jean-François, 136
Sardou, Victorien, 131
Sarraute, Nathalie, 144
Sartre, Jean-Paul, 2, 10, 107
satire, 18–23, 61–70, 83–86, 115–18, 160
Scarron, Paul, 57–58, 139–140
Scève, Maurice, 8, 10, 15, 43, 52, 53, 56, 73, 87, 94, 99, 136, 154, 155, 157, 164, 170, 171, 176, 177
Schelandre, Jean de, 136
Schiller, Johann Christoph Friedrich, 159, 168
Scudéry, Georges de, 135, 140
Segalen, Victor, 100
Seghers, Pierre, 7, 45
Segrais, Jean Regnault de, 136
Selve, Lazare de, 105, 134, 136
Senghor, Léopold Sédar, 86, 145

seventeenth century, 8, 24, 53, 57–59, 80–82, 105–6, 132, 136–37, 139–41, 157–59, 166–72, 174–76
Shakespeare, William, 48, 149, 159, 168
Shelley, Percy Bysshe, 99, 101, 173
sonnet, 34–39, 115–21
Soumet, Alexandre, 162, 165
Spender, Stephen, 143
Spenser, Edmund, 6, 9, 86, 172
Sponde, Jean de, 4, 8, 43, 52, 53, 55, 105, 109, 115–18, 120–22, 135, 136, 157, 158, 164, 172, 176
Stendhal (Henri Beyle), 167
Stivell, Alan, 146
structuralism, 9, 10, 11, 143, 169, 173
style, levels of, 23–25, 51–70, 108, 119, 153, 159, 164, 165, 170–71
Sully Prudhomme, René François Armand, 96, 147
Supervielle, Jules, 42, 54, 55, 85, 145, 165, 166, 171
Surrealism, 2, 3, 47–48, 163, 165, 166, 169
Swift, Jonathan, 86
Swinburne, Algernon Charles, 99
Symbolism, 1–4, 41–46, 50, 52–55, 99–101, 166, 175

Tasso, Torquato, 9, 139, 140, 141, 168, 169
Tassoni, Alessandro, 141
Tate, Allen, 173
Tchikaya U Tam'si, Gérald Félix, 86, 145
Tel Quel, 86, 165–66
Tennyson, Alfred Lord, 173
Theocritus, 168
Thibaut IV, Count of Champagne, I King of Navarre, 8, 31–33, 39, 45, 135, 139
Thomas Aquinas, Saint, 86
Thomas of England, 130, 152, 176. See also Tristan et Iseut, 139
Thomson, James, 168
Tibullus, 161
Todorov, Tzvetan, 10
Tolkien, J. R. R., 172
Tolstoy, Leo, Count, 100
tragedy, 56, 126, 138, 161, 167
Tristan l'Hermite, François, 95, 158, 164

trobar clus, 52, 53, 54, 127, 146, 164, 170, 177
trobar leu, 54, 177
trobar plan, 53, 170
trobar ric, 52, 53, 127, 164, 170
Turold, 96, 122, 155. See also Chanson de Roland
Twain, Mark, 173
twentieth century, 1–11, 42–43, 45, 47–48, 85–86, 100, 102, 106–7, 125–26, 139, 142–48, 165–73, 175–78
Tyard, Pontus de, 135, 176
typology, Christian, 79–80, 87–88, 92, 105, 107–8, 121, 167
Tzara, Tristan, 51

Urfé, Honoré d', 135, 141; L'Astrée, 95, 132
U.S.S.R., poetry in, 144

Valéry, Paul, 2, 3, 4, 8, 11, 42, 43, 45, 46, 55, 73, 86, 100, 101, 139, 143, 148, 165, 167, 175, 176
Vauquelin, Nicolas, seigneur des Yveteaux, 135, 136
Vauquelin de La Fresnaye, Jean, 136
Vega Carpio, Lope Félix de, 159
Verhaeren, Emile, 50, 73, 163, 165
Verlaine, Paul, 3, 5, 43, 44, 45, 52, 54, 73, 106, 147, 177, 182
Vian, Boris, 45, 46, 166
Viau, Théophile de, 8, 15, 43, 52, 58, 73, 95, 134, 136, 138, 158, 164, 166, 172, 176, 177
Viélé-Griffin, Francis, 50
Vigny, Alfred de, 4, 5, 8, 43, 52, 72, 73, 85, 96, 101, 106, 135, 139, 153, 161–65, 172
Villehardouin, Geoffroi de, 126
Villon, François, 4, 5, 8, 10, 15, 18–20, 45, 48, 52, 53, 66–70, 101, 107, 109, 139, 142, 147, 150, 154, 168–70, 172, 173, 176, 177
Virgil, 25, 26, 40, 56, 62, 86, 91–96, 107, 113, 139–41, 161, 162, 168
Voltaire (François-Marie Arouet), 11, 22–23, 43, 49, 55–57, 73, 74–77, 83–85,

96, 101, 106, 122, 126, 133, 137–39,
141, 148, 149, 160, 161, 167, 172, 177

Wagner, Richard, 44
Walpole, Horace, 149
Weckherlin, Georg Rodolf, 50
Whitman, Walt, 49, 172

Wilde, Oscar, 50, 99
Wordsworth, William, 9, 100, 101

Young, Edward, 168

Zesen, Philipp von, 50
Zola, Emile, 16, 86